COLLECTOR'S ENCYCLOPEDIA OF

DEPRESSION GLASS

TWELFTH EDITION

America's #1 Best Selling Glass Book!

BY GENE FLORENCE

COLLECTOR BOOKS
A Division of Schroeder Publishing Co., Inc.

The current values in this book should be used only as a guide. They are not intended to set prices, which vary from one section of the country to another. Auction prices as well as dealer prices vary greatly and are affected by condition as well as demand. Neither the Author nor the Publisher assumes responsibility for any losses that might be incurred as a result of consulting this guide.

On the Cover:
Top left: Queen Mary candlesticks double branch, Royal Ruby, $32.50 each.
Top right: Iris iridescent demitasse cup and saucer, rare color, $325.00.
Bottom center: Block Optic roll-edge bowl, green, $60.00.

Searching For A Publisher?

We are always looking for knowledgeable people considered to be experts within their fields. If you feel that there is a real need for a book on your collectible subject and have a large comprehensive collection, contact us.

Cover design by: Beth Summers
Book design by: Gina Lage

ACKNOWLEDGMENTS

I appreciate all the information readers and collectors have provided me through their writing, calling, and talking to me at shows! Thanks for bringing those newly found pieces to shows so that I can verify them and for sending measurements and photographs confirming new discoveries! Photographs are priceless when authenticating a new piece. (If you have trouble photographing glass, take it outside in natural light, place the glass on a neutral surface {concrete works}, and forget the camera has a flash attachment. A bright, cloudy day works best.) Please enclose a **SASE** (self addressed stamped envelope) that is **large** enough to send back your pictures, if you wish them returned!

There have been approximately **thirty-seven previously uninventoried pieces added to the listings** since the eleventh edition! (Those of you who feel that nothing new is ever found should look closely at your favorite pattern!) Similarly, there have been seven deletions from the book of pieces that have never been found that were listed in catalogues or had mysteriously appeared in my listings.

Over forty measurements have been corrected in this book. These corrections have occurred due to original catalogue misinformation, entry mistakes, or errors in measurement in the past. Realize, too, that the size of the **same patterned** plate or tumbler **can** vary from each moulding generation, especially if the pattern were made for a long time. American Sweetheart plates vary every time you measure one. Be sure to read about measurements on page 4.

I have taken much delight in the shows that Depression Glass clubs and private show promoters have invited me to guest. I have received invaluable information and knowledge from them, and hopefully, contributed to them.

An unequivocal thanks is always due family. Cathy, my wife, continues as chief editor, critic, and proofreader and spends days trying to make sure you understand what I wanted to say. Marc, my son, has taken over shipping my book orders from Lexington while he attends the University of Kentucky. Chad, my eldest, who has now married, is still available to help load and unload boxes for photography sessions.

It is difficult to write acknowledgments for this book without remembering Grannie Bear who spent hours organizing and helping price previous books. For those who have not heard, my mom, Grannie Bear, died suddenly in July, 1993. Her help is painfully missed! Dad has since remarried.

Thanks, too, to Cathy's mom, Sibyl, who helped sort and pack glass for photography. Thanks to Charles for all the shelves built to hold glass. I'm grateful to all the family who tried to keep everything under control at home while we traveled.

Glass and information for this book were furnished by Earl and Beverly Hines, Dick and Pat Spencer, Sam and Becky Collings, Dan Tucker and Lorrie Kitchen, Calvin and Gwen Key, Matt and Angela Koester, Bill and Millie Downey, Charles Griggs, and numerous readers from across the U.S.A., Puerto Rico, Canada, England, New Zealand, and Australia!

Photographs for this book were made by Richard Walker of New York and Charley Lynch of Collector Books. They both provided multiple photographs during a five day session of shooting glass. Glass arranging, unpacking, sorting, carting, and repacking was accomplished by Jane White, Zibbie Walker, and Cathy Florence. Van loading and unloading was facilitated by some of Collector Books shipping crew. As far as I know, no one has left Collector Books that helped on this project as happened on the last book.

In addition, Jane White and many of the crew mentioned previously helped on other photography shoots over the two year period since the eleventh edition. There is no way anyone would believe what we do to get you these photographs short of being there. Thanks to the special people in the Editing Department at Collector Books: Lisa Stroup, who is working as Editor, and Gina Lage who transferred all my computer disks into a book and caught some mistakes that Cathy and I missed!

This twelfth book was written in Florida. Sitting here writing and watching the alligators and fishing boats trolling by sure beats looking at the wall in my Kentucky office, or shoveling snow or scraping ice! I am finally free to be at our home in Florida which is mostly a pleasant experience. The mosquitoes still like my windows at night when the lights are shining out. The fishing has been sporadic at best, but I wouldn't be doing **any** fishing in Kentucky at this time. As it is today, I have crappie in my fish cage to clean and fresh fish for supper tonight. Who could ask for more?

The phone rings less here; although, today, I have had four (make that five) calls since I started on this section. One call was from a subscriber of *Reader's Digest* who tracked me down through an article about Depression Glass in that magazine. Our glassware has been a favorite subject in both women's and collecting magazines recently.

I do my best; but there is no way I could accomplish any of this without you! As we go to press with the twelfth edition, thank you for making this America's #1 best selling glass book! Educate your friends about Depression Glass! In the grand scheme of things, it still appears that only a few of us know anything about its worth. I am amazed almost daily by letters from people who have just heard about it!

FOREWORD

Depression Glass as defined in this book is the colored glassware made primarily during the Depression years in the colors of amber, blue, black, crystal, green, pink, red, yellow, and white. There are other colors and some glass made before, as well as after, this time; but primarily, the glass within this book was made from the 1920's through the end of the 1930's. This book is mostly concerned with the inexpensively made dinnerware turned out by machine in quantity and sold through smaller stores or given away as promotional or premium items for other products of that time. Depression Glass was often packed in cereal boxes, flour sacks, or given as gifts at the local movie theaters, gasoline stations, and grocery stores.

There have been changes in the collecting of Depression Glass since my first book was released in 1972. Prices have soared; seemingly plentiful patterns have been assembled into vast collections and removed from the market. Smaller Depression patterns and previously ignored crystal wares have attracted buyers; truly, **anything** that is Depression Glass, whether it is a known pattern or not, suddenly has added value and collectability. Collectors have become more knowledgeable and sophisticated in their collecting. Many are enhancing their collections of "A to W" (Adam to Windsor) with patterns of hand-made glassware made during the same time. This broadening interest of collectors prompted me to research and write six more books in the field of Depression Glass, one on ELEGANT glassware of the time, one on the glass KITCHENWARE items of the Depression, and four others on the VERY RARE glassware of the Depression era. Additionally, collectors have been acquiring later made patterns encompassing the 1940's through the early 1960's that has led to my latest book, *Collectible Glassware from the 40's, 50's, 60's...*, which is now in its third edition. To correctly date glassware from that later period, it was necessary to move some patterns previously exclusive to this book in the era encompassed by the 50's book. All patterns manufactured after 1940 are now in that book covering the period after the Depression years.

Information for this book comes through years of research, experience, fellow dealers, collectors, and over 1,125,000 miles of travel pursuant to glassware. However, some of the most interesting material has come from generous readers who shared catalogues, magazines, photographs of glass, and their specific information with me. These contributions to the body of knowledge I especially value.

PRICING

All prices in this book are retail prices for mint condition glassware. This book is intended to be only a guide to prices as there are some regional price differences that cannot reasonably be dealt with herein!

You may expect dealers to pay from 30% to 50% less than the prices quoted. Glass that is in less than mint condition, i.e., chipped, cracked, scratched, or poorly molded, will bring only a **small percentage** of the price of glass that is in mint condition.

Prices have become fairly well standardized due to national advertising by dealers and Depression Glass shows that are held from coast to coast. Several nationally known dealers have assisted in updating prices for this book. However, **there are still some regional differences in prices due partly to glass being more readily available in some areas than in others.** Companies distributed certain pieces in some areas that they did not in others. Generally speaking, however, prices are about the same among dealers from coast to coast.

Prices **tend to increase dramatically** on rare items and, in general, they have increased as a whole due to more and more collectors entering the field and people becoming more aware of the worth of Depression Glass. However, I receive letters regularly from new collectors who have just "discovered" Depression Glass!

One of the more important aspects of this book is the attempt made to illustrate as well as realistically price those items that are in demand. The desire is to give you the most accurate guide to collectible patterns of Depression Glass available.

MEASUREMENTS

To illustrate why there are discrepancies in measurements, I offer the following sample from just two years of Hocking's catalogue references:

Year		Ounces		Ounces		
1935	Pitcher	37, 58, 80	Flat Tumbler	5, 9, 13½	Footed Tumbler	10, 13
1935	Pitcher	37, 60, 80	Flat Tumbler	5, 9, 10, 15	Footed Tumbler	10, 13
1936	Pitcher	37, 65, 90	Flat Tumbler	5, 9, 13½	Footed Tumbler	10, 15
1935	Pitcher	37, 60, 90	Flat Tumbler	5, 9, 13½	Footed Tumbler	10, 15

All measurements in this book are exact as to some manufacturer's listing **or** to actual measurement. You may expect variance of up to ½" or 1–5 ounces. This may be due to mould variations or changes by the manufacturer as well as rounding off measurements for catalogue listings.

CONTENTS

ADAM JEANNETTE GLASS COMPANY, 1932–1934

Colors: Pink, green, crystal, some yellow, and Delphite blue. *(See Reproduction Section.)*

The quantity of Adam for sale is rapidly diminishing! For years, there was enough being found to keep the prices reasonable on everything except scarce items. Now, even formerly common pieces are no longer available.

There are more collectors of pink Adam than there are for the more expensive green. Green Adam is less abundant, and therefore, prices remain higher. However, more collectors buying pink Adam are now causing those prices to **increase faster** than for green. Generally, prices of pink have a way to go to catch those of green; but individual items, such as tumblers and serving pieces, are selling in the same price range as green! The pink vase is the most elusive piece of Adam unless you include the Adam/Sierra butter dish. Many pink vases tilt or appear lopsided and some collectors are unwilling to pay a high price for these less than perfect vases.

Speaking of the Adam/Sierra butter dish, **both** pattern designs are on the top. Adam is found on the outside of the top and Sierra is found on the inside of the lid. These tops have been found on **both** Adam and Sierra butter bottoms; those respective butter bottoms contain only one pattern. To be a real Adam/Sierra combination butter it has to have **both** patterns on that top! Several times I have seen an Adam butter top on a Sierra bottom or a Sierra top on an Adam bottom priced as the rare butter. Sorry! That isn't it. There would be many more of these rarely found butters if that held true.

Green Adam **is** much harder to find than the pink. Yet, prices for green have remained steady for years. A little increase has been seen in prices for butter dishes, candy jars, candlesticks, and shakers. If you start collecting green Adam, buy those pieces first — if you can find them for sale!

As with some other Jeannette patterns, the sugar and candy lids are interchangeable. This was a savings idea for Jeannette and a blessing for collectors today. Sugar and candy lids are always more difficult to find than the bottoms.

Inner rims of all Adam pieces need to be carefully checked. That advise goes double for cereal bowls. Damage to these came from both using and stacking them over the years. If you are willing to buy pieces that are rough inside, you should not expect to pay mint condition prices. Damaged glass is a problem in collecting. **You** have to decide if you are willing to accept **less than perfect** glass. If it ever comes time to resell, I guarantee you will be happier with the prices obtained for mint glassware. Prices in this book are for mint (like new) condition glass. Admittedly, some damaged glass can be nicely repaired by competent workmen, but not all glass grinders and repairmen are competent! Ask to see samples of their work before you turn your glass over to them.

Adam lamps are scarce. In the Floral pattern on page 85, you can see a pink lamp that is designed the same way Adam lamps were. A sherbet was frosted in order to hide the wiring and a notch was cut into the top edge of the sherbet to accommodate a switch. A metal cover was fitted to the top of the frosted sherbet through which a tall bulb was connected to the switch that fit the notch. The prices listed are for working lamps. That **bulb assembly** is hard to find. The notched, frosted sherbets are available and could even be made today without much difficulty!

The Adam butter dish is the **only** piece that has been reproduced! Do not use the information given in the Reproduction Section in the back of the book for any other pieces in the pattern. You can not apply the directions of the arrows on the butter to any other pieces in Adam. **It only applies to the butter.** This goes for all reproductions I have listed in the back. Only apply the telltale clues to the piece I describe. Transferring information to some other item in the pattern will not work!

	Pink	Green		Pink	Green
Ash tray, 4½"	30.00	25.00	**Cup	23.00	21.00
Bowl, 4¾" dessert	16.00	16.00	Lamp	250.00	275.00
Bowl, 5¾" cereal	40.00	40.00	Pitcher, 8", 32 oz.	40.00	45.00
Bowl, 7¾"	22.00	25.00	Pitcher, 32 oz. round base	47.50	
Bowl, 9", no cover	30.00	42.50	Plate, 6" sherbet	9.00	9.50
Bowl, cover, 9"	25.00	42.50	***Plate, 7¾" square salad	15.00	15.00
Bowl, 9" covered	55.00	85.00	Plate, 9" square dinner	30.00	28.00
Bowl, 10" oval	30.00	30.00	Plate, 9" grill	20.00	20.00
Butter dish bottom	25.00	65.00	Platter, 11¾"	28.00	32.00
Butter dish top	55.00	245.00	Relish dish, 8" divided	20.00	22.50
Butter dish & cover	80.00	310.00	Salt & pepper, 4" ftd.	70.00	100.00
Butter dish combination			****Saucer, 6" square	7.00	7.00
with Sierra Pattern	825.00		Sherbet, 3"	30.00	37.50
Cake plate, 10" ftd.	25.00	30.00	Sugar	17.50	20.00
*Candlesticks, 4" pr.	85.00	95.00	Sugar/candy cover	25.00	40.00
Candy jar & cover, 2½"	85.00	95.00	Tumbler, 4½"	30.00	27.50
Coaster, 3¼"	22.00	20.00	Tumbler, 5½" iced tea	60.00	50.00
Creamer	20.00	20.00	Vase, 7½"	250.00	55.00

* Delphite $225.00   ** Yellow $100.00   *** Round pink $60.00; yellow $100.00   **** Round pink $75.00; yellow $85.00

AMERICAN PIONEER LIBERTY WORKS, 1931–1934

Colors: Pink, green, amber, and crystal.

American Pioneer pattern incorporates plain fields of glass, narrow ridges, and bumpy hobs, a diversity of design akin to the peoples represented by its name. The look is one of quiet elegance.

Green American Pioneer is the most coveted color, but you should realize that there are three distinct shades available. Color variances do not deter collectors of American Pioneer as much as they do collectors of other patterns. So few pieces are seen that they are happy to acquire any new item no matter if it is a slightly different shade of green.

Crystal or amber have fewer admirers, but collectors of amber have told me that there is little being found except for basic luncheon pieces. To date, only one set of amber covered pitchers (urns, shown on page 10) has ever been found! Liners for urns are regular 6" and 8" plates. That should make it easier to find those liners except for the 6" **pink** plate for the small urn, which is also rare.

The dresser set is the most valuable commodity in this pattern. Only one has been found in pink and just a few in green. These sets have become more difficult for Depression Glass collectors to own due, in part, to the many perfume and cologne bottle collectors also searching for them. Often items in a Depression Glass pattern become more valuable because collectors from some other area of collecting are searching for that particular item. It makes for spirited competition and some frustration if you are looking for such a piece.

There are two styles of American Pioneer cups being found. Some cups have more rim flair than others which makes one style have a 4" diameter (2¼" tall) the other a 3⅜" diameter (2⅜" tall).

Two different sizes of cocktails have only been found in amber! One holds 3 oz. and stands 3¹³⁄₁₆" high while the other holds 3½ oz. and stands 3¹⁵⁄₁₆" tall.

Candy jar lids are interchangeable in American Pioneer even though the jars hold different quantities of candy! This was another of those cost cutting procedures by a glass company, often done during this economically depressed time.

You may have difficulty in matching lids for covered bowls. One collector just told me that he believes there are three different covered bowl sizes instead of the two I have previously listed. If you find a different size from those listed, please let me know. The same goes for any additional items in American Pioneer not listed. I do appreciate the information you share with me; and I make a point to pass that information along to other readers.

		Crystal, Pink	Green			Crystal, Pink	Green
*	Bowl, 5" handled	20.00	20.00		Lamp, 5½" round, ball		
	Bowl, 8¾" covered	95.00	125.00		shape (amber $80.00)	75.00	
	Bowl, 9" handled	22.00	27.50		Lamp, 8½" tall	100.00	110.00
	Bowl, 9¼" covered	95.00	125.00		Mayonnaise, 4¼"	57.50	90.00
	Bowl, 10¾" console	55.00	65.00		Pilsner, 5¾", 11 oz.	100.00	100.00
	Candlesticks, 6½" pr.	70.00	90.00	**	Pitcher, 5" covered urn	150.00	210.00
	Candy jar and cover, 1 lb	85.00	100.00	***	Pitcher, 7" covered urn	175.00	225.00
	Candy jar and cover, 1½ lb.	95.00	125.00		Plate, 6"	12.50	15.00
	Cheese and cracker set (in-			*	Plate, 6" handled	12.50	15.00
	dented platter and comport)	50.00	60.00	*	Plate, 8"	10.00	12.00
	Coaster, 3½"	30.00	30.00	*	Plate, 11½" handled	18.00	20.00
	Creamer, 2¾"	25.00	20.00	*	Saucer	4.00	5.00
*	Creamer, 3½"	20.00	22.00		Sherbet, 3½"	16.00	20.00
*	Cup	10.00	12.00		Sherbet, 4¾"	32.50	37.50
	Dresser set (2 cologne, powder				Sugar, 2¾"	20.00	22.00
	jar, on indented 7½" tray)	375.00	325.00	*	Sugar, 3½"	20.00	22.00
	Goblet, 3¹³⁄₁₆", 3 oz., cocktail (amber)	40.00			Tumbler, 5 oz. juice	30.00	35.00
	Goblet, 3¹⁵⁄₁₆", 3½ oz., cocktail (amber)	40.00			Tumbler, 4", 8 oz.	30.00	50.00
	Goblet, 4", 3 oz. wine	35.00	45.00		Tumbler, 5", 12 oz.	40.00	50.00
	Goblet, 6", 8 oz. water	40.00	45.00		Vase, 7", 4 styles	85.00	100.00
	Ice bucket, 6"	50.00	60.00		Vase, 9", round		225.00
	Lamp, 1¾", w/metal pole 9½"		60.00		Whiskey, 2¼", 2 oz.	45.00	

  * Amber — Double the price of pink unless noted
  ** Amber $250.00
  *** Amber $300.00

Please refer to Foreword for pricing information

AMERICAN SWEETHEART MacBETH-EVANS GLASS COMPANY, 1930–1936

Colors: Pink, Monax, red, blue; some Cremax and color trimmed Monax.

The photograph of red American Sweetheart below was initially set up to be the cover of the eleventh edition of *The Collectors Encyclopedia of Depression Glass*; but there was a problem with picture proportions fitting the cover. I hope you enjoy seeing it here. This set-up was created by Pat Spencer. The red was emphasized with Heisey stems and candlesticks.

Observe the red sherbet shown on the left. This sherbet was made from a similarly shaped mould, but does not carry American Sweetheart design. As with the pink pitchers discussed on page 14, these are **not** considered to be American Sweetheart, only **shaped** like American Sweetheart. You will also find 8" plates and 6" cereal bowls without the design in both red and blue. Several years ago, I saw a plain red 18" console bowl in a Columbus, Ohio, antique show. That bowl was water stained and too highly priced for a bowl with that much damage. Perhaps you could find a blue one.

Red and blue American Sweetheart sets were originally sold in fifteen piece groups consisting of four each cups, saucers, and 8" plates with a creamer, sugar, and 12" salver. Additional pieces in these colors were **very limited** in distribution. Observe the latest price increases on the larger pieces in these colors. The few items that have been marketed in recent months have had huge prices on them and some have been **sold** at the prices listed on page 12.

Blue American Sweetheart continues to captivate more collectors than red. More people appear to prefer blue glass to red; and the abundance of red found in comparison to blue irritates most collectors searching for it, today. Over the years, blue has remained the truly desired color in all Depression Glass patterns claiming a blue color. Bargains can still be found. I recently bought a 15½" salver labeled "Cambridge" from an antique mall (priced $115.00 firm) which was really American Sweetheart.

If you are a new collector trying to learn terminology, take note that Cremax is a beige-like color when compared to Monax which is a white made by MacBeth-Evans. The Monax with the grayish-blue edge pictured on the bottom of page 12 is called "Smoke" by collectors. Much of Monax American Sweetheart has a bluish cast to its edges. To be the rarely found "Smoke" color however, it will always have a black trim at the edge. I received a letter last spring from the lady who had bought a set of Smoke from me in the late 1970's. Those of you with some of my earlier editions have seen that set photographed. She was selling her glass and the "Smoke" set was already consigned to be auctioned. The only "Smoke" 9" round berry that I have ever seen was a part of that set. Unfortunately, it was cracked from being overheated in the back window of a car.

I have tried to show a variety of other color-trimmed and decorated pieces of Monax (page 13) rather than plain Monax. You will sometimes find pieces trimmed in pink, green, yellow, black, or 22K gold. Gold was often used as a glass "trim" at the time. Unfortunately, there is no premium for gold trim; in fact, many dealers have difficulty selling it because it is hard to find a full set with gold that is not worn. The gold (only) can be removed by using a pencil eraser on it. Don't use a scouring pad since you will damage the glass! I only point this out because badly worn gold trimmed items will not sell, but plain Monax will.

The 8" Monax plate with the "Indian Park, Mohawk Trail" advertisement is the only one I have owned, but I have heard of other ads on these plates. If you have such an advertising plate, please let me know what it advertises.

	Red	Blue	Cremax	Smoke & Other Trims
Bowl, 6" cereal			10.00	37.50
Bowl, 9" round berry			35.00	150.00
Bowl, 9½" soup				100.00
Bowl, 18" console	850.00	1,000.00		
Creamer, ftd.	100.00	115.00		85.00
Cup	75.00	105.00		75.00
Lamp shade			450.00	
Lamp (floor with brass base)			695.00	
Plate, 6" bread and butter				18.00
Plate, 8" salad	65.00	75.00		27.50
Plate, 9" luncheon				37.50
Plate, 9¾" dinner				70.00
Plate, 12" salver	130.00	185.00		90.00
Plate, 15½" server	300.00	375.00		
Platter, 13" oval				175.00
Saucer	20.00	25.00		15.00
Sherbet, 4¼" ftd. (design inside or outside)				70.00
Sugar, open ftd.	100.00	115.00		85.00
Tid-bit, 2 tier, 8" & 12"	195.00	245.00		
Tid-bit, 3 tier, 8", 12" & 15½"	575.00	650.00		

Please refer to Foreword for pricing information

AMERICAN SWEETHEART (Cont.)

American Sweetheart pink and Monax prices are increasing, but not as fast as they were two years ago. Pink shakers, pitchers, flat and cream soup bowls, and serving pieces have had major price adjustments. For the neophyte collector, a cream soup is a two-handled bowl that was used for consommé or creamed soups. A pink cream soup can be seen in the center of the bottom picture. Soups were not sold in basic sets which means that today, there are fewer of these found. At least there is no sugar lid in pink to find; so collectors of pink get off easier in that respect.

Pink pitchers appear in two sizes and tumblers in three. Many collectors buy only the water tumbler since the juice and iced tea tumblers are more difficult to find. The smaller pitcher, shown at the bottom of page 15, is not as abundant as its larger counterpart; however, not all collectors try to find both pitchers. That keeps the smaller pitcher more reasonably priced for the quantity of these found. Please remember that there are pitchers **shaped** like American Sweetheart that do not have the moulded design of American Sweetheart. You can see one of these in the top (right) photograph on page 15. It is **not** American Sweetheart (or Dogwood, which has to have the silk screened Dogwood design), but is the blank made by MacBeth-Evans to go with the plain, no design tumblers they made. The **design has to be moulded** into the pitcher for it to truly be American Sweetheart. These plain pitchers sell in the $30.00–35.00 range and plain tumblers $6.00–8.00 each.

There are many reasons for price increases; one is desirability, a major asset for this pattern. Beginning collectors are impressed with the numerous colors and the fact that American Sweetheart has not been reproduced. There is also an abundant supply of Monax (white color) in basic pieces such as cups, saucers, plates, sugar and creamers that can still be found at reasonable prices. Monax plates were widely distributed, and can be found in almost all parts of the country making them an excellent starting point for new collectors. Rare pieces of Monax and pink offer a definite challenge to collectors who have already bought all the basics.

Harder to find Monax items are experiencing price hikes! Most notable advances include sugar lids, cream soups, flat soups, and shakers. Sugar lids have doubled in price in two years after staying nearly the same for ten years! This happens on occasion to rarely found pieces. Collectors avoid buying the higher priced pieces for years; and suddenly, everyone collecting the pattern decides now is the time to splurge. The only problem with that is that there are not enough pieces to go around; so prices rise because of the demand. A couple of collectors, needing one or two pieces to complete a set, decide to pay "whatever it takes." Some dealer is willing to raise the price to the "whatever it takes" level. Word gets out that a piece sold for "X" dollars, and the next piece is priced the same or higher. The price is now established at the next level!

Shakers have just begun to be scarce for those same reasons, but their price rise seems to be slower. Remember the early days when $15.00 for a pair of **rare** Depression shakers seemed like a fortune? Now, $100.00 to $200.00 seems a fair price for many hard to find shakers.

Sets of pink or Monax can still be collected with patience. Tid-bit sets, consisting of two or three plates drilled with center holes and joined with a metal handle, can be spotted in both colors. The origin of many of these sets has been questioned over the years. A few may have been made at the factory, but others were put together by someone in the St. Louis area in the early 1970's. If you wish to buy a tid-bit, just remember that it is almost impossible to tell newly made from old. Because of this, I do not list prices for tid-bits unless they are made up of hard to find plate sizes. Most original tid-bits sell in the $50.00 range for two tiers and $75.00 for three.

Sherbets came in two sizes. Although the sherbet on the right in the top picture looks much larger than the one on the left, there is only ½" difference in diameter. The smaller, 3¾", is more difficult to find than the larger; but many collectors seek only one size, making price parity closer than rarity indicates. Rarity does not always set price. Demand does! A rarely found item that no one wants will remain reasonably priced because no one is buying it!

	Pink	Monax		Pink	Monax
Bowl, 3¾" flat berry	45.00		Plate, 15½" server		210.00
Bowl, 4½" cream soup	75.00	105.00	Platter, 13" oval	50.00	65.00
Bowl, 6" cereal	15.00	13.50	Pitcher, 7½", 60 oz.	675.00	
Bowl, 9" round berry	45.00	60.00	Pitcher, 8", 80 oz.	575.00	
Bowl, 9½" flat soup	60.00	75.00	Salt and pepper, ftd.	450.00	325.00
Bowl, 11" oval vegetable	60.00	75.00	Saucer	4.00	2.50
Bowl, 18" console		395.00	Sherbet, 3¾" ftd.	20.00	
Creamer, ftd.	13.00	10.00	Sherbet, 4¼" ftd.		
Cup	17.50	10.00	(design inside or outside)	16.00	18.00
Lamp shade		450.00	Sherbet in metal holder		
Plate, 6" or 6½" bread & butter	5.00	4.00	(crystal only)	3.50	
Plate, 8" salad	11.00	8.00	Sugar, open, ftd.	12.00	8.00
Plate, 9" luncheon		11.00	* Sugar lid		300.00
Plate, 9¾" dinner	37.50	25.00	Tid-bit, 2 tier, 8" & 12"	55.00	55.00
Plate, 10¼" dinner		25.00	Tid-bit, 3 tier, 8", 12" & 15½"		275.00
Plate, 11" chop plate		15.00	Tumbler, 3½", 5 oz.	85.00	
Plate, 12" salver	20.00	17.50	Tumbler, 4¼", 9 oz.	75.00	
			Tumbler, 4¾", 10 oz.	100.00	

*Two style knobs.

Please refer to Foreword for pricing information

AUNT POLLY U.S. GLASS COMPANY, Late 1920's

Colors: Blue, green, and iridescent.

With Aunt Polly pattern displayed on shelves, you should be able to match all pieces pictured with those in the price list. For some reason, the two-handled candy on the far right of row 2 has been omitted from my listings in the past. Desirability of Aunt Polly is influenced by its lack of cups or saucers. Prices would ascend if any were ever found. That same dilemma exists for other U.S. Glass patterns such as Strawberry, Cherryberry, and Swirl.

In the seventeen years since I discovered that U. S. Glass was the manufacturer of Aunt Polly (and her sister patterns mentioned above) not one additional piece of blue has been discovered! The covered candy is shown in green next to the sugar in row 4. This candy lid is interchangeable with the sugar lid, giving sugar and creamer collectors an extra avenue for finding lids in green and iridescent. This is an expensive candy dish but perfect lids are difficult to find today! Candy dishes have only, so far, been found in green and iridescent colors.

There are two variations of the blue creamer shown. One has a more pronounced lip than the other. These lips were formed by hand using a wooden tool; that probably accounts for these irregularities.

There is an Aunt Polly look-alike shown in two colors. The blue tumbler next to the plate and the Vaseline colored tumbler in the row 5 are moulded differently from the normally found tumblers. The paneled lines are wider and there is no design in the bottom. The ground bottoms on these items may indicate prototypes that were redesigned, because the Vaseline colored tumbler is a typical U. S. Glass color of the late 1920's. Vaseline is a collectors' name for the glowing, yellow-green shown by that tumbler. Most companies had their own name for this color, be it canary or yellow. A petroleum jelly product lent the glass this commonly mentioned name.

This pattern tends to mould imperfections such as irregular seams and pieces of extra glass. If you are obstinate about mint condition glass, I advise you to look for another pattern.

The oval vegetable, sugar lid, shakers, and butter dish have always caused problems. Finding the blue butter top or bottom creates a headache; paradoxically, butter bottoms in green or iridescent are plentiful. All the U.S. Glass butter bottoms are interchangeable. The bottom has a starred design and fits Cherryberry, Strawberry, and U. S. Swirl as well as Aunt Polly tops. That is the reason that the **butter top** prices are so much more than the bottoms in green and iridescent. There is no blue color in the other U.S. Glass patterns, however; so there were always fewer butter bottoms to be obtained in blue.

Blue is still **the** most collected color, but a few collectors of iridized and green remain. The primary difficulty in collecting green is the diversity of shades. Green is found from almost yellow in appearance to the vivid green you see in the photograph on the next page. Only recently have I noticed color variations in the blue. I bought a separate sugar lid only to find that it was much lighter in color than my sugar bowl.

	Green, Iridescent	Blue		Green, Iridescent	Blue
Bowl, 4¾" berry	8.00	17.50	Creamer	30.00	45.00
Bowl, 4¾", 2" high	15.00		Pitcher, 8" 48 oz.		165.00
Bowl, 5½" one handle	14.00	20.00	Plate, 6" sherbet	6.00	14.00
Bowl, 7¼" oval, handled pickle	15.00	40.00	Plate, 8" luncheon		20.00
Bowl, 7⅞" large berry	20.00	42.50	Salt and pepper		210.00
Bowl, 8⅜" oval	40.00	100.00	Sherbet	10.00	14.00
Butter dish and cover	225.00	210.00	Sugar	25.00	30.00
Butter dish bottom	90.00	90.00	Sugar cover	50.00	150.00
Butter dish top	135.00	120.00	Tumbler, 3⅝", 8 oz.		28.00
Candy, cover, 2-handled	65.00		Vase, 6½" ftd.	30.00	45.00
Candy, ftd., 2-handled	25.00	30.00			

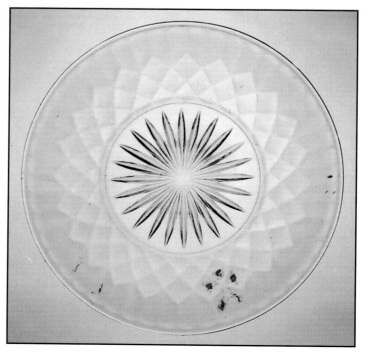

Please refer to Foreword for pricing information

"AURORA" HAZEL ATLAS GLASS COMPANY, Late 1930's

Colors: Cobalt blue, pink, green, and crystal.

For such a small pattern, "Aurora" has several pieces that could become financial drains on your budget. The little 4½" deep bowl has sailed out of sight, especially if you want six, eight, or twelve. Creamers and tumblers are also disappearing from dealer's stocks. I once said this was an economically priced blue pattern, but it has escaped those bonds.

Regardless of how many little bowls we find, not one lasts the first day of a show! Frequently, it is a dealer who buys it before the doors even open to the public. Cobalt blue magnetizes collectors in ways that no other color seems to do. Even with the price of the little bowl now being $40.00, an eight place setting would not involve borrowing against the house as some other cobalt blue sets will; so, if you like cobalt blue, here is a smaller pattern to check out!

Several readers have suggested that patterns with a tall creamer and no sugar should have the creamer listed as a milk pitcher. If you prefer calling it that, do so.

Most pieces have also been found in pink, and these command as high a price as the blue due to scarcity. You will not be able to put a large set together in pink since the small bowl, creamer, and tumbler have, so far, never been seen in that color. There are few collectors of pink, however.

Both green and crystal cereal bowls, cups and saucers have been found. Canadian readers report finding green "Aurora" cereal bowls. So far, only collectors of cup and saucers have been very excited over them. If you find any other "Aurora" pieces in these (or other) colors, please let me know.

	Cobalt, Pink		Cobalt, Pink
Bowl, 4½" deep	40.00	Plate, 6½"	12.00
* Bowl, 5⅜" cereal	15.00	*** Saucer	6.00
Creamer, 4½"	22.50	Tumbler, 4¾", 10 oz.	22.00
** Cup	15.00		

*Green $7.00 or crystal $5.00   **Green $7.50   ***Green $2.50

"AVOCADO," NO. 601 INDIANA GLASS COMPANY, 1923–1933

Colors: Pink, green, crystal, and white. *(See Reproduction Section.)*

I stated that all sixteen pieces made in "Avocado" (meaning **types** of pieces) were pictured last time. I had a letter stating that I couldn't add because there were seventeen pieces in the photo. As a former (mathematics) teacher, I guess I should have stated all sixteen pieces of **green** manufactured plus one crystal bowl!

"Avocado" remains costly, but continues to sell in large lots rather than a piece here and there. Evidently, many people who collect this pattern know that it is expensive and are willing to shell out big bucks whenever they find it! However, unless someone sells a collection, little "Avocado" is being found.

Price for the green pitcher has risen again; but prices for tumblers have been fairly steady. That may be because so few are being seen. Crystal pitchers have been found, but I have not heard of crystal tumblers. Several sets of milk glass pitcher and tumblers have surfaced. These are quickly bought by both pitcher collectors and "Avocado" collectors. These white items were a part of Indiana's experimenting with that color in the mid-1950's. You will also find a few Pyramid and Sandwich pieces in white.

Prices for crystal are not advancing as are other colors. So far, there are only a few collectors for it. The deep bowl is the piece most often seen.

Green is the predominant color collected. Green tumblers hurdled over the $200.00 mark with hardly a stumble. Reproduced green items are much darker than the original green shown here. I have preached since 1974 about the reproductions and how to tell the differences so that you will not be taken in by a fake. Any color not in the listing in this book is a Tiara reproduction. For example, if you spot any pieces in yellow, they are of **recent** vintage!

Reproduced pink items have an orange cast to the color, but this does vary. Buyers beware! Know your dealer and his reputation for knowledge and integrity. Pink prices have finally recovered from those reproduced pitchers and tumblers that were introduced in 1974; but it is doubtful they will ever catch the prices of green which is where they were when the repro bug hit!

	Crystal	Pink	Green		Crystal	Pink	Green
Bowl, 5¼" 2-handled	10.00	25.00	32.00	* Pitcher, 64 oz.	350.00	750.00	1,000.00
Bowl, 6" ftd. relish	9.00	25.00	25.00	*** Plate, 6⅜" sherbet	5.00	14.00	16.00
Bowl, 7" 1 handle preserve	8.00	20.00	25.00	** Plate, 8¼" luncheon	7.00	17.00	20.00
Bowl, 7½" salad	12.00	35.00	55.00	Plate, 10¼" 2-handled cake	14.00	35.00	55.00
Bowl, 8" 2-handled oval	11.00	22.00	27.50	Saucer, 6⅜"		22.00	24.00
Bowl, 9½", 3¼" deep	22.00	100.00	130.00	*** Sherbet		50.00	55.00
*** Creamer, ftd.	12.00	30.00	35.00	*** Sugar, ftd.	12.00	32.00	34.00
Cup, ftd., 2 styles		30.00	35.00	* Tumbler	25.00	155.00	250.00

* Caution on pink. The orange-pink is new!
* White: Pitcher $400.00; Tumbler $30.00.
** Apple design $10.00. Amber has been newly made.
*** Remade in dark shade of green.

Please refer to Foreword for pricing information

BEADED BLOCK IMPERIAL GLASS COMPANY, 1927–1930's

Colors: Pink, green, crystal, ice blue, vaseline, iridescent, amber, red, opalescent, and milk white.

Beaded Block is a pattern that collectors of other sets buy to add extra serving or display pieces to their Depression patterns. The multitude of colors of Beaded Block is matched by few other patterns in this book. It is the one Depression pattern that gets labeled by unenlightened antique dealers as "Carnival," "Vaseline," or "Pattern" glass. Imperial originally made this in the late 1920's and early 1930's. I say "originally" because Imperial had a reissue of pink and iridized pink in the late 1970's and early 1980's. These pieces are easily spotted since they are marked IG in the bottom. When I visited the factory in 1981, I was told that the white was made in the early 1950's and the IG mark (for Imperial Glass) was first used about that time. Only a few marked pieces are found, but they include the white bowl shown in the bottom photograph.

A two-part candy in the shape of a large pear is being found occasionally. I was told by a collector that it was an apple, but it looks like a pear to me. These have been found in yellow, green, and even amber. You can see a green one in the top picture. The white bowl in the bottom photo seems to be a base for a pear in case you find a top in white. I have seen these candy jars priced from $35.00 to $650.00. I do know that the green pictured here and the yellow shown in *Very Rare Glassware of the Depression Years, Fourth Series* sold for $250.00 each. A lady celebrating her fortieth birthday bought the green one.

There remain an abundance of square plates, but most of the round plates must have been transformed into bowls, which was how bowls were made in Beaded Block. The edges of plates were rolled up to make a bowl. That makes for size variances in this pattern and a major headache for collectors. Sizes listed in the Imperial catalogues vary greatly as to actual sizes found today. **The sizes listed here were all obtained from actual measurements and not from the catalogue.** These measurements were taken from a collection of twenty years. The 2-handled jelly which most companies called a cream soup measures from 4¾" to 5". Be sure to read the section on measurements at the bottom of page 4!

Several more pink Beaded Block pitchers have finally been found! Like the white pitcher, pink ones are surfacing after I mentioned they were rare in the last book. I have had reports of seven white pitchers now, but only four pink ones! Green pitchers are being found in such quantities that the price has adjusted downward again!

That supply of red lily bowls found in the central Ohio area has finally dissipated and that seems to have been the only place that they were distributed. In fact, no other red Beaded Block pieces have emerged except that 4½" lily bowl.

The 6" vases shown in cobalt and pink are not Beaded Block, but are often sold as such. They have no beading and no scalloped edge as do all the other pieces except candy bottoms. Imperial called these tall pieces "footed jellies." These were attained at groceries with a product inside. One found with the original label still attached reads "Good Taste Mustard Seed, 3½ oz., Frank Tea & Spice Co., Cin., O." I imagine the edge had to be smooth to take a lid. Obviously these zipper-like designs were a part of some other Imperial line. Remember, these are "go-with" pieces and not truly Beaded Block.

Collecting a set of Beaded Block in a specific color is a venture. That is why most collectors buy all colors.

	*Crystal, Pink, Green, Amber	Other Colors
Bowl, 4⅞"-5" 2-handled jelly	7.50	16.00
** Bowl, 4½" round lily	9.50	19.00
Bowl, 5½" square	7.50	11.00
Bowl, 5½" 1 handle	7.50	12.00
Bowl, 6" deep round	11.00	19.00
Bowl, 6¼" round	8.00	16.50
Bowl, 6½" round	8.00	16.50
Bowl, 6½" 2-handled pickle	13.00	19.00
Bowl, 6¾" round, unflared	11.50	17.00
Bowl, 7¼" round, flared	11.50	18.00
Bowl, 7½" round, fluted edges	21.00	25.00
Bowl, 7½" round, plain edge	18.50	23.00
Bowl, 8¼" celery	13.00	18.50
Creamer	16.00	27.50
*** Pitcher, 5¼", pint jug	80.00	
Plate, 7¾" square	7.00	10.00
Plate, 8¾" round	18.00	25.00
Stemmed jelly, 4½"	9.50	18.00
Stemmed jelly, 4½", flared top	11.00	19.00
Sugar	14.50	25.00
Vase, 6" bouquet	12.00	24.00

* All pieces 25% to 40% lower.
** Red $125.00
*** White $175.00, pink $160.00

BLOCK OPTIC, "BLOCK" HOCKING GLASS COMPANY, 1929–1933

Colors: Green, pink, yellow, crystal, and some amber and blue.

The eleventh edition listed a newly discovered Block Optic 2" tall, 11¾" diameter, amber, rolled-edge console bowl that was found with matching candlesticks. I figured it was only a matter of time until some would show up in pink or green. They did, and you can see a green one in the bottom photograph on page 23. You will have to wait for the pink one since I bought it at an antique mall in Henderson, KY. Years go by without new pieces being found in a pattern, and all of a sudden one turns up in a pattern that major collectors thought they'd acquired every piece known. Now, these same collectors (who thought they had completed sets) are searching for a console bowl, grill plates, and 3½" short wines. That short wine was finally found in green, but you will have to check the *Very Rare Glassware of the Depression Years, Fourth Series* to see it. (Note that the true grill plate in the bottom picture has the same rings and designed center as does the dinner plate.)

New collectors were asking about the 5¾" blown vase that has not been pictured since an early book. It took years to corral another one, but you can see it at the bottom of page 24. This blown vase is shaped like the Cameo one.

The 4¼" diameter bowl with a height of 1½" is the one shown in the center of the bottom photograph on page 23. This bowl is difficult to find and appears to be made thicker than most Block Optic. The 7" salad bowl has taken a big jump in price! The price listing is not a mistake! Several have sold at the price listed; but some collectors are vowing to do without.

Block Optic has been the pattern of choice for many new collectors of Depression Glass since it was widely distributed and a piece or two seems to have remained in everyone's family. When beginners used to ask me to recommend a starting pattern, I would mention Block Optic because it was economically priced and a novice could find it and afford it. Today, the price is no longer as economical as it once was! Of course, groceries and cars are not either! As far as collectability goes, Block remains high on the list of collector demand. There is yet an abundant supply of almost all basic pieces; and infrequently found items are not completely "sky high" as has happened with some green Depression patterns.

Be aware that there are at least five styles of cups and that there are **four different shapes of creamer and sugars.** Several exacting collectors state that there are even more varieties than these. Let me know what you find!

There are variations in handles and slight differences in style to make **a total of five different styles of creamers and sugars** that can be collected in Block Optic. There are four basic **shapes** but five **styles.** In yellow, only the fancy handled, rounded type has been found. There are three styles of pink creamer/sugar sets, flat bottomed and two styles of cone shaped pairs. One of the cone shaped styles has a base that is plain whereas the other type has a rayed base. (This is true of many of Hocking's patterns. Some tumblers or stems also show variations of plain and ribbed bases.) In green creamers/sugars, there are two cone shaped styles with one of these having pointed handles, the flat bottomed variety, and the rounded style with plain handles evidenced by the frosted pair in the bottom photo. I have never seen a green fancy handled set. Let me know if you have such a pair!

Regarding the frosted green cup, saucer, creamer, and sugar shown in the bottom picture, Hocking, as well as other companies, satinized (frosted by using camphoric acid) many of their dinnerware lines. Evidently, these were special orders or special promotions since many were hand decorated with flowers or fruit. For years, many collectors shied away from these pieces for some reason; but lately, I've begun to notice more collectors buying satinized wares. Frosted items still command only a fraction of the price of their unfrosted counterparts. Even though these pieces are more scarce, lack of demand has lessened the price. That is one of the lessons beginners need to learn as soon as possible about collectibles. Rarity does not always determine price! Demand is the determining factor of price!

Note the Deco decorated pink candy on the bottom of page 25. I have seen more than one of these in my travels; thus, these candies may also have been a special order or promotional item at one time. No more pink 3½" short wines have surfaced; and many of the stems in this pattern have encountered large price increases in the last few years. New collectors and the dearth of stems available have contributed to this. Be aware that many pink stems are very light in color and do not match the normally found pink ones very well. Not only are stems scarce, but when have you seen any serving pieces in pink?

There is enough crystal Block Optic being found that you could put a basic set together if you were inclined to do so. You will have to tell dealers you are searching for crystal as many do not normally stock that at shows. Presently only the butter dish has a premium value. Other crystal pieces sell for a little less than prices of green.

A tumble-up set has been found that explains how they were marketed. A stopper in a bottle was marked "Bareé Fragrant Bath Salts Paris, New York." (That is how the decanter in Mayfair was also sold years ago. It, too, contained bath salts and the stopper was used as a measuring device.) That stopper and the tumblers for the tumble-up are scarce today. Slippery hands and bath tubs are extremely dangerous to glass items!

Some green Block is found with a black foot or stem. As far as I can determine, that black is fired-on and cannot be removed! These used to be ignored. Recently, we've had two different requests from collectors searching for these black trimmed items.

A reader in California sent some interesting information about the green butter dish top. In the twenty years I have been buying Depression Glass, I have seen 15 to 20 green Block butter tops for every bottom. I had assumed that the heavy top had destroyed many of the bottoms since it is somewhat difficult to grasp. However, it seems that the tops were also sold as a butter holder for ice boxes. This top slid into a metal holder eliminating the need for a glass bottom!

BLOCK OPTIC, "BLOCK" (Cont.)

	Green	Yellow	Pink
Bowl, 4¼" diam., 1⅜" tall	8.00		10.00
Bowl, 4½" diam., 1½" tall	27.50		
Bowl, 5¼" cereal	14.00		25.00
Bowl, 7¼" salad	150.00		
Bowl, 8½" large berry	25.00		30.00
* Bowl, 11¾" rolled-edge console	60.00		60.00
** Butter dish and cover, 3" x 5"	47.50		
Butter dish bottom	27.50		
Butter dish top	20.00		
*** Candlesticks, 1¾" pr.	100.00		75.00
Candy jar & cover, 2¼" tall	50.00	60.00	50.00
Candy jar & cover, 6¼" tall	55.00		125.00
Comport, 4" wide mayonnaise	30.00		65.00
Creamer, 3 styles: cone shaped, round, rayed-foot & flat (5 kinds)	13.00	13.00	13.00
Cup, four styles	7.00	8.00	7.00
Goblet, 3½" short wine	400.00		400.00
Goblet, 4" cocktail	35.00		35.00
Goblet, 4½" wine	35.00		35.00
Goblet, 5¾", 9 oz.	22.50		30.00
Goblet, 7¼", 9 oz. thin		35.00	
Ice bucket	40.00		45.00
Ice tub or butter tub, open	45.00		90.00
Mug	32.50		
Pitcher, 7⅝", 54 oz., bulbous	70.00		70.00
Pitcher, 8½", 54 oz.	40.00		40.00
Pitcher, 8", 80 oz.	75.00		75.00
Plate, 6" sherbet	3.00	3.00	3.00
Plate, 8" luncheon	5.00	5.00	5.00
Plate, 9" dinner	22.00	40.00	33.00
Plate, 9" grill	25.00	40.00	25.00
Plate, 10¼" sandwich	25.00		25.00
Salt and pepper, ftd.	35.00	75.00	75.00
Salt and pepper, squatty	90.00		
Sandwich server, center handle	65.00		50.00
Saucer, 5¾", with cup ring	10.00		8.00
Saucer, 6⅛", with cup ring	10.00		8.00
Sherbet, non-stemmed (cone)	4.00		
Sherbet, 3¼", 5½ oz.	6.00	9.00	7.50
Sherbet, 4¾", 6 oz.	15.00	15.00	15.00
Sugar, 3 styles: as creamer	12.50	12.50	12.50
Tumbler, 2⅝", 3 oz.	20.00		22.50
Tumbler, 3½", 5 oz. flat	20.00		22.50

	Green	Yellow	Pink
Tumbler, 9½ oz. flat, 3¹³⁄₁₆" flat	15.00		15.00
Tumbler, 10 or 11 oz., 5" flat	20.00		15.00
Tumbler, 12 oz., 4⅞" flat	25.00		25.00
Tumbler, 15 oz., flat, 5¼",	40.00		35.00
Tumbler, 3¼", 3 oz. ftd.	25.00		25.00
Tumbler, 9 oz. ftd.	18.00	22.00	15.00
Tumbler, 6", 10 oz. ftd.	30.00		30.00
Tumble-up night set	62.50		
Tumbler, 3" only	50.00		
Bottle only	12.50		
Vase, 5¾" blown	275.00		
Whiskey, 1⅝", 1 oz.	35.00		40.00
Whiskey, 2¼", 2 oz.	27.50		27.50

* Amber $50.00
** Green clambroth $195.00, blue $450.00, crystal $100.00
*** Amber $100.00

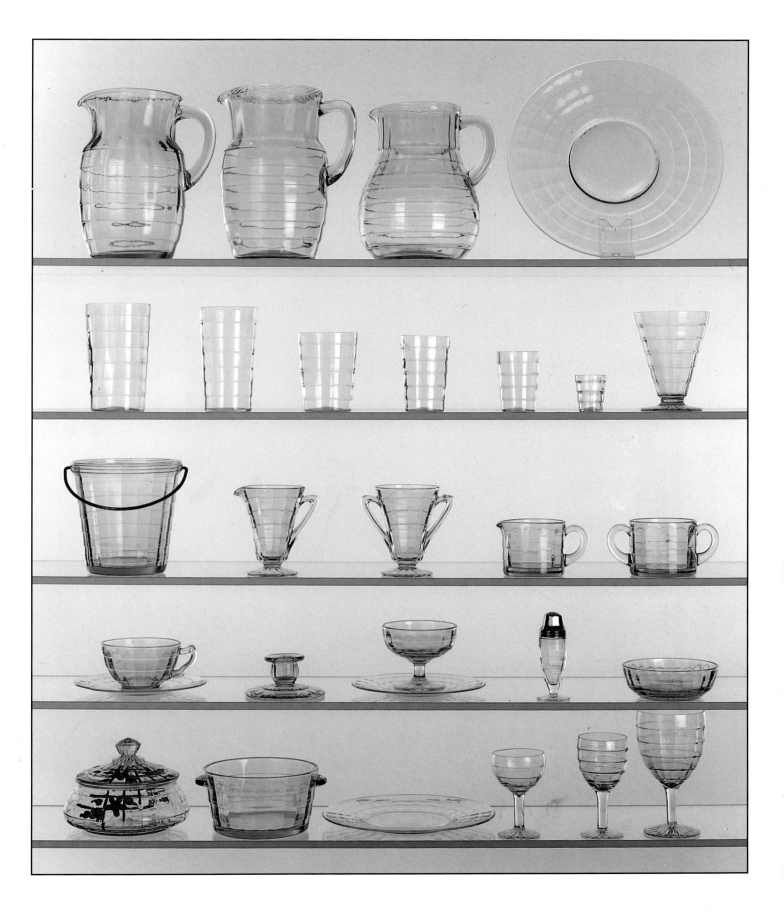

"BOWKNOT" MANUFACTURER UNKNOWN, Probably late 1920's

Color: Green.

The seven pieces in this little pattern called "Bowknot" have attracted the interest of some current collectors and that has caused scme price hikes on items already scarce. "Bowknot" remains a mystery pattern as to its manufacturer and the exact dates it was made. One of the significant things to look for in "Bowknot" is inner rim roughness on bowls and sherbets. Add to that a cup with no saucer and two different style tumblers with no pitcher and you have a real Columbo-type mystery. That cup has driven collectors mad for years trying to discover why there is only a cup with no other piece to accompany it.

You can see the cereal bowl, which I had a devil of a time finding without damage! The price has vaulted on perfect pieces. Many dealers who set up at glass shows do not carry some of the smaller patterns such as "Bowknot." I find "Bowknot" pieces among the first to depart from my booth.

I still receive letters from amateur collectors who feel that they have found the first "Bowknot" creamer and sugar. Fostoria patterns "June" and "Romance" have a bow; but neither of these patterns were made in green. If you find a **green** "Bowknot" creamer or sugar or any green piece not listed in this pattern, give me a call or send a picture!

	Green		Green
Bowl, 4½" berry	16.00	Sherbet, low ftd.	16.00
Bowl, 5½" cereal	20.00	Tumbler, 5", 10 oz.	20.00
Cup	8.00	Tumbler, 5", 10 oz. ftd.	20.00
Plate, 7" salad	12.00		

Please refer to Foreword for pricing information

CAMEO, "BALLERINA," or "DANCING GIRL" HOCKING GLASS COMPANY, 1930–1934

Colors: Green, yellow, pink, and crystal w/platinum rim. (*See Reproduction Section.*)

Cameo, as we know it, was made by the Hocking Glass Company in the early 1930's; but apparently the pattern originated from a Monongah Glass Company design called "Springtime." This company was bought by Hocking and many of their patterns were changed or continued by Hocking. To see the Springtime pattern as it existed before being machine-made, I have shown a crystal cocktail on the bottom of this page beside the rarely seen sandwich server. Monongah's glass was plate etched and is of exceptional quality when compared to our Cameo. Many Depression Glass collectors are glad that little ballerina continued to dance on Hocking's wares for several years!

Yellow Cameo is shown at the top of page 29. Many yellow items are quite difficult to obtain including the butter dish and milk pitcher. Yellow Cameo cups, saucer/sherbet plates, footed tumblers, grill, and dinner plates were heavily promoted by Hocking. These five pieces are still bountiful today. In fact, until recently, they were difficult to sell. Prices on commonly found yellow pieces have begun to rise, albeit, slowly. It's a particularly attractive yellow pattern; so if you like it, now may be the time to acquire a basic set!

I receive numerous letters and calls about Cameo saucers each year. Now that I have put the measurements in for green, I am getting calls on yellow. The yellow saucers (which have never been seen) would have the **same center measurement** as the green ones! The real Cameo saucer has an indented cup ring. Hocking made very few of these indented saucers. They ordinarily made a dual purpose saucer/sherbet plate for their patterns. If you will look on the bottom of page 31, the difference can be seen in front. The saucer on the right has a **distinct** indented ring (1¾" center) while the saucer/sherbet plate (2¾" center) on the left does not (although the cup may hide that fact). That footed oil lamp base with a threaded top (below the photograph of yellow) is the only one that has ever surfaced.

You should also note the color variations in the cups as well as the handle styles in that picture. The cups on the left have plain handles (abbreviated "ph" in glass ads) and the cup on the right has a fancy handle (abbreviated "fh" in glass ads).

Green Cameo continues as one of the most desirable Depression Glass patterns. There is an adequate supply of easily found items, enough to obtain a basic set. Many collectors can not afford every piece made. They do not try to find all stems and every tumbler; instead they purchase only one or two sizes of tumblers and stems.

Enjoy the photograph of pink Cameo on page 30. Pink is rarely seen. It is also costly as you can tell by perusing the prices. New collectors should be forewarned of prices and difficulty in obtaining pink. Pink shakers have been reproduced. See the reproduction section in the back of the book.

Cameo has two styles of grill plates. (A grill plate is a sectioned or divided plate that keeps the food separated. They were used mostly in restaurants and "grills" of that day.) Both styles are shown on the top of page 29 and the bottom of page 30. One has tab handles and one does not. Both styles are common in yellow. In green, however, the grill with the tab or closed handles is harder to find. The 10½" rare, rimmed dinner or flat cake plate is just like the heavy edged grill plate only without the dividers! The regular dinner plate has a large center as opposed to the small centered sandwich plate. The less expensive sandwich plate is often priced as the more expensive dinner plate, so be sure to avoid buying into that trap.

The darker green bottles with Cameo design are marked underneath "Whitehouse Vinegar." These originally came from the grocery with vinegar — and a cork. Glass stoppers are found atop water bottles. These stoppers do not have a Cameo pattern on them, but are plain paneled.

All the **miniature** pieces in Cameo are **new**! No smaller Cameo (or children's dishes) was ever made during the Depression era. See the Reproduction Section in the back of the book for information on this. A new importer is making a sometimes weakly patterned shaker in pink, cobalt blue, and a darker shade of green than the original color. If new tops are the first thing you notice — beware!

27

CAMEO, "BALLERINA," or "DANCING GIRL" (Cont.)

	Green	Yellow	Pink	Crystal, Plat		Green	Yellow	Pink	Crystal, Plat
Bowl, 4¼" sauce				5.50	Jam jar, 2" and cover	160.00			160.00
Bowl, 4¾" cream soup	115.00				Pitcher, 5¾", 20 oz.				
Bowl, 5½" cereal	30.00	30.00	150.00	6.50	syrup or milk	210.00	2,000.00		
Bowl, 7¼" salad	55.00				Pitcher, 6", 36 oz. juice	57.50			
Bowl, 8¼" large berry	35.00		150.00		Pitcher, 8½", 56 oz. water	50.00		1,500.00	500.00
Bowl, 9" rimmed soup	55.00		100.00		Plate, 6" sherbet	4.00	3.00	90.00	2.00
Bowl, 10" oval vegetable	30.00	40.00			Plate, 7" salad				3.50
Bowl, 11", 3-legged					Plate, 8" luncheon	10.00	11.00	33.00	4.00
console	70.00	90.00	50.00		Plate, 8½" square	40.00	250.00		
Butter dish and cover	200.00	1,500.00			Plate, 9½" dinner	18.00	9.00	75.00	
Butter dish bottom	120.00	500.00			Plate, 10" sandwich	13.00		40.00	
Butter dish top	80.00	1,000.00			** Plate, 10½" rimmed dinner	90.00		150.00	
Cake plate, 10", 3 legs	20.00				Plate, 10½" grill	8.00	6.00	50.00	
Cake plate, 10½" flat	90.00		150.00		Plate, 10½" grill				
Candlesticks, 4" pr.	95.00				with closed handles	65.00	6.00		
Candy jar, 4" low					Plate, 10½" with closed				
and cover	70.00	75.00	475.00		handles	12.00	12.00		
Candy jar, 6½" tall					Platter, 12", closed handles	20.00	40.00		
and cover	150.00				Relish, 7½" ftd., 3 part	30.00			150.00
Cocktail shaker (metal					* Salt and pepper, ftd. pr.	67.50		775.00	
lid) appears in crystal only				500.00	Sandwich server,				
Comport, 5" wide					center handle	4,950.00			
mayonnaise	30.00		195.00		Saucer with cup ring	175.00			
Cookie jar and cover	50.00				Saucer, 6" (sherbet plate)	4.00	3.00	90.00	
Creamer, 3¼"	22.00	20.00			Sherbet, 3⅛" molded	13.00	40.00	75.00	
Creamer, 4¼"	27.50		110.00		Sherbet, 3⅛" blown	15.00		75.00	
Cup, 2 styles	14.00	7.50	75.00	5.50	Sherbet, 4⅞"	34.00	42.50	100.00	
Decanter, 10"					Sugar, 3¼"	20.00	18.00		
with stopper	145.00			195.00	Sugar, 4¼"	25.00		110.00	
Decanter, 10"					Tumbler, 3¾", 5 oz. juice	27.50		90.00	
with stopper, frosted					Tumbler, 4", 9 oz. water	25.00		80.00	9.00
(stopper represents ⅓					Tumbler, 4¾", 10 oz. flat	27.50		95.00	
value of decanter)	32.00				Tumbler, 5", 11 oz. flat	27.50	47.50	90.00	
Domino tray, 7"					Tumbler, 5¼", 15 oz.	65.00		125.00	
with 3" indentation	130.00				Tumbler, 3 oz. ftd. juice	57.50		125.00	
Domino tray, 7"					Tumbler, 5", 9 oz. ftd.	25.00	16.00	110.00	
with no indentation			250.00	120.00	Tumbler, 5¾", 11 oz. ftd.	60.00		125.00	
Goblet, 3½" wine	750.00		800.00		Tumbler, 6⅜", 15 oz. ftd.	450.00			
Goblet, 4" wine	62.00		200.00		Vase, 5¾"	185.00			
Goblet, 6" water	47.00		160.00		Vase, 8"	35.00			
Ice bowl or open butter,					Water bottle (dark green)				
3" tall x 5½" wide	155.00		650.00	250.00	Whitehouse vinegar	17.50			

* Beware Reproductions
** Same as flat cake plate

Please refer to Foreword for pricing information

CHERRYBERRY U.S. GLASS COMPANY, Early 1930's

Colors: Pink, green, crystal; some iridized.

Gathering Cherryberry began with collectors searching for Strawberry. Scant notice of this pattern existed, except for those who were buying Strawberry and were invariably running into cherries instead of strawberries. Now, Cherryberry has become a significant Depression Glass pattern with a few Carnival Glass devotees invading our ranks to latch on to the iridescent pitchers, tumblers, and butter dishes, the most prized iridized pieces. Not only do collectors of Cherryberry and Carnival Glass appreciate these, but collectors of butters and pitchers pursue them, also.

Crystal is much rarer than pink or green; yet, there are few collectors buying it.

The color vicissitudes of green in the photograph are not caused by the printing or photography. This is another problem in Cherryberry. The green can be found from a very yellow hue to a blue one. There is not as much color variance with the pink, but there is some.

This is another of the U.S. Glass patterns that has no cup or saucer and has a plain butter base. If all these U.S. Glass patterns are "sister" patterns, then Strawberry and Cherryberry are twins. You can only tell them apart by careful scrutiny of the fruits.

	Crystal, Iridescent	Pink, Green		Crystal, Iridescent	Pink, Green
Bowl, 4" berry	6.50	8.50	Olive dish, 5" one-handled	9.00	15.00
Bowl, 6¼", 2" deep	37.50	50.00	Pickle dish, 8¼" oval	9.00	15.00
Bowl, 6½" deep salad	16.00	20.00	Pitcher, 7¾"	160.00	165.00
Bowl, 7½" deep berry	17.00	20.00	Plate, 6" sherbet	6.00	9.00
Butter dish and cover	145.00	165.00	Plate, 7½" salad	8.00	14.00
Butter dish bottom	77.50	90.00	Sherbet	6.50	9.00
Butter dish top	67.50	75.00	Sugar, small open	12.00	17.00
Comport, 5¾"	16.00	24.00	Sugar, large	15.00	25.00
Creamer, small	12.00	17.00	Sugar cover	30.00	55.00
Creamer, 4⅝" large	15.00	37.50	Tumbler, 3⅝", 9 oz.	20.00	33.00

CHERRY BLOSSOM JEANNETTE GLASS COMPANY, 1930–1939

Colors: Pink, green, Delphite (opaque blue), crystal, Jadite (opaque green), and red. *(See Reproduction Section.)*

Not long ago dealers were refusing to acquire Cherry Blossom since you couldn't sell it at any price due to the abundance of reproductions. What a contrast today! Time and education about the differences in old and new have made collecting Cherry Blossom a viable option again. Most pieces have increased in price since the last book, but nothing compares with the price increase on the two-handled bowl!

Prices have inflated to ante-repro days except for the pink shakers which still have a long way to go. The problem with shakers is not only the large number of reproductions made, but that many collectors are willing to purchase these imitations in order to have a pair of shakers for their sets. I continue to get many calls and letters on pink Cherry shakers. The stories I've heard told at auctions and estate sales boggles the mind. Why would anyone offer you something worth $1,000.00 for only a few hundred…or less? Very few pairs of original pink shakers were ever found; so the likelihood of your finding another old pair is fairly remote, particularly at a bargain price. I've learned never to say "never," however. People **are** still discovering unusual Depression Glass even at this late date!

The 9" platter is the hardest piece to find after the shakers. I have only seen one green one! Measure this platter outside edge to outside edge. The 11" platter measures only 9" on the inside rims.

Be sure to check all inner rims of Cherry Blossom since there is a proclivity for them to have chips and nicks. This was caused as much from stacking as from utilization. You can safely stack dishes with proper sized paper plates between them. This is especially true at glass shows where stacks of plates are often handled over and over.

Pieces of Cherry Blossom that are harder to acquire include the aforementioned 9" platter, mugs, soup and cereal bowls, and the 10" green grill plate. The three-footed bowl and flat iced teas have also joined that list.

Crystal Cherry Blossom appears at times. Normally, it is the two-handled bowl that sells in the $15.00 range. It is scarce, but there is not enough crystal found to be collectible as a set. A few red pieces have been found, but the reproduction red wiped out collectors' desire for these.

The letters AOP in listings and advertisements stand for "all over pattern" on the footed tumblers and rounded pitcher. The footed large tumblers and the AOP pitcher come in two styles. One style has a scalloped or indented foot while the other is merely round with no indentations. PAT stands for "pattern at the top" illustrated by the flat bottomed tumblers and pitchers.

There are some known experimental pieces of Cherry such as a pink cookie jar, some pink five-part relish dishes, orange with green trim slag bowls, and amber children's pieces. Pricing on experimental items is difficult to determine; but keep your eye out for any of these pieces, and don't pass them up if the price is right — for you! There is always some market demand for rare items of Depression Glassware.

CHERRY BLOSSOM JEANNETTE GLASS COMPANY, 1930–1939 (Cont.)

	Pink	Green	Delphite
Bowl, 4¾" berry	15.00	17.50	14.00
Bowl, 5¾" cereal	35.00	37.50	
Bowl, 7¾" flat soup	60.00	55.00	
* Bowl, 8½" round berry	45.00	45.00	50.00
Bowl, 9" oval vegetable	37.50	37.50	45.00
Bowl, 9" 2-handled	45.00	65.00	25.00
** Bowl, 10½", 3 leg fruit	80.00	80.00	
Butter dish and cover	72.50	82.50	
Butter dish bottom	15.00	22.50	
Butter dish top	57.50	60.00	
Cake plate (3 legs) 10¼"	27.50	27.50	
Coaster	14.00	13.00	
Creamer	18.00	18.00	18.00
Cup	18.00	19.00	18.00
Mug, 7 oz.	250.00	175.00	
*** Pitcher, 6¾" AOP, 36 oz. scalloped or round bottom	55.00	55.00	85.00
Pitcher, 8" PAT, 42 oz. flat	52.50	52.50	
Pitcher, 8" PAT, 36 oz. footed	52.50	52.50	
Plate, 6" sherbet	8.00	8.00	10.00
Plate, 7" salad	18.00	21.00	
**** Plate, 9" dinner	22.00	23.00	20.00
***** Plate, 9" grill	25.00	25.00	

	Pink	Green	Delphite
Plate, 10" grill		85.00	
Platter, 9" oval	795.00	975.00	
Platter, 11" oval	37.50	40.00	40.00
Platter, 13" and 13" divided	65.00	65.00	
Salt and pepper (scalloped bottom)	1,250.00	975.00	
Saucer	6.00	6.00	6.00
Sherbet	16.00	18.00	15.00
Sugar	13.00	16.00	18.00
Sugar cover	17.00	18.00	
Tray, 10½" sandwich	25.00	25.00	20.00
Tumbler, 3¾", 4 oz. footed AOP	15.00	18.00	20.00
Tumbler, 4½", 9 oz. round foot AOP	32.00	33.00	20.00
Tumbler, 4½", 8 oz. scalloped foot AOP	32.00	33.00	20.00
Tumbler, 3½", 4 oz. flat PAT	20.00	30.00	
Tumbler, 4¼", 9 oz. flat PAT	18.00	22.00	
Tumbler, 5", 12 oz. flat PAT	55.00	70.00	

* Yellow – $375.00

** Jadite – $300.00

*** Jadite – $300.00

**** Translucent green – $200.00

***** Jadite – $65.00

CHERRY BLOSSOM — CHILD'S JUNIOR DINNER SET

	Pink	Delphite
Creamer	45.00	47.50
Sugar	45.00	47.50
Plate, 6"	11.00	13.00 (design on bottom)
Cup	35.00	35.00
Saucer	6.25	7.25
14 Piece set	300.00	325.00

Original box sells for $25.00 extra with pink sets.

Please refer to Foreword for pricing information

CHINEX CLASSIC MacBETH-EVANS DIVISION OF CORNING GLASS WORKS, Late 1930's–Early 1940's

Colors: Ivory, ivory w/decal decoration.

Chinex addicts are still trying to match all those different decorations. It is tough enough to find Chinex; but to find the piece you need only to have it adorned with a decal other than the one you need is frustrating. The blue and pink trimmed pieces with a red flower are not being found consistently, nor is the brown trimmed castle scene. My favorite is the blue trimmed castle decal. I have found a butter top as you can see in the bottom photo. What I do not know is whether the top has a castle decal or just a blue trim. I suspect that it will have the castle decal, since the butter top shown in the top picture has a floral design on it. Unfortunately, I have not been able to find the bottom for that one either. The floral decal on that top is like those pieces on the left of the photograph. If you have either one of these butter bottoms, let's make a deal!

More Chinex is found in the Pittsburgh area than any other part of the country. Undoubtedly, the fact that MacBeth-Evans was just down the road has a great deal to do with this. I have found most of the items shown either in that area or from dealers who shop there. This pattern grows on you. I have enjoyed finding the many pieces shown on page 37.

One collector was very disturbed with me for depicting the attractiveness of the pastel trimmed, red flower design (shown in the eleventh edition). He blamed me for the higher prices he was paying because new collectors were buying it before he could find it. He was right that more collectors did start to search and more dealers began to stock it. What he should have recognized is that the **value** of his collection was increasing with each new person buying it!

The plainer, undecorated beige pieces are still awaiting collectors' notice. Undecorated Chinex works wonderfully in the microwave according to a Midwestern collector. I must admit that I have never tried it; so remember to test it first by putting it in for a **short** time (a few seconds) and checking for hot spots just as you would any other dish not designed **specifically** for microwave usage. After removing the piece from the microwave, be sure to place it on a place mat or some surface that is not cold. A sudden temperature change may crack it.

Castle decal items are the most fascinating to collectors; darker blue is more popular than the lighter blue or brown trimmed.

Remember, butter bottoms look like Cremax instead of Chinex. The butter tops have the scroll-like design that distinguishes Chinex, but this scroll design is missing from the butter bottoms. The bottom has a plain "pie crust" edge. Also, the floral or castle designs will be inside the base of the butter, and apparently on the outside of the top, too.

	Browntone or Plain Ivory	Decal Decorated	Castle Decal
Bowl, 5¾" cereal	5.50	8.00	15.00
Bowl, 7" vegetable	14.00	25.00	35.00
Bowl, 7¾" soup	12.50	20.00	35.00
Bowl, 9" vegetable	11.00	25.00	35.00
Bowl, 11"	17.00	35.00	45.00
Butter dish	55.00	75.00	125.00
Butter dish bottom	12.50	27.50	45.00
Butter dish top	42.50	47.50	80.00
Creamer	5.50	10.00	18.00
Cup	4.50	6.50	15.00
Plate, 6¼" sherbet	2.50	3.50	7.50
Plate, 9¾" dinner	4.50	8.50	20.00
Plate, 11½" sandwich or cake	7.50	13.50	25.00
Saucer	2.50	4.50	6.50
Sherbet, low ftd.	7.00	11.00	25.00
Sugar, open	5.50	9.00	17.50

CIRCLE HOCKING GLASS COMPANY, 1930's

Colors: Green, pink, and crystal.

Green Circle sets can be assembled over time, but it will take more than luck to put a pink set together. Let me know if you have accomplished that task. For some reason, I have seen little pink in the areas where I have looked; maybe you will have better luck than I.

Circle is observed more closely by collectors of kitchenware (especially reamer collectors) than it is by Depression Glass enthusiasts. The 80 oz. Circle pitcher with a reamer top is highly desired by reamer enthusiasts. There are probably more of these reamer topped pitchers sitting in reamer collections than there are in sets of Circle. A significant dilemma with the pitcher and reamer is that color variations of these pitchers make it difficult to find a reamer that matches the green hue of the pitcher. The pitcher shown here is more yellow when contrasted with the other green pieces. (Hopefully, that yellow hue will show when the book is printed.)

Two styles of cups add to the eccentricities of Circle. The flat bottomed style fits a saucer/sherbet plate while the rounded cup takes an indented saucer. I am still looking for an indented saucer for my pink cup. I have never heard of tumblers, pitchers, or bowls in pink. I assume only a luncheon set was made, but two styles of cups makes one wonder what else might be available.

Both bowls, 9⅜" and 5¼", have ground bottoms. The 5" flared bowl is shown on the right front of the photograph. Observe how it is a distinctly darker shade of green when compared to the other pieces.

I had previously doubted the existence of a 9½" dinner plate, but I received a letter from a lady who says she has three 9½" plates. She is the only one who ever wrote. The green dinner would have a larger surface area in the center of the plate than the 10" sandwich plate pictured in the back.

You can find green colored stems with crystal tops more easily than you can find plain green stems; however, few collectors value crystal topped items at present. I, personally, like the two-toned variations better than all green.

	Green, Pink		Green, Pink
Bowl, 4½"	8.00	Plate, 6" sherbet/saucer	1.50
Bowl, 5¼"	10.00	Plate, 8¼" luncheon	4.00
Bowl, 5" flared, 1¾" deep	12.00	Plate, 9½"	12.00
Bowl, 8"	16.00	Plate, 10" sandwich	12.00
Bowl, 9⅜"	18.00	Saucer w/cup ring	2.50
Creamer	9.00	Sherbet, 3⅛"	4.00
Cup (2 styles)	5.00	Sherbet, 4¾"	6.00
Decanter, handled	45.00	Sugar	7.00
Goblet, 4½" wine	12.50	Tumbler, 3½", 4 oz. juice	8.00
Goblet, 8 oz. water	11.00	Tumbler, 4", 8 oz. water	9.00
Pitcher, 60 oz.	32.00	Tumbler, 5", 10 oz. tea	16.00
Pitcher, 80 oz.	27.50	Tumbler, 15 oz. flat	20.00

CLOVERLEAF HAZEL ATLAS GLASS COMPANY, 1930–1936

Colors: Pink, green, yellow, crystal, and black.

Arrangements of Cloverleaf collections are always well received by collectors and the public when displays are exhibited at shows. Cloverleaf is a pattern easily recognized by non collectors.

There seem to be equal numbers of collectors for yellow, black, and green. Very few are turning to pink or crystal since they are limited to a luncheon set. Only a pink flared 10 oz. tumbler exists besides the basic luncheon pieces. That pink tumbler is quite sparsely distributed and is not found in crystal at all. Crystal makes a pleasant table display with colored accoutrements.

At present all Cloverleaf colors are selling well with yellow leading the way. In yellow, the candy dish, shakers, and bowls do not seem to be available at any price. In green, the 8" bowl and tumblers are selling briskly.

Black Cloverleaf prices have slowed somewhat with the ash trays suddenly being ignored. I have noticed that this is true in many patterns. Evidently, the non-smokers are being heard for a change or the smokers are finally wising up; and it is affecting the sale of smokers' items even in the glassware business. However, one man at a show recently told me that since he read of the virtual shunning of smoking accessories in my book, he made up his mind right then he was going to start a collection of them! The black sherbet plate and saucer are the same size. The saucer has no Cloverleaf pattern in the center. These sherbet plates still turn up in stacks of saucers occasionally; so keep your eyes open!

Some black Cloverleaf pieces in the photograph on page 41 are gold decorated, probably for a special promotion. I have included these hoping the Cloverleaf pattern will show better in the picture. In my first book in 1972, we highlighted the designs with Bon Ami; but that made for unnatural white clover leaves.

Actually, Cloverleaf was to some extent limited in distribution nationally. In 1978, I bought a large collection of Cloverleaf in Ohio. It had been gathered from dealers all over the country, but major portions of the accumulation had come from Ohio and Pennsylvania. A yellow candy bottom marked "large sherbet – $2.00" became my favorite piece of this collection since the tag had been left on it when it was bought. (Someone buying my New Era plates with the "flower pot saucer" labels will get a laugh years from now — if those tags are not removed.)

I have been reminded to point out that the Cloverleaf pattern comes on both the inside and outside of the pieces. That does not seem to make a difference in value or collectability. In order for the black to show the pattern, moulds had to be designed with the pattern on the outside. On transparent pieces, the pattern could be on the bottom or the inside and it would still show. In black, the pattern on the bottom of a plate makes it look like a plain black plate; so it was moved to the top. Over the years, transparent pieces also were made using the moulds designed for the black; so, you now find these pieces with designs on both sides.

CLOVERLEAF HAZEL ATLAS GLASS COMPANY, 1930–1936 (Cont.)

	Pink	Green	Yellow	Black
Ash tray, 4", match holder in center				67.50
Ash tray, 5¾", match holder in center				77.50
Bowl, 4" dessert	14.00	20.00	25.00	
Bowl, 5" cereal		27.50	32.50	
Bowl, 7" deep salad		40.00	50.00	
Bowl, 8"		55.00		
Candy dish and cover		50.00	100.00	
Creamer, 3⅝" ftd.		10.00	17.50	18.00
Cup	7.00	8.00	10.00	18.00
Plate, 6" sherbet		5.00	7.00	37.50
Plate, 8" luncheon	7.00	8.00	14.00	15.00
Plate, 10¼" grill		20.00	22.50	
Salt and pepper, pr.		32.00	100.00	85.00
Saucer	4.00	4.00	5.00	7.00
Sherbet, 3" ftd.	6.00	7.00	11.00	20.00
Sugar, 3⅝" ftd.		10.00	17.50	18.00
Tumbler, 4", 9 oz. flat		52.50		
Tumbler, 3¾", 10 oz. flat flared	22.00	38.00		
Tumbler, 5¾", 10 oz. ftd.		22.50	32.00	

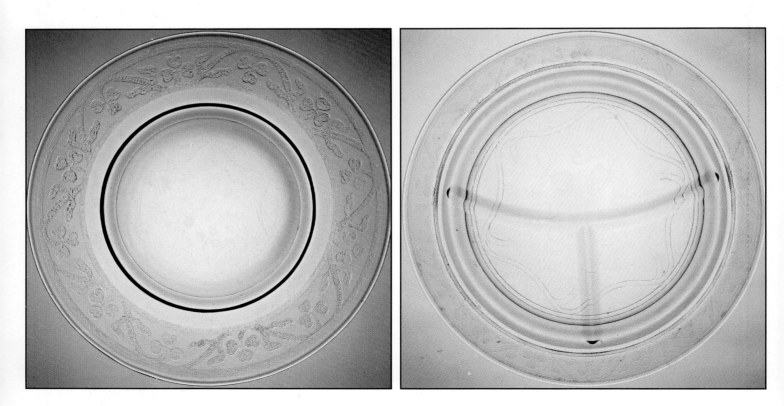

COLONIAL, "KNIFE AND FORK" HOCKING GLASS COMPANY, 1934–1936

Colors: Pink, green, crystal, and opaque white.

Green Colonial has begun to sell again! For a while collectors were turning to the pink and crystal instead of the higher priced green. There are more green pieces available since there are no stems to be found in pink. The problem in collecting colors other than green is limited availability. Green may have been more heavily promoted in this pattern while Hocking promoted Mayfair pattern in pink. My inventory of green Colonial has been depleted at the last few shows I have attended. Color preference in collecting has been cyclical for the twenty-six years that I have been watching Depression Glass. Green is now in favor!

Prices for crystal stems are more than half of green. For years these sold about half the price of green because there were few collectors of crystal Colonial. There is a scarcity of crystal stemware. I had a letter from a Floridian who sent photos of her crystal Colonial stems. She had a 5" high stem that fit between the wine and the claret. The edge was rolled inward. It may have been a claret with the top rim treated differently. She did not send ounce capacities. I suspect it would hold close to four ounces. Since I have no catalogue listing for it, does anyone else have one of these?

Only footed tumblers are found in pink; do not mistake them for stems. All three sizes of footed tumblers are shown in the top photograph on page 43. The 3¾" straight side berry is shown in the foreground. This bowl is rarely seen and is only found in pink! It is surrounded by the two-handled cream soup and cereal. Behind that bowl is the 3" sherbet that has also only been found in pink.

In the top photo on page 44 is the first **beaded top** green Colonial pitcher to appear. The pink one was found in the Cincinnati area in 1975. I bought this one about thirty miles north of there almost twenty years later.

Soup bowls (both cream and regular), cereals, unclouded shakers, and dinner plates are still difficult to obtain in all colors of Colonial. Cereal bowls may be the most difficult cereals to obtain in all of Depression Glass. Fortunately, they are not yet the most expensive.

Mugs occasionally surface in pink; but only three have been discovered in green. Those were found in Ohio for $1.00 each in the early 1970's and sold years later at a very large profit! Bargains still turn up, but not as often as they once did!

From the few days time I wrote the above paragraph to the time I re-entered copy from Cathy's editing, I received a letter from a collector in Northern Kentucky who found another green mug! The price increased dramatically as he had to pay $5.00 for this one! That is what's so exciting about Depression Gass! There are new finds all the time — by someone!

The 11 oz. tumbler measures 2¾" across the top while the 12 oz. measures exactly 3" across the top. These two tumblers are often confused. It is easier to measure across the top than to measure the contents! The spooner stands 5½" tall while the sugar without a lid is only 4½" high.

The cheese dish lid is only ¼" shorter than the butter top, not the ½" previously thought. The butter top is 4" tall and the cheese top is only 3¾" tall. The cheese dish is a wooden board with a indented groove on which the lid rests. I will show it to you again in the thirteenth edition since I just repurchased one that was first shown in my third book. The cheese top has a more flattened look when you have the two tops together. So far, the cheese has only been found in green; but the pink butter is already impossible to find without looking for a cheese dish!

	Pink	Green	Crystal		Pink	Green	Crystal
Bowl, 3¾" berry	45.00			Plate, 6" sherbet	6.00	8.00	4.00
Bowl, 4½" berry	15.00	16.00	9.00	Plate, 8½" luncheon	9.00	9.00	4.50
Bowl, 5½" cereal	55.00	85.00	30.00	Plate, 10" dinner	50.00	60.00	30.00
Bowl, 4½" cream soup	65.00	65.00	65.00	Plate, 10" grill	25.00	25.00	15.00
Bowl, 7" low soup	60.00	60.00	25.00	Platter, 12" oval	30.00	21.00	15.00
Bowl, 9" large berry	25.00	30.00	22.00	Salt and pepper, pr.	135.00	135.00	60.00
Bowl, 10" oval vegetable	32.00	35.00	20.00	Saucer/sherbet plate (white 3.00)	6.00	8.00	4.00
Butter dish and cover	600.00	55.00	40.00	Sherbet, 3"	22.00		
Butter dish bottom	420.00	32.50	25.00	Sherbet, 3⅜"	11.00	15.00	7.00
Butter dish top	180.00	22.50	15.00	Spoon holder or celery	125.00	120.00	75.00
Cheese dish		225.00		Sugar, 5"	25.00	15.00	10.00
Cream/milk pitcher, 5", 16 oz.	55.00	22.00	17.50	Sugar cover	50.00	20.00	15.00
Cup (white 7.00)	12.00	12.00	8.00	Tumbler, 3", 5 oz. juice	18.00	25.00	15.00
Goblet, 3¾", 1 oz. cordial		27.00	20.00	** Tumbler, 4", 9 oz. water	20.00	20.00	15.00
Goblet, 4", 3 oz. cocktail		25.00	16.00	Tumbler, 5⅛" high, 11 oz.,	35.00	42.00	22.00
Goblet, 4½", 2½ oz. wine		25.00	16.00	Tumbler, 12 oz. iced tea	45.00	50.00	24.00
Goblet, 5¼", 4 oz. claret		25.00	18.00	Tumbler, 15 oz. lemonade	65.00	75.00	45.00
Goblet, 5¾", 8½ oz. water	37.50	28.00	22.00	Tumbler, 3¼", 3 oz. ftd.	15.00	22.00	12.00
Mug, 4½", 12 oz.	475.00	795.00		Tumbler, 4", 5 oz. ftd.	30.00	40.00	20.00
+ Pitcher, 7", 54 oz.	50.00	55.00	30.00	*** Tumbler, 5¼", 10 oz. ftd.	45.00	45.00	27.50
*+ Pitcher, 7¾", 68 oz.	65.00	70.00	33.00	Whiskey, 2½", 1½ oz.	12.00	15.00	11.00

*Beaded top $1,000.00   **Royal ruby $100.00   ***Royal ruby $150.00   +With or without ice lip

43

COLONIAL BLOCK HAZEL ATLAS GLASS COMPANY, Early 1930's

Colors: Green, crystal, black, pink, and rare in cobalt blue; white in 1950's.

Colonial Block is not seen as frequently as some collectors would like. For years, only people who collected butter dishes, candy jars, or sugar and creamers were aware of this small Hazel Atlas pattern. Today, few expensive item collectors are left. It has become prohibitive to collect only butter dishes or salt and peppers as was common twenty years ago. Often, too little of this pattern is displayed at glass shows to pique the interest of new collectors.

I have talked to several collectors who are trying to put sets of pink together, and they are having a difficult time! Sets of green are easier to assemble. Both 4" and 7" bowls, butter tub, sherbets, and the pitcher are the pieces most often lacking in collections.

Several pink Colonial Block collectors report that they have never seen a pink pitcher; enjoy the one shown! That goblet by the green pitcher is Colonial Block and not Block Optic as it is often mislabeled. Many Block Optic collectors use these goblets with their sets since they are less costly. The heavier Colonial Block goblets are definitely more durable when compared to the thinner Block Optic.

Most pieces of Colonial Block are marked HA, but not all. The **H** is atop the **A** which confuses some novice collectors who believe that this is the symbol for Anchor Hocking. The anchor is a symbol used by Anchor Hocking and that was not used until after the 1930's.

U.S. Glass made a pitcher similar to Colonial Block. There is little difference in them except most Hazel Atlas pitchers are marked. Collectors today are not as rigid in their collecting standards as they once were. Many collectors will buy either pitcher to go with their set. That is why items that are similar to a pattern, but not actually a part of it, are referred to as "go-with" or "look-alike" pieces. Usually, these items are more reasonably priced.

The cobalt blue Colonial Block creamer is shown in my *Very Rare Glassware of the Depression Years, Second Series*. So far, no sugar bowl has been forthcoming. It's a shame more cobalt blue was not made!

A few black and frosted green Colonial Block powder jars are being found. We photographed a black powder jar, but this picture was chosen instead. The white creamer, sugar and lid are the only white pieces to surface so far.

More green sherbets have been found recently! How a piece like that can go undiscovered for years is one of those astounding things that keep me excited and writing about glass! Let me hear what you find.

	Pink, Green	White			Pink, Green	White
Bowl, 4"	6.50		Creamer		12.00	7.00
Bowl, 7"	17.00		Goblet		12.50	
Butter dish	45.00		Pitcher		40.00	
Butter dish bottom	12.50		* Powder jar with lid		17.50	
Butter dish top	32.50		Sherbet		9.00	
Butter tub	40.00		Sugar		10.00	5.50
Candy jar w/cover	37.50		Sugar lid		10.00	4.50

*Black $22.50

COLONIAL FLUTED, "ROPE" FEDERAL GLASS COMPANY, 1928–1933

Colors: Green and crystal.

Colonial Fluted was a utilitarian pattern that was widely distributed; you will find pieces with heavy wear marks. Knives scratch the surface of most glassware. Today, you need to choose your menus carefully, if you serve on your collection. I wouldn't recommend a hearty grilled steak!

The "**F**" in a shield found at center of many Colonial Fluted pieces is the trademark used by the Federal Glass Company. Not all pieces are marked.

Colonial Fluted is usually a starter set for beginning collectors; some find it an ideal bridge set. In fact, much of the original advertising for this pattern was for bridge parties. Crystal is seldom collected, except for decal pieces with hearts, spades, diamonds, and clubs.

Colonial Fluted is priced moderately enough to use. Most guests recognize this old glass as antique and treat it very gently.

There is no dinner plate in Colonial Fluted pattern. There is a dinner sized plate made by Federal with the roping around the outside of the plate, but without the fluting that goes very well with this. It is shown in the back of the photograph along with the grill plate that also goes well with this pattern. It has no roping. Both of these pieces can expand the number of items in your set without their looking out of place.

Colonial Fluted can be blended with other sets, a present trend with collectors.

	Green		Green
Bowl, 4" berry	6.00	Plate, 6" sherbet	2.50
Bowl, 6" cereal	9.00	Plate, 8" luncheon	5.00
Bowl, 6½", deep (2½") salad	20.00	Saucer	2.00
Bowl, 7½" large berry	16.00	Sherbet	6.00
Creamer	6.50	Sugar	5.00
Cup	5.00	Sugar cover	16.00

Please refer to Foreword for pricing information

46

COLUMBIA FEDERAL GLASS COMPANY, 1938–1942

Colors: Crystal, some pink.

You will find examples of Columbia butter dishes with varicolored, flashed decorations and floral decals. Some were even satinized (frosted) and others were flashed with color after the satinized finish was applied. Federal must have promoted these fervently and it apparently worked since there are so many found today! It is the only butter dish in this book that has not increased at least twenty-five percent in the last ten years.

Two sizes of Columbia tumblers have now been confirmed, the 2⅞", 4 ounce juice and 9 ounce water. Both are pictured. I have had periodic reports of other sizes and have had others shown to me at Depression Glass shows. So far, these have all turned out to be Duncan and Miller Hobnail and not Columbia. You can find water tumblers with advertisements of dairy products on them. Cottage cheese seems to have been the most popular product therein.

Pink Columbia sells extremely well for a pattern that has only four different pieces. At a recent glass show, a dealer had pink Columbia prices higher than I have ever seen. I noticed those pieces did not sell even if they are scarce! Of course, a collector who searched the show could have bought pieces for about book price — and some did!

The snack tray is shown behind the pink cup and saucer on the right. Many collectors have not known what to look for since it is an unusual piece and shaped differently from most Columbia. The picture in the tenth edition showed the tray so well that collectors are finding these to the point that supply is over running demand right now. These snack plates were found with Columbia cups in a boxed set over twenty years ago in northern Ohio. The box was labeled "Snack Sets" by Federal Glass Company. No mention was made of Columbia on the box. Snack trays are also being found with Federal cups **other than Columbia**. I have been told that they turn up regularly in Colorado.

Prices continue to increase on crystal bowls and tumblers and all pink items.

Satinized, pastel banded, and floral decaled luncheon sets have been found. Even though these sets are considered rare, they are difficult to sell, unless you find a complete set.

	Crystal	Pink		Crystal	Pink
Bowl, 5" cereal	16.00		Cup	8.50	22.50
Bowl, 8" low soup	20.00		Plate, 6" bread & butter	3.50	13.00
Bowl, 8½" salad	18.00		Plate, 9½" luncheon	10.00	30.00
Bowl, 10½" ruffled edge	20.00		Plate, 11" chop	10.00	
Butter dish and cover	20.00		Saucer	3.50	10.00
Ruby flashed (22.00)			Snack plate	35.00	
Other flashed (21.00)			Tumbler, 2⅞", 4 oz., juice	20.00	
Butter dish bottom	7.50		Tumbler, 9 oz., water	27.50	
Butter dish top	12.50				

CORONATION, "BANDED RIB," "SAXON" HOCKING GLASS COMPANY, 1936–1940

Colors: Pink, green, crystal, and Royal Ruby.

Coronation tumblers are regularly confused with the seldom found Old Colony ("Lace Edge") tumblers. Observe the fine ribs above the middle of the Coronation tumbler. These ribs are missing on a "Lace Edge" footed tumbler. Look in the store display photograph on page 155 or on the bottom of page 157 to see the differences. (Notice that the real name of the pattern we have called "Lace Edge" is shown in those store displays as **Old Colony** and that is **now** the pattern listing name in this book.) Many collectors buy Coronation tumblers and use them with Old Colony since they cost a third as much. Both are the same shape and color and both were made by Hocking. Just don't confuse the two since there is quite a price disparity! Of course, if you see Old Colony tumblers priced as Coronation, you might want to make that purchase!

The pitchers are rarely seen, but a couple have been sold for the price listed below. That is the one piece missing from most collections of Coronation. Years ago, these were bought by collectors of pitchers and tumblers. Few were bought by Coronation collectors because they have always been relatively expensive. Now, avid Coronation collectors are willing to pay the price, but no pitchers are being found to satisfy that market.

Notice that the handles on Royal Ruby Coronation bowls are open; handles on the pink are closed, and handles on the green are nonexistent. If you should find another style of handle on a different color, please let me know.

It has been a dozen years since I first verified green Coronation. The green pieces at the bottom of page 49 are from Anchor Hocking's morgue and the ones in the top picture are the only ones I have been able to unearth outside it. The larger green tumbler in the lower photograph is 5$\frac{7}{16}$" tall and holds 14$\frac{1}{4}$ oz. For new readers the lower photo was taken by Anchor-Hocking of glassware in their morgue. The morgue is so named since it has examples of past (dead production) patterns made by the company. Unfortunately, this was not well kept. Many examples have "walked" or were thrown or given out over the years. It is now under lock! Who knew Depression Glass was going to be so significant?

Dealers uneducated about Depression Glass still mark big prices on those commonly found red, handled, berry bowls. They have always been plentiful and some years ago a large accumulation was discovered in an old warehouse. They are hard to sell; yet, I see them priced for two to three times their worth. They are usually marked "rare" or "old" or "pigeon blood." That "pigeon blood" terminology comes from old time collectors who used that term to describe dark red glass.

Royal Ruby Coronation cups were sold on crystal saucers. Those crystal saucer/sherbet plates and cups are the only known crystal pieces found in Coronation. No Royal Ruby saucer/sherbet plates have ever been seen. I would not go so far as to say that red saucers do not exist. If I have learned anything in the last 25 years, it is never to say some piece of glass was never made. Royal Ruby is the name of the red glass that was made by Hocking and only their red glassware can be called Royal Ruby.

	Pink	Royal Ruby	Green
Bowl, 4¼" berry	4.50	6.50	
Bowl, 4¼", no handles			30.00
Bowl, 6½" nappy	6.00	12.00	
Bowl, 8" large berry, handled	8.50	15.00	
Bowl, 8", no handles			150.00
Cup	5.50	6.50	
Pitcher, 7¾", 68 oz.	500.00		
Plate, 6", sherbet	2.00		
Plate, 8½" luncheon	4.50	8.00	40.00
* Saucer (same as 6" plate)	2.00		
Sherbet	4.50		65.00
Tumbler, 5", 10 oz. ftd.	20.00		150.00

* Crystal $.50

CREMAX MacBETH-EVANS DIVISION OF CORNING GLASS WORKS, Late 1930's–Early 1940's

Colors: Cremax, Cremax with fired-on color trim.

I have received numerous letters over the years asking me to include the blue Cremax with the commonly found ivory color. I have finally found enough for the small photograph below. Notice the distinctly different hues of blue as well as the two different shapes. The Delphite colored blue has the same shapes as what we are familiar with but the robin egg blue has a flat sugar and creamer and a slightly smaller cup. I have been told by collectors that the robin egg blue was distributed by Corning almost exclusively in Canada. That may be accurate since most of the pieces I have found have been in northern states. For now, price both shades of blue about the same as the pieces with decals.

The green castle decal seems to be the most difficult decal to find. I had never seen that in green until I found the one piece pictured in the top photo on page 51. Besides the red floral decorations that collectors seek, there is not much activity in this pattern. Like Chinex, this should be **usable** in the microwave; but be sure to test it before putting it in for a long time. A Cremax set could be collected without putting a strain on the checkbook.

I found an 11½" Cremax sandwich plate decorated with the same red floral design as is found on Petalware. If you have pieces with additional decorations, let me hear about those and I'll pass the information to collectors.

Demitasse sets are being found in sets of eight. Some have been on a wire rack. The usual make-up of these sets has been two sets each of four colors: pink, yellow, blue, and green. I have finally obtained some of these to show you.

Regularly the bottom to the butter dish in Chinex is thought to be Cremax. The scalloped edges of the butter bottom are just like the edges on Cremax plates; however, the only tops to the butter ever found have the Chinex scroll-like pattern. If you find only the bottom of a butter, it is a Chinex bottom!

Another dilemma surrounds the name Cremax. The beige-like **color** made by MacBeth-Evans is also called Cremax. Be cognizant of that.

	Cremax	Blue, Decal Decorated		Cremax	Blue, Decal Decorated
Bowl, 5¾" cereal	3.50	7.50	Plate, 9¾" dinner	4.50	9.50
Bowl, 9" vegetable	8.00	15.00	Plate, 11½" sandwich	5.50	12.00
Creamer	4.50	8.00	Saucer	2.00	3.50
Cup	4.00	5.00	Saucer, demitasse	5.00	9.00
Cup, demitasse	13.00	22.00	Sugar, open	4.50	8.00
Plate, 6¼" bread and butter	2.00	4.00			

"CROW'S FOOT," PADEN CITY GLASS COMPANY, LINE 412 & LINE 890, 1930's

Colors: Ritz blue, Ruby red, amber, amethyst, black, pink, crystal, white, and yellow.

Adding "Crow's Foot" to the eleventh edition aroused more collector interest in this pattern. "Crow's Foot" is the most commonly used blank for Paden City etchings. The squared shape is Line #412, and the round is Line #890.

A red punch bowl has been found and is shown below. Keep your eyes peeled as you never know what will turn up in a pattern! The tumblers remain elusive with red tumblers creating special problems for collectors wishing a vivid red color. Many "Crow's Foot" pieces tend to run amberina instead of true red. Some collectors will do without before they add a piece showing yellow color. Amberina is a collector's term for the yellowish tint in pieces that were supposed to be red. It was a mistake and not a color that glass manufacturers tried to make! However, there are now collectors for this amberina colored ware!

	Red	Black/Blue	Other Colors		Red	Black/Blue	Other Colors
Bowl, 4⅞", square	25.00	30.00	12.50	Cup, ftd. or flat	10.00	12.50	5.00
Bowl, 8¾" sq.	45.00	55.00	25.00	Gravy boat, flat	85.00	100.00	40.00
Bowl, 6"	30.00	35.00	15.00	Gravy boat, pedestal	125.00	140.00	65.00
Bowl, 6½", rd., 2½" high, 3½" base	45.00	50.00	22.50	Mayonnaise, 3 ftd.	45.00	55.00	22.50
Bowl, 8½", square, 2-hdld.	50.00	60.00	27.50	Plate, 5¾"	2.25	3.50	1.25
Bowl, 10", ftd.	65.00	75.00	32.50	Plate, 8", round	9.00	11.00	4.50
Bowl, 10", square, 2-hdld.	65.00	75.00	32.50	Plate, 8½", square	7.00	9.00	3.50
Bowl, 11", oval	35.00	42.50	17.50	Plate, 9¼", round, small dinner	30.00	35.00	15.00
Bowl, 11", square	60.00	70.00	30.00	Plate, 9½", rd., 2-hdld.	65.00	75.00	32.50
Bowl, 11", square, rolled edge	65.00	75.00	32.50	Plate, 10⅜", rd., 2-hdld.	50.00	60.00	25.00
Bowl, 11½", 3 ftd., round console	85.00	100.00	42.50	Plate, 10⅜", sq., 2-hdld.	40.00	50.00	20.00
Bowl, 11½", console	75.00	85.00	37.50	Plate, 10½", dinner	90.00	100.00	40.00
Bowl, cream soup, ftd./flat	20.00	22.50	10.00	Plate, 11", cracker	45.00	50.00	22.50
Bowl, Nasturtium, 3 ftd.	175.00	200.00	90.00	Platter, 12"	27.50	32.50	15.00
Bowl, whipped cream, 3 ftd.	55.00	65.00	27.50	Relish, 11", 3 pt.	85.00	100.00	45.00
Cake plate, sq., low pedestal ft.	85.00	95.00	42.50	Sandwich server, rd., center-hdld.	65.00	75.00	32.50
Candle, round base, tall	75.00	85.00	37.50	Sandwich server, sq., center-hdld.	35.00	40.00	17.50
Candle, square, mushroom	37.50	42.50	20.00	Saucer, 6", round	2.50	3.00	1.00
Candlestick, 5¾"	25.00	30.00	12.50	Saucer, 6", square	3.00	3.50	1.50
Candy w/cover, 6½", 3 part (2 styles)	50.00	60.00	25.00	Sugar, flat	11.00	13.50	5.50
Candy, 3 ftd., rd., 6⅛" wide, 3¼" high	150.00	185.00	75.00	Sugar, ftd.	11.00	13.50	5.50
Cheese stand, 5"	25.00	30.00	12.50	Tumbler, 4¼"	75.00	85.00	37.50
Comport, 3¼" tall, 6¼" wide	27.50	32.50	15.00	Vase, 10¼", cupped	85.00	100.00	45.00
Comport 4¾" tall, 7⅜" wide	50.00	60.00	35.00	Vase, 10¼", flared	65.00	75.00	32.50
Comport, 6⅝" tall, 7" wide	60.00	75.00	30.00	Vase, 11¾", flared	125.00	175.00	65.00
Creamer, flat	12.50	15.00	6.50	Vase, 4⅝" tall, 4⅛" wide	60.00	70.00	40.00
Creamer, ftd.	12.50	15.00	6.50				

CUBE, "CUBIST" JEANNETTE GLASS COMPANY, 1929–1933

Colors: Pink, green, crystal, amber, white, ultramarine, canary yellow, and blue.

Cube is a pattern design that captures the eye of non-collectors. Cube is often confused with Fostoria's American by neophyte collectors. Cube is less vibrant and wavy in appearance when compared to the brighter, clearer quality of Fostoria's American pattern. The crystal Cube 3⁹⁄₁₆" creamer and 3" sugar on the 7½" round tray are the pieces most often confused.

No Fostoria American was made in pink. If you find a Cube-like pitcher shaped differently than the ones pictured on page 55, you probably are the victim of Indiana's Whitehall pattern which is in current production. Other pieces of Cube-like pink and a darker shade of green are also being made. Cube tumblers are flat as pictured.

Recently, I found a pink Whitehall pitcher with three Cube tumblers priced for $115 for the set. I asked the owner if she would sell only the tumblers since the pitcher was made by Indiana and not Jeannette. She said she had to have $45 for the tumblers if she sold them separately, so I let her do just that!

Prices for pink Cube pitchers and tumblers continue to increase. Most collectors are looking for four, six, or eight tumblers; consequently, it usually takes longer to find all these than the pitcher. Be sure to check the pointed sides of the tumblers and pitchers since they damaged on the sides long before the heavy rims chipped!

Green Cube is more difficult to find than the pink, but there are more collectors for pink. A major difficulty in collecting pink is finding it with the right hue of pink. The pink varies from a light pink to an orange-pink. This shows how difficult it was for glass factories in the Depression era to consistently mass produce quality glassware. As glass tanks got hotter, the pink color got lighter. The orange shade of pink is almost as troublesome to sell as it is difficult to match. There are also two distinct shades of green. For now, the darker shade of green is not as desirable as the normally found green. Both colors of Cube make for problems when ordering by mail if you want your colors to match. That is why it is preferable to attend shows and see what you are getting. You might even be willing to pay a little more for that convenience! However, I have noticed that as Depression Glass is getting more difficult to find, collectors are becoming less choosy about matching colors.

The Cube powder jar is three footed and shown to the left side of the bottom picture. There have been a few experimental colors found in these jars. Canary yellow and blue are two colors that have appeared in recent years. Occasionally, these jars are found with celluloid or plastic lids. Powder jars were not made with those lids at the factory. These may have been substitutes when tops were broken. Another possibility is that powder bottoms were bought from Jeannette and non-glass lids were made up elsewhere to fit the bottoms. In any case, prices below are for intact, original glass lids. The powder jars with other types of lids sell for half or less. As with most items having lids, it was the top that was most often destroyed, leaving far too many bottoms.

	Pink	Green
Bowl, 4½" dessert	6.50	7.00
* Bowl, 4½" deep	7.00	
** Bowl, 6½" salad	9.50	14.00
Butter dish and cover	60.00	60.00
Butter dish bottom	20.00	20.00
Butter dish top	40.00	40.00
Candy jar and cover, 6½"	27.50	30.00
Coaster, 3¼"	7.00	7.50
*** Creamer, 2⅝"	2.00	
Creamer, 3⁹⁄₁₆"	6.00	9.00
Cup	7.50	9.00
Pitcher, 8¾", 45 oz.	200.00	225.00
Plate, 6" sherbet	3.50	4.00
Plate, 8" luncheon	6.50	7.00
Powder jar and cover 3 legs	25.00	25.00
Salt and pepper, pr.	35.00	35.00
Saucer	3.00	3.00
Sherbet, ftd.	7.00	7.50
*** Sugar, 2⅝"	2.00	
Sugar, 3"	7.00	8.00
Sugar/candy cover	14.00	14.00
Tray for 3⁹⁄₁₆" creamer and sugar, 7½" (crystal only)	4.00	
Tumbler, 4", 9 oz.	65.00	70.00

* Ultramarine – $30.00
** Ultramarine – $65.00
*** Amber or white – $3.00; crystal $1.00

Please refer to Foreword for pricing information

"CUPID" PADEN CITY GLASS COMPANY, 1930's

Colors: Pink, green, light blue, peacock blue, black, canary yellow, amber, and crystal.

Collectors of "Cupid" are scouring every nook and cranny to find any piece of this pattern. Have you noticed that cupids are again in fashion in the stores? People have been known to buy **one** piece of "Cupid" just to own an appealing piece of glass. You do not have to own every piece of "Cupid" to enjoy what you have! You can be a collector with only a few pieces that you like!

There are several new pieces of "Cupid" to report. A gold decorated flat sugar and creamer can be seen in my *Very Rare Glassware of the Depression Years, Fourth Series*. It is truly amazing at the variety of pieces that are still being discovered!

In the eleventh edition, I mentioned that after fourteen years another piece of blue had been found! It was another 10½" plate. Since then, I have found a blue mayonnaise in Oregon and a 6¼" comport in Texas. Unfortunately, the mayonnaise did not have the 8" liner; if you find one, please let me know! "Cupid" seems to have traveled to all parts of the country, but never in any quantity!

We also found a green creamer and sugar set in Texas. Unfortunately, all photographs for this edition were long since made; but there will be several new pieces to show in the next book.

Samovars are rarely found, but are fetching "big bucks" when they are! You can see one on page 57 and another on page 59. The green one on page 57 is missing some of the metal hardware, but it was priced at $15 when I bought it years ago. A collector approached me at a recent show where a green samovar was displayed and priced well above the price I have listed. He asked me what I thought about buying it. This always puts me in a quandary as I have a price listed at what several have sold. Ultimately, only **you** can determine whether a piece of glass is worth that price to you. The dealer sets an asking price, and you have to decide if you will pay that price. No one can tell you what to pay! A reader recently found a green one at half the book price!

New discoveries in Paden City glassware are the norm rather than unusual! Most pieces were shown in catalogues with no etchings; and until a piece shows up with a Paden City etching, there is no way to know if it exists in that pattern.

Prices on this Paden City "Cupid" pattern continue to ascend. I heard from a West Coast dealer who sold a green ice bucket for $250.00. **Keep in mind that one sale at a high price does not mean that everyone would be willing to pay that price.**

Those center-handled pieces were called sandwich trays and the odd, center-handled bowls of Paden City were called candy trays.

A cobalt vase with silver overlay was brought to me in Miami a few years ago. It was the wrong color and shape to be "Cupid," yet it had the design! I looked at the bottom and saw the words "Made in Germany" there. The collector was shocked when I showed him since he had never noticed those words. Hold on! This is not the only piece. Cathy and I have found two other vases since then. One is yet a different shaped cobalt vase and the other is a stately lavender. They both have silver overlays of the exact "Cupid" pattern found on the Paden City pieces. You can see the cobalt blue vase on page 59. A cobalt lamp with silver overlay which was reported from Arizona is probably German also. How this happened is beyond me; but with Europe's doors opening wider, we may see some other mysteries unveiled in the future. If anyone knows anything about these pieces, I'd enjoy hearing from you.

	Green/Pink		Green/Pink
Bowl, 8½" oval-ftd.	195.00	Creamer, 5" ftd.	90.00
Bowl, 9¼" ftd. fruit	175.00	Ice bucket, 6"	190.00
Bowl, 9¼" center-handled	165.00	Ice tub, 4¾"	195.00
Bowl, 10¼", fruit	150.00	** Lamp, silver overlay	395.00
Bowl, 10½", rolled edge	135.00	*** Mayonnaise, 6" diameter,	
Bowl, 11" console	135.00	fits on 8" plate, spoon, 3 pc.	145.00
Cake plate, 11¾"	150.00	**** Plate, 10½"	100.00
Cake stand, 2" high, ftd.	150.00	Samovar	795.00
Candlestick, 5" wide, pr.	150.00	Sugar, 4¼" ftd.	90.00
Candy w/lid, ftd., 5¼" high	225.00	Sugar, 5" ftd.	90.00
Candy w/lid, 3 part	200.00	Tray, 10¾" center-handled	135.00
Casserole, covered (black) silver overlay	400.00	Tray, 10⅞" oval-ftd.	165.00
* Comport, 6¼"	75.00	Vase, 8¼" elliptical	450.00
Creamer, 4½" ftd.	90.00	Vase, fan-shaped	225.00

* blue — $150.00

** possibly German

*** blue – $250.00

**** blue – $150.00

Please refer to Foreword for pricing information

"CUPID"

58

DELLA ROBBIA #1058 WESTMORELAND GLASS COMPANY, LATE 1920's–1940's

Colors: Crystal w/applied lustre colors, milk glass.

I received several dozen letters from collectors thanking me for including Della Robbia in my eleventh edition. There were many collectors of Della Robbia who had no idea what pieces were made. Its popularity has extended to new collectors and supplies of many pieces are beginning to be sorely depleted. My listing is only a beginning from catalogue information that I own. Hopefully, you will let me know of additional pieces or of other catalogue information to which you may have access.

You will find Della Robbia in crystal, milk glass, and crystal with applied lustre colors. Notice that the fruits on each piece are apples, pears, and grapes. A similar pattern has bananas in the design; do not confuse the patterns.

Note that Della Robbia is Pattern #1058. On page 64 at the bottom of the catalogue reprint are candlesticks and a console bowl in Pattern #1067. They are not priced in my listings and neither is the Zodiac plate on page 65 because they are not Della Robbia!

There are two distinct color variations in the fruit decorations. All apples are red; pears, yellow; and grapes, purple; but the intensity of the colors applied is distinct. Look at the pictures on page 61 and compare them to the pieces at the bottom of page 62. The darker colored fruits on page 61 are the variation that is most in demand. The dilemma with this darker color is that the applied lustre scuffs very easily. Presumably, there is no difference in these color varieties, but most collectors prefer not to mix the two.

The dinner plates in pristine condition will cause you sleepless nights as you search for them. All serving pieces need to be carefully examined for wear. Remember the prices below are for mint condition pieces and not ones that are worn or scuffed.

The punch set on page 62 is rarely seen; but if you ever tried to cart around an 18" plate, you will understand why you see so few of these for sale at shows.

For the listings, I should discuss some terminology of Westmoreland. Cupped means turned in from the outside as opposed to belled which is turned out from the inside. The flanged pieces have an edge that is parallel to the base of the piece.

The sweetmeat is the comport shown to the right rear of the bottom photograph on page 61. In the same picture is the 14" footed salver or cake plate. The indentation in the center must have made for interesting cakes. I guess they had bundt pans before I was aware of them! The two-part candy with the ruffled bottom is the one shown on the left in that shot. Its catalogue description is "candy jar, scalloped edge, w/cover."

The moulds of a Della Robbia pitcher and tumbler were used to make some carnival colored water sets. These were made for Levay just as were pieces of red English Hobnail. In any case, they were made in light blue and amethyst carnival and maybe another color. If you have more information than this, share it please!

Basket, 9"	175.00	Plate, 6", finger liner	10.00
Basket, 12"	275.00	Plate, 6⅛", bread & butter	10.00
Bowl, 4½", nappy	27.50	Plate, 7¼", salad	20.00
Bowl, 5", finger	32.00	Plate, 9", luncheon	32.50
Bowl, 6", nappy, bell	35.00	Plate, 10½", dinner	75.00
Bowl, 6½", one hdld. nappy	30.00	Plate, 14", torte	80.00
Bowl, 7½", nappy	40.00	Plate, 18"	165.00
Bowl, 8", bell nappy	45.00	Plate, 18", upturned edge, punch bowl liner	165.00
Bowl, 8", bell, hdld.	60.00	Platter, 14", oval	145.00
Bowl, 8", heart, hdld.	95.00	Punch bowl set, 15 pc.	600.00
Bowl, 9", nappy	65.00	Salt and pepper, pr.	50.00
Bowl, 12", ftd.	110.00	Salver, 14", ftd., cake	125.00
Bowl, 13", rolled edge	115.00	Saucer	10.00
Bowl, 14", oval, flange	165.00	Stem, 3 oz., wine	25.00
Bowl, 14", punch	195.00	Stem, 3¼ oz., cocktail	22.00
Bowl, 15", bell	185.00	Stem, 5 oz., 4¾", sherbet, high foot	22.00
Candle, 4"	32.00	Stem, 5 oz., sherbet, low foot	20.00
Candle, 4", 2-lite	75.00	Stem, 6 oz., champagne	22.00
Candy jar w/cover, scalloped edge	80.00	Stem, 8 oz., 6", water	30.00
Candy, round, flat, chocolate	70.00	Sugar, ftd.	15.00
Comport, 6½", 3⅝" high, mint, ftd.	27.50	Tumbler, 5 oz., ginger ale	25.00
Comport, 8", sweetmeat, bell	95.00	Tumbler, 8 oz., ftd.	30.00
Comport, 12", ftd., bell	110.00	Tumbler, 8 oz., water	22.00
Comport, 13", flanged	110.00	Tumbler 11 oz., iced tea, ftd.	32.00
Creamer, ftd.	15.00	Tumbler 12 oz., iced tea, bell	35.00
Cup, coffee	17.50	Tumbler 12 oz., iced tea, bell, ftd.	35.00
Cup, punch	15.00	Tumbler 12 oz., 5³⁄₁₆", iced tea, straight	38.00
Pitcher, 32 oz.	195.00		

Westmoreland's Handmade,
Hand=Decorated Crystal

WESTMORELAND GLASS COMPANY
GRAPEVILLE, PENNSYLVANIA

Handmade Glassware
of Quality
SINCE 1889

"Della Robbia" in deep Lustre Colors

1058/9"
Plate

1058
Candy Jar

1058
Sherbet

1058
Ice Tea

1058
Goblet

1058
Mint

1058
Nappy, Heart

1058
Sugar/Cream

757
Basket

1058/14"
Plate

1058
Candle

1058
Bowl, Bell

1058
Candle

1067
Candle

1067
Bowl

1067
Candle

1067
Plate

"Della Robbia" Pattern in Crystal with Applied Lustre Colors.

"Della Robbia"

"Zodiac"
Plate

TOP ROW: *1058/9"/L126. Plate, Luncheon.*
1058/7½"/L126. Plate, Salad.
1058/8 oz./L126. Goblet.
1058/11 oz./L126. Ice Tea, Footed.
1058/8 oz./L126. Tumbler, Footed.
1058/L126/3¼ oz. Cocktail.
1058/L126. Sherbet, Low Foot.

SECOND ROW: *1058/L126. Sugar and Cream*

Set, Individual. "Della Robbia."
1058/L126. Salt, with Chrome Top.
1058/L126. Pepper, with Chrome Top.
1058/L126. Cup and Saucer.
1058/8 oz./L126. Tumbler.
1058/6½"/L126. Nappy, Cupped, Handled.

THIRD ROW: *1058/6½"/L126. Mint, Footed.*
1058/4"/L126. Candlestick.

1058/12"/L126. Bowl, Bell.
1058/½ lb./L126. Candy Jar and Cover.
1058/4¼"/L126. Nappy, Round.

BOTTOM ROW: *1058/14"/L126. Plate, Torte.*
1058/8"/L126. Nappy, Heart Shape, Handled.
25/15"/L126. Plate, "Zodiac." Pictures the
twelve signs of the Zodiac. An attractive serv-
ing piece for sandwiches or canapes.

— 2 —

DIAMOND QUILTED, "FLAT DIAMOND" IMPERIAL GLASS COMPANY, Late 1920's–Early 1930's

Colors: Pink, blue, green, crystal, black; some red and amber.

In the eleventh edition I said that pink and green Diamond Quilted are the only colors that you could collect in a large set. I received a letter from a lady who insisted I had a set of blue and black photographed; so those colors could be collected, also. Yes, they can be collected, but not in a **large** set. (I really had not meant to quibble over set size.) What you see here is twenty-five years of gathering those colors, less than one piece a year! I have tried to show you as much Diamond Quilted in colors besides pink and green. This will give you an idea of the other colors and items that are available.

Unfortunately, Diamond Quilted has no dinner-sized plate. Lack of a dinner plate stops a few collectors from further pursuit who are planning on using their prized set. I have always said that you should collect what you like. With some creativity, you can enjoy a less than perfect sized pattern.

There is a Hazel Atlas quilted diamond pitcher and tumbler set made in pink, green, cobalt blue, and a light blue similar to the blue shown here that is often confused with Imperial's Diamond Quilted. The quilting on Hazel Atlas pieces ends in a **straight line** around the top of each piece. Notice **Imperial's** Diamond Quilted pattern ends **unevenly** in points. You may also notice that the diamond designs on Hazel Atlas pieces are flat as opposed to those Imperial ones that are curved.

Punch bowls remain the elusive prize of this pattern. Two different people told me that they started collecting Diamond Quilted after spotting a punch bowl for the first time. As more and more of the harder to find pieces are disappearing into collections, there are fewer rare pieces being offered for sale. Until these collections are sold, those rarely found items are not seen again. Believe me, they're just becoming increasingly valuable as they remain in those collections, too!

Flat black pieces have the design on the bottom. Thus, the design on the plate can only be seen if it is turned over as it was in the photograph. Other black items have the pattern on the inside. A black creamer is shown satinized with painted flowers. It is the only piece I have seen with such treatment.

Blue is the color many people would like to collect, but little blue is being found. Amber and red are seen even less often.

The candle shown in the catalogue ad at the bottom of the page is sometimes confused as Windsor Diamond. Console sets at 65¢ and a dozen candy dishes in assorted colors for $6.95 would be quite a bargain today. No, I do not have any for sale at that price. This ad is from a 1930's catalogue and not my store. I mention that since I get letters every year from people trying to order glass from these old catalogue ads placed throughout the book! They even send their Visa or Master Card number and ask that I send several sets. Nobody ever orders just **one** set. It has to be multiples! One lady said she understood if I had to add postal charges to the order. Considering the ad states the six sets weigh thirty pounds, she was being generous!

	Pink, Green	Blue, Black		Pink, Green	Blue, Black
Bowl, 4¾" cream soup	10.00	20.00	Pitcher, 64 oz.	50.00	
Bowl, 5" cereal	7.50	15.00	Plate, 6" sherbet	4.00	5.00
Bowl, 5½" one handle	7.50	18.00	Plate, 7" salad	6.00	9.00
Bowl, 7" crimped edge	9.00	18.00	Plate, 8" luncheon	6.00	12.00
Bowl, 10½", rolled edge console	20.00	60.00	Punch bowl and stand	425.00	
Cake salver, tall 10" diameter	55.00		Plate, 14" sandwich	12.50	
Candlesticks (2 styles), pr.	25.00	50.00	Sandwich server, center handle	25.00	50.00
Candy jar and cover, ftd.	60.00		Saucer	3.00	5.00
Compote, 6" tall, 7¼" wide	45.00		Sherbet	5.00	14.00
Compote and cover, 11½"	75.00		Sugar	8.00	17.50
Creamer	8.00	17.50	Tumbler, 9 oz. water	9.00	
Cup	9.50	17.50	Tumbler, 12 oz. iced tea	9.00	
Goblet, 1 oz. cordial	12.00		Tumbler, 6 oz. ftd.	8.50	
Goblet, 2 oz. wine	12.00		Tumbler, 9 oz. ftd.	12.50	
Goblet, 3 oz. wine	12.00		Tumbler, 12 oz. ftd.	15.00	
Goblet, 6", 9 oz. champagne	11.00		Vase, fan, dolphin handles	50.00	75.00
Ice bucket	50.00	85.00	Whiskey, 1½ oz.	8.00	
Mayonnaise set: ladle, plate, comport	36.00	56.00			

DIANA FEDERAL GLASS COMPANY, 1937–1941

Colors: Pink, amber, and crystal.

Pink Diana is still the color to collect. Some amber and a little crystal sell occasionally, but it is the pink that is often snatched up as soon as a piece is spotted by collectors. Collectors of crystal Diana have found out what collectors of the other colors noticed years ago. There are very few tumblers available. Tumblers, candy dishes, shakers, sherbets, and even platters are rarely being found in any of Diana's colors.

Only pink has continued to make price advances recently, but that could be a gauge that other colors are soon to adopt that upward swing. Those price increases are not anything as drastic as four to five years ago when many new collectors started gathering this pattern about the same time. This was one of the used-to-be less expensive patterns! It is not as available as it once was and collectors have been paying through clenched teeth to finish sets that they have started.

Of course that goes for many other Depression Glass patterns as well. The prices listed below are **actual selling** prices and **not advertised prices**. There is a **major difference** between an advertised price for an item and the price actually accepted by both buyer and seller. Rarely have I heard of something selling for more than advertised, but often I've heard of less! Today, dealers coast to coast are willing to share with me pricing information obtained on glassware. That's been a great help!

I have added the price for the 9" salad bowl which was inadvertently left out of earlier editions. There are very few demitasse sets being found. These sets in crystal are more plentiful (as well as the sprayed-on cranberry or red sets). Flashed red sets are selling in the $10.00 to $12.00 range. Pink demitasse sets are found occasionally, but you will have to search long and hard for a pink set of six on a rack.

There is little demand yet for frosted or satinized pieces that have shown up in crystal or pink. Some crystal frosted pieces have been trimmed in colors, predominantly red. A set of the frosted items with different colored trims is not as strange looking as you might imagine. I'll try to show you a few pieces in the next edition. Finding any of these specialty items is a dilemma unless you buy a whole set at one time.

New collectors often confuse Diana with other swirled patterns such as Swirl and Twisted Optic. The centers of Diana pieces are swirled where the centers of other patterns are plain. That elusive sherbet is shown in amber in the center of the bottom photo and in pink in the foreground of the top photograph. The spirals on this sherbet are often mistaken for Spiral by Hocking. This is the sherbet shown in original advertisements for this pattern. As with many other patterns, pieces advertised along with a pattern are often accepted as that pattern. A prime example is the Moderntone tumbler.

	Crystal	Pink	Amber
* Ash tray, 3½"	2.50	3.50	
Bowl, 5" cereal	4.00	9.00	12.00
Bowl, 5½" cream soup	5.00	22.00	16.00
Bowl, 9" salad	6.00	20.00	20.00
Bowl, 11" console fruit	5.50	40.00	17.50
Bowl, 12" scalloped edge	7.00	27.50	17.50
Candy jar and cover, round	15.00	40.00	35.00
Coaster, 3½"	2.50	7.00	10.00
Creamer, oval	3.50	12.00	9.00
Cup	3.00	14.00	7.00
Cup, 2 oz. demitasse and 4½" saucer set	13.00	45.00	
Plate, 6" bread & butter	1.50	4.00	2.00
Plate, 9½"	5.00	16.00	9.00
Plate, 11¾" sandwich	5.00	25.00	10.00
Platter, 12" oval	5.50	27.50	13.00
Salt and pepper, pr.	25.00	70.00	100.00
Saucer	1.50	5.00	2.00
Sherbet	3.00	11.00	9.00
Sugar, open oval	3.00	12.00	8.00
Tumbler, 4⅛", 9 oz.	22.00	42.00	26.00
Junior set: 6 cups and saucers with round rack	100.00	300.00	

* Green $3.00

DOGWOOD, "APPLE BLOSSOM," "WILD ROSE" MacBETH-EVANS GLASS COMPANY, 1929–1932

Colors: Pink, green, some crystal, Monax, Cremax, and yellow.

Pink Dogwood remains the color most in demand; and that is a good thing since green is not found with regularity. I haven't owned a pink Dogwood large bowl or platter in almost five years. I once bought a stack of nine platters. Those really were the good old days! One of the reasons that the large fruit bowls are so difficult to find is that these were sold to someone who frosted the bowls, drilled a hole in the center and made ceiling globes out of them. These globes sell in the $75.00 range. There is a growing trend among collectors to own Depression Glass shades.

There is still an adequate supply of pitchers and most sizes of tumblers available in both colors. Price is the detriment. Only the pink juice tumbler is rarely found, but the price has gotten so high on that piece that few collectors are willing to buy more than one. I attended a show last year where a dealer had a dozen of these for sale. Putting out a dozen of a rarely found piece may not be an excellent marketing scheme. **Even rarely found items do not look rare if a dozen of them are staring back at you!**

On page 71 the four items on the left in front of the grill plate are all go-with items and not actually Dogwood. The champagne has a moulded dogwood-like design but was not made by MacBeth-Evans. This usually sells in the $20.00 to $25.00 range. The ash tray was packed with many MacBeth-Evans patterns and was once erroneously thought to be Royal Lace. This one has an advertisement for the glass company itself. The center-handled mint tray is a Mt. Pleasant piece but has etched dogwood blossoms and these sell around $30.00 to Dogwood collectors desiring a new item. The little shot glass has the same shape as all the Dogwood tumblers, but is missing the Dogwood silk screening. It is **not** Dogwood without the design! The same goes for the larger tumblers like it. There are pitchers shaped like Dogwood that do not have the silk screen design of Dogwood. These are **not** Dogwood, but are the blanks made by MacBeth-Evans to go with the plain, no design tumblers (like the shot glass shown) that they made. The pattern has to be silk screened onto the pitcher to be considered Dogwood and to command those prices. Many collectors have bought these blanks to use with their sets, however; and that's perfectly fine. It is also easier on the pocketbook to replace a $5.00 tumbler than one that costs $50.00 should it become broken through use.

Few pieces of yellow are being found, but there is not much demand for it either. It is a rare color in Dogwood!

Cremax is another rare color of Dogwood that does not excite many collectors. You can see four pieces of Cremax in the top picture including the 8½" berry, 5½" cereal, cup, and 6" plate. I recently bought a saucer for the cup so I will be able to show that in the next book. The Monax salver (12" plate) shown in the center was once thought of as hard to find; but, over the years, it has turned out to be more of a novelty than rare. In fact, you can buy them today for less than you could fifteen years ago. I used to sell them in the $25.00 range, but have recently had a couple that are not selling at $15.00!

The pink sugar and creamer portray the thick, footed style while the green creamer and sugar show the thin, flat style. Pink is found in both styles, but the green is only found in the thin variety. The thin creamers were made by adding a spout to the cups. Some of these thin creamers have a very undefined spout. Although there are thick and thin pink cups, the saucers for both style cups are the same.

Grill plates come in two varieties. Some have the Dogwood pattern all over the plate as the pink one does, and others have the pattern only around the rim of the plate as on the green one pictured. Sherbets, grill plates (rim pattern only), and the large fruit bowls are also difficult to accumulate in green Dogwood. Note the two distinct hues of green pitchers. I included both to show that color variations can be a problem if that bothers you!

Sherbets come in two styles. Some have a Dogwood blossom etched on the bottom; some do not. I have been told that this discrepancy can drive mail order dealers to drink. Please be sure to specify which style you are trying to match if that is important to you. It really makes no difference in price since they are only from different moulds.

See the *Very Rare Glassware of the Depression Years, Second Series* for a picture of the only known Dogwood coaster!

	Pink	Green	Monax Cremax		Pink	Green	Monax Cremax
* Bowl, 5½" cereal	30.00	30.00	5.00	Plate, 9¼" dinner	35.00		
Bowl, 8½" berry	55.00	100.00	36.00	Plate, 10½" grill AOP or			
Bowl, 10¼" fruit	425.00	250.00	95.00	border design only	20.00	20.00	
Cake plate, 11" heavy				Plate, 12" salver	27.50		15.00
solid foot	650.00			Platter, 12" oval (rare)	495.00		
Cake plate, 13" heavy				Saucer	7.00	8.00	20.00
solid foot	110.00	100.00	175.00	Sherbet, low footed	35.00	95.00	
Coaster, 3¼"	495.00			Sugar, 2½" thin, flat	18.00	45.00	
Creamer, 2½" thin, flat	18.00	45.00		Sugar, 3¼" thick, footed	18.00		
Creamer, 3¼" thick, footed	20.00			Tumbler, 3½", 5 oz.			
Cup, thick	17.00		40.00	decorated	260.00		
Cup, thin	15.00	35.00		Tumbler, 4", 10 oz. decorated	37.50	85.00	
Pitcher, 8", 80 oz. decorated	165.00	495.00		Tumbler, 4¾", 11 oz.			
Pitcher, 8", 80 oz. (American				decorated	42.50	95.00	
Sweetheart Style)	550.00			Tumbler, 5", 12 oz. decorated	55.00	100.00	
Plate, 6" bread and butter	8.00	9.00	21.00	Tumbler, moulded band	20.00		
* Plate, 8" luncheon	7.00	8.00					

* Yellow – $55.00

Please refer to Foreword for pricing information

DORIC JEANNETTE GLASS COMPANY, 1935–1938

Colors: Pink, green, some Delphite, and yellow.

Prices of the harder-to-find items continue to escalate in green Doric and price is affecting the number of collectors willing to jump on its bandwagon. Long time collectors of green will pay whatever it takes to complete their sets. Most are still searching for cereal bowls, footed tumblers, cream soups, and the larger pitcher. Those pieces in pink are not common either, but they can all be found with diligent searching except for the cream soup that has never been spotted in pink. Cream soups, or consommés as some companies called them, are always two-handled. Novice collectors sometimes confuse these with cereal bowls.

Even though green Doric collecting is a task, it probably will not deplete your checking account at one time since you may need years to complete a set unless you get extraordinarily lucky! Prices for green continue to dominate, but some items in pink are beginning to catch up.

Doric collectors should know that there are mould seams on many pieces. They are especially distinctive on footed tumblers and cereals. This deters collectors who are searching for perfection. On the other hand, many collectors have never seen cereal bowls or footed tumblers! I, personally, would not let a little roughness keep me from owning these if I saw them for sale! Perfection is desirable in glass collecting, but it can be carried to extremes. For instance, carrying a magnifier to a glass show is not considered to be normal behavior; but I have seen it done, recently!

Since moving to Florida, I have observed more green Doric than any place I have traveled. One of the major difficulties in buying glass in Florida, however, is cloudy glass. Evidently, well water created mineral deposits on the glass. Nothing I know of will remove this; you could make a fortune if you could figure out a way to easily remove these deposits. I know I have heard of everything from Tidy Bowl to Efferdent! I recently had a letter from someone who proposed that I send some of my books as payment for letting me know what commonly found cleaner would remove this cloudiness. Had she sent a sample and asked for the books, I would have tried it and sent her the books — if it had worked! As far as I know, it cannot be done short of polishing it out over a period of time. In any case, a number of the Doric tumblers I've seen in Florida are cloudy or "sick" as most dealers call this condition. Don't get duped into buying cloudy glass unless it is very inexpensive or you have that magic cure!

The yellow pitcher in the bottom photo is still the only one known. Pay attention to its price! Speaking of Doric pitchers, the large footed ones come with or without an ice lip as shown in the pink. Candy and sugar lids in this pattern are **not** interchangeable as are some of Jeannette's lids. The candy lid is taller and more domed. I received a picture of a candy bottom last week asking what unlisted piece had been found. Sometimes you might be able to solve a problem like that from looking closely at the pictures in the book.

I still get a lot of letters about Delphite (opaque blue) pieces. The sherbet and cloverleaf candy are common in Delphite. All other Delphite pieces are rare in Doric; however, there are few collectors to date; thus, the price is still reasonable for so rare a color. Only the pitcher creates much of a stir in Delphite. There is demand for it!

An iridized, three-part candy was made in the 1970's and sold for 79 cents in our local dish barn. All other colors of the three-part candy are old.

The top shown on the pink shaker is the original nickel plated top; the one on the green is a newly made aluminum top. Original tops are favored when available, but there is an option (new tops) to having no tops.

	Pink	Green	Delphite		Pink	Green	Delphite
Bowl, 4½" berry	7.00	8.00	40.00	Plate, 6" sherbet	4.00	5.00	
Bowl, 5" cream soup		375.00		Plate, 7" salad	18.00	20.00	
Bowl, 5½" cereal	45.00	65.00		Plate, 9" dinner			
Bowl, 8¼" large berry	14.00	17.00	125.00	(serrated 125.00)	12.50	17.50	
Bowl, 9" 2-handled	15.00	15.00		Plate, 9" grill	15.00	20.00	
Bowl, 9" oval vegetable	27.50	32.50		Platter, 12" oval	22.00	25.00	
Butter dish and cover	70.00	85.00		Relish tray, 4" x 4"	9.50	8.50	
Butter dish bottom	25.00	32.50		Relish tray, 4" x 8"	11.00	15.00	
Butter dish top	45.00	52.50		Salt and pepper, pr.	32.50	35.00	
Cake plate, 10", 3 legs	21.00	21.00		Saucer	3.50	4.50	
Candy dish and				Sherbet, footed	12.00	14.00	6.00
cover, 8"	35.00	37.50		Sugar	12.00	12.50	
*Candy dish, 3-part	7.00	7.00	8.00	Sugar cover	13.00	22.50	
Coaster, 3"	18.00	18.00		Tray, 10" handled	12.50	15.00	
Creamer, 4"	12.00	14.00		Tray, 8" x 8" serving	18.00	20.00	
Cup	9.00	10.00		Tumbler, 4½", 9 oz.	60.00	95.00	
Pitcher, 5½", 32 oz. flat	35.00	40.00	1,000.00	Tumbler, 4", 10 oz.			
Pitcher, 7½", 48 oz.				footed	60.00	85.00	
footed (yellow at $2,000.00)	435.00	825.00		Tumbler, 5", 12 oz.,			
				footed	75.00	110.00	

*Candy in metal holder – $40.00. Iridescent made recently. Ultramarine $15.00.

Please refer to Foreword for pricing information

DORIC AND PANSY JEANNETTE GLASS COMPANY, 1937–1938

Colors: Ultramarine; some crystal and pink.

Ultramarine Doric and Pansy may be scarce in America, but glass dealers in England and Canada continue to find large quantities. Until two years ago, I had only owned six or seven butter dishes in this pattern. I have bought more than that in the last two years! No wonder we always thought Doric and Pansy was rare. It is in the continental United States, but not so outside these boundaries! The price on the butter dish has experienced a down turn with so many butters now on the market.

Sugars and creamers are also being found along with those butter dishes; however, their price has not been as dramatically affected since they were not so highly priced as the butters. Tumblers and large and small berry bowls are not being found in the accumulations abroad. The tumbler pictured is rarely found. The normally found tumbler is shaped like the flat pink Doric tumbler on the left on page 73. I recently purchased the regular tumbler to use for the photograph in the next book. There have also been no reported findings of the children's sets in England or Canada!

Watch out for weak patterned shakers. These should fetch less (20 or 25 percent) than the price listed. If the only way you can tell that the shaker is Doric and Pansy comes from color and shape instead of pattern, then leave it alone. Weak pattern and cloudiness occur with the shakers coming from England, also. Remember cloudy shakers are not worth mint prices either.

An additional problem facing collectors of ultramarine Doric and Pansy is color variation. Many pieces have a distinct green cast instead of blue. Few collectors collect the green shade of Ultramarine. Unless you are able to buy the greener hue as a large lot, you may have trouble if you try to resell it. However, there is a plus side to this greener shade. Oft times you can purchase it at a fantastic price, and who is to know what it may be worth years hence.

Only berry and children's sets have been found in pink. Crystal creamer and sugar sets can be found, but have few collectors. These sets are usually purchased by collectors of sugar and creamers rather than Doric and Pansy collectors. Only a luncheon set in crystal can be amassed.

	Green, Teal	Pink, Crystal		Green, Teal	Pink, Crystal
Bowl, 4½" berry	17.50	8.00	Plate, 6" sherbet	10.00	7.50
Bowl, 8" large berry	77.50	20.00	Plate, 7" salad	35.00	
Bowl, 9" handled	32.50	14.00	Plate, 9" dinner	30.00	7.50
Butter dish and cover	450.00		Salt and pepper, pr.	400.00	
Butter dish bottom	70.00		Saucer	5.00	4.00
Butter dish top	380.00		Sugar, open	110.00	65.00
Cup	16.00	9.00	Tray, 10" handled	25.00	
Creamer	115.00	70.00	Tumbler, 4½", 9 oz.	80.00	

DORIC AND PANSY
"PRETTY POLLY PARTY DISHES"

	Teal	Pink		Teal	Pink
Cup	45.00	32.50	Creamer	45.00	32.50
Saucer	8.00	7.00	Sugar	45.00	32.50
Plate	10.00	8.00	14-Piece set	345.00	255.00

Please refer to Foreword for pricing information

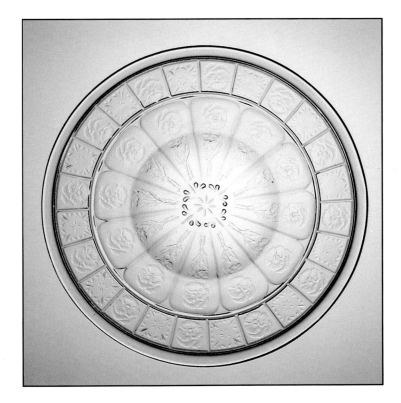

ENGLISH HOBNAIL WESTMORELAND GLASS COMPANY, 1920's–1940's

Colors: Pink, turquoise blue, cobalt blue, green, and red.

English Hobnail spans two eras of my books. To have some semblance of working order, I have placed crystal and amber into the *Collectible Glassware of the 40's, 50's, 60's...* and am including the rest of the colors in this book. It will take several editions to straighten out each piece that exists in the colors. There are various pages of catalogue listings from the later years of Westmoreland's production (when only amber and crystal were being run) in the *Collectible Glassware of the 40's, 50's, 60's...*; refer to that for an identification guide.

At present, I am incorporating two prices. Pink and green will make up one column and blue will make up the other. A piece in cobalt blue will bring twenty-five to thirty percent more than the turquoise blue price listed. Very little cobalt English Hobnail is being found. Turquoise blue has more collectors than the cobalt because so many more pieces can be found in that shade of blue.

Turquoise blue appears more regularly, but remember that some pieces of this color were produced in the late 1970's. The later-made production seems to be of poorer quality and color when compared to the older pieces. Collectors use the term ice blue and turquoise blue interchangeably; so do not get confused on that issue. A large collection of turquoise English Hobnail was put on the market a few years ago. En masse, it was appealing and magnetized a crowd at the show. The turquoise blue vase and lamp are especially nice as an accessory items.

A set of English Hobnail can be gathered in pink or green with time and patience. This, too, is a pattern that has many color vicissitudes. Pink is the easiest color to find, but there are two distinct shades of pink. There are three different greens, from a light yellow green to a deep, dark green. Some collectors mix shades of color, but others cannot abide mixing them. That only becomes a dilemma when you have searched for ages for a specific piece, and find it, in the wrong hue.

For new collectors, I offer the following to distinguish English Hobnail from Miss America. The centers of English Hobnail pieces have rays of varying distances. Notice the upright pieces in the photographs for this six point star effect. In Miss America, shown on page 132, the center rays all end equidistant from the center. The hobs on English Hobnail are more rounded and feel smoother to the touch; goblets flare and the hobs go directly into a plain rim area. On Miss America the hobs are sharper to touch and the goblets do not flair at the rim; both goblets and tumblers of Miss America have three sets of rings above the hobs before entering a plain glass rim.

	Pink/Green	*Ice Blue		Pink/Green	*Ice Blue
Ash tray, 3"	20.00		Bowl, 6½", grapefruit	20.00	
Ash tray, 4½"		22.50	Bowl, 6½", round nappy	20.00	
Ash tray, 4½", sq.	25.00		Bowl, 7", round nappy	22.00	
Bon bon, 6½", handled	25.00	37.50	Bowl, 8", cupped, nappy	30.00	
Bottle, toilet, 5 oz.	22.50	45.00	Bowl, 8", ftd.	45.00	
Bowl, 3", cranberry	15.00		Bowl, 8", hexagonal ftd., 2-handled	75.00	110.00
Bowl, 4", rose	45.00		Bowl, 8", pickle	27.50	
Bowl, 4½", finger	15.00		Bowl, 8", round nappy	32.50	
Bowl, 4½", round nappy	13.00	27.50	Bowl, 9", celery	30.00	
Bowl, 4½", sq. ftd., finger	15.00	35.00	Bowl, 10", flared	37.50	
Bowl, 5", round nappy	15.00	32.50	Bowl, 11", rolled edge	37.50	80.00
Bowl, 6", crimped dish	17.50		Bowl, 12", celery	32.50	
Bowl, 6", round nappy	1600		Bowl, 12", flange or console	40.00	
Bowl, 6", square nappy	16.00		Candlestick, 3½", rd. base	17.50	30.00

*Cobalt blue – twenty-five to thirty percent higher

	Pink/Green	*Ice Blue		Pink/Green	*Ice Blue
Candlestick, 9", rd. base	35.00		Plate, 8", rd.	12.50	
Candy dish, 3 ftd.	50.00		Plate, 8½", rd.	12.50	25.00
Candy, ½ lb. and cover, cone shaped	40.00	85.00	Plate, 10", rd.	32.50	65.00
Cigarette box and cover, 4½" x 2½"	27.50	50.00	Plate, 14", rd., torte	45.00	
Cigarette jar w/cover, rd.	22.50	60.00	Puff box, w/ cover, 6", rd.	27.50	77.50
Compote, 5", round, ftd.	25.00		Saucer, demitasse, rd.	15.00	
Compote, 6", honey, rd. ftd.	30.00		Saucer, rd.	4.00	5.00
Compote, 8", ball stem, sweetmeat	55.00		Shaker, pr., rd. ftd.	77.50	
Creamer, hexagonal, ftd.	22.50	45.00	Stem, 2 oz., sq. ftd., wine	30.00	60.00
Creamer, sq. ftd.	42.50		Stem, 3 oz., rd. ftd., cocktail	20.00	35.00
Cup	18.00	25.00	Stem, 5 oz., sq. ftd., oyster cocktail	16.00	
Cup, demitasse	50.00		Stem, 8 oz., sq. ftd., water goblet	30.00	50.00
Ice tub, 4"	47.50	80.00	Stem, sherbet, rd. low foot		12.00
Ice tub, 5½"	65.00	100.00	Stem, sherbet, sq. ftd., low	12.00	
Lamp, 6¼", electric	50.00		Stem, sherbet, rd. high foot	1500	
Lamp, 9¼", electric	110.00		Stem, sherbet, sq. ftd., high	15.00	35.00
Marmalade w/cover	40.00	65.00	Sugar, hexagonal, ftd.	22.50	45.00
Mayonnaise, 6"	20.00		Sugar, sq. ftd.	45.00	
Nut, individual, ftd.	13.00		Tid-bit, 2 tier	42.50	75.00
Pitcher, 23 oz., rounded	145.00		Tumbler, 5 oz., ginger ale	18.00	
Pitcher, 32 oz., straight side	165.00		Tumbler, 8 oz., water	22.00	
Pitcher, 38 oz., rounded	210.00		Tumbler, 10 oz., ice tea	25.00	
Pitcher, 60 oz., rounded	285.00		Tumbler, 12 oz., ice tea	27.50	
Pitcher, 64 oz., straight side	295.00		Urn, 11", w/cover (15")	325.00	
Plate, 5½", rd.	9.50		Vase, 7½", flip	65.00	
Plate, 6", sq. finger bowl liner	9.00		Vase, 7½", flip jar w/cover	85.00	
Plate, 6½", rd.	10.00		Vase, 8½", flared top	115.00	225.00
Plate, 6½, rd. finger bowl liner	9.50		Vase, 10" (straw jar)	85.00	

*Cobalt blue – 25 to 30 percent higher

FIRE-KING DINNERWARE "PHILBE" HOCKING GLASS COMPANY, 1937–1938

Colors: Blue, green, pink, and crystal.

The crystal cup and saucer in Fire-King Dinnerware are shown for the first time. Note that it also has the platinum band that was on the blue one pictured previously. That blue cup and saucer set were found in Washington Court House, Ohio, along with several other pieces in the middle 1970's. I was unable to get the blue cup and saucer for the photograph. You'll have to find an earlier edition for that.

Collectors who try to have one piece of every pattern in my book, find that Fire-King Dinnerware is usually one of the very last examples they find. It rates with "Cupid" as the two toughest patterns to capture! You can see additional pieces pictured in my *Very Rare Glassware of the Depression Years, Second Series* including the blue candy dish, tall water goblet, and green cookie jar.

Speaking of green, has anyone found a candy lid? I have had two green candy bottoms and one complete blue, but I have never found the green top!

This blue is very similar to Mayfair's blue. Many pieces have that added platinum trim as can be seen in the photograph. All the platinum banded blue pieces, except the pitcher, turned up in 1975 at the flea market mentioned above. I have never seen blue Mayfair trimmed in platinum. This seems strange since these patterns were contemporaries.

On my first trip to Anchor Hocking in June 1972, there was a large set of "Philbe" in a window display in the showroom. Until then, all I knew was that it had the same shape as Cameo and the color of blue Mayfair. I discovered then that the footed tumblers and goblet even had the Mayfair shape.

Many of the pieces shown here are the only ones ever found. Of the four pitchers shown on the right, only one other pink juice and a blue water without platinum band have been found. The usually found blue items include footed tumblers of which the tea seems twice as abundant as the water.

Oval vegetable bowls are the only commonly found piece of pink although you couldn't prove it by my picture. That oval bowl is also available in green and crystal. I have only found and sold seven pieces in the past two years and five of them were bought at one time! So "commonly found" may be a misnomer.

Green grill plates or luncheon plates might end up in your collection with more ease than anything else in "Philbe." For once, any color 6" saucer/sherbet plate is rarer than these plates.

	Crystal	Pink, Green	Blue		Crystal	Pink, Green	Blue
Bowl, 5½" cereal	18.00	40.00	60.00	Plate, 10½" salver	22.50	55.00	80.00
Bowl, 7¼" salad	26.00	50.00	85.00	Plate, 10½" grill	22.50	45.00	75.00
Bowl, 10" oval				Plate, 11⅝" salver	22.50	62.50	95.00
vegetable	50.00	80.00	150.00	Platter, 12" closed			
Candy jar, 4" low,				handles	30.00	125.00	175.00
with cover	215.00	725.00	795.00	Saucer, 6" (same as			
Cookie jar with cover	600.00	950.00	1,500.00	sherbet plate)	30.00	55.00	75.00
Creamer, 3¼" ftd.	37.50	110.00	130.00	Sugar, 3¼" ftd.	40.00	110.00	130.00
Cup	55.00	110.00	140.00	Tumbler, 4", 9 oz.			
Goblet, 7¼", 9 oz.				flat water	40.00	105.00	130.00
thin	75.00	175.00	225.00	Tumbler, 3½" ftd.			
Pitcher, 6", 36 oz.				juice	40.00	150.00	175.00
juice	295.00	625.00	895.00	Tumbler, 5¼", 10 oz.			
Pitcher, 8½", 56 oz.	395.00	925.00	1,175.00	ftd.	30.00	70.00	90.00
Plate, 6" sherbet	30.00	55.00	75.00	Tumbler, 6½", 15 oz.			
Plate, 8" luncheon	20.00	37.50	47.50	ftd. iced tea	40.00	75.00	75.00
Plate, 10" heavy							
sandwich	22.50	65.00	100.00				

FLORAL, "POINSETTIA" JEANNETTE GLASS COMPANY, 1931–1935

Colors: Pink, green, Delphite, Jadite, crystal, amber, red, and yellow.

NEWS FLASH! We have been discovered by the "weed" set. Cathy recently took a call from someone who was extremely anxious that I let my readers know that this so called "Poinsettia" pattern was, in fact, a hemp plant — the growing of which, she further explained, was very important to the war effort. The war dates are a little fuzzy in time, but other than that, we're always glad to get readers input.

Green Floral pieces rarely found in the United States continue to be uncovered in England and Canada. As with Doric and Pansy, it is the more unusual and previously thought to be rare pieces that are being found. Many Canadians have ancestry in England who are continuing the search over there. All the pieces shown in the photograph at the bottom of page 83 have been discovered in England. Many of these pieces have only been found in England! Some discoveries were brought back to the United States by furniture dealers. Now, many dealers have contacts in England searching for American made glassware as well as fine European antiques.

The green Floral, flat bottomed pitchers and flat bottomed tumblers are some of the pieces whose prices are moderating because of these discoveries. Notice the color hues of green Floral in the pictures. Floral found in Canada and England is usually a slightly lighter green color, and flat pieces all have ground bottoms which may mean that this was an early production of the pattern. This Floral is also slightly paneled. Observe the oval vegetable bowl in the background which was placed on its side so you could see this paneled effect. The green cup has a ground bottom and is slightly footed. The base is larger than the normally found saucer and will not fit its indentation! If you have relatives in England that missed the Mayflower, better send them one of my books! Better yet, try a European vacation searching England for Depression Glass.

Lemonade pitchers are still being found in the Northwest, but not as often as in previous years. Last year, a collector on his way to a show in Medford, Oregon, stopped in a junque shop and bought a pink lemonade pitcher for $50. He asked me if I would pay 60% of the price listed in my book as he had read that I would buy at that price. I agreed and we were both happy. Those pink pitchers substantially outnumber the green; that is one reason for price differences in these colors.

Floral is one of Jeannette's patterns in which the sugar and candy lids **are** interchangeable.

There are two varieties of pink Floral platters. One has a normal flat edge as shown in the back right of the top photo; the other has a sharp inner rim like the platter in Cherry Blossom. Few collectors deem both necessary to their collections!

For new collectors, in the pink picture atop page 85, the 9" comport is the piece in the center and the ice tub is the oval, tab-handled piece on its immediate right. For a description of the lamp shown in the top photograph, be sure to read about a similarly made lamp under Adam on page 6.

Smaller Floral shakers have **now been reproduced** in pink, cobalt blue, and a very dark green color. Cobalt blue and the dark green Floral shakers are of little concern since they were originally never made in these colors. The green is darker than the original green shown here but not as deep a color as forest green. The new pink shakers, however, are not only a very good pink, but they are also a fairly good copy! There are many minor variations in design and leaf detail to someone who knows glassware well, but there is one easy way to tell the Floral reproductions. Take off the top and look at the threads where the lid screws onto the shaker. On the old there are a **pair of parallel threads** on each side or at least a pair on one side that end right before the mould seams down each side. The new Floral has **one continuous line** thread that starts on one side and continues around the shaker until it ends above the beginning line on the other side. There is approximately one inch of overlapped thread making two lines for that inch; but the whole thread is **one continuous line** and not two separate ones as on the old. No other Floral reproductions have been made as of May 1995.

Unusual items in Floral (so far) include the following:
- a) an entire set of **Delphite**
- b) a **yellow** two-part relish dish
- c) **amber** and **red** plate, cup, and saucer
- d) green and crystal juice pitchers w/ground flat bottoms (shown)
- e) ftd. vases in green and crystal, flared at the rim (shown); some hold **flower frogs with the Floral pattern on the frogs** (shown)
- f) a crystal lemonade pitcher
- g) lamps (shown in green and pink)
- h) a green **grill** plate
- i) an octagonal vase with patterned, octagonal foot (shown)
- j) a **ruffled edge** berry and master berry bowl
- k) pink and green Floral **ice tubs** (shown)
- l) oval vegetable with cover
- m) **rose bowl** and **three ftd. vase** (shown)
- n) two styles of **9" comports** in pink and green
- o) 9 oz. flat tumblers in green (shown)
- p) 3 oz. ftd. tumblers in green (shown)
- q) 8" round bowl in **beige** and **opaque red**
- r) **caramel** colored dinner plate
- s) **cream soups** (shown in pink)
- t) **beige** creamer and sugar
- u) green **dresser set** (shown)
- v) **beige**, 8½" bowl (like Cherry Blossom)

FLORAL, "POINSETTIA" JEANNETTE GLASS COMPANY, 1931–1935 (Cont.)

	Pink	Green	Delphite	Jadite
Bowl, 4" berry (ruffled $65.00)	16.00	18.00	35.00	
Bowl, 5½" cream soup	725.00	725.00		
* Bowl, 7½" salad (ruffled $125.00)	16.00	18.00	60.00	
Bowl, 8" covered vegetable	37.50	45.00	75.00 (no cover)	
Bowl, 9" oval vegetable	18.00	20.00		
Butter dish and cover	82.50	87.50		
Butter dish bottom	22.50	25.00		
Butter dish top	60.00	62.50		
Canister set: coffee, tea, cereal sugar, 5¼" tall, each				50.00
Candlesticks, 4" pr.	70.00	80.00		
Candy jar and cover	35.00	40.00		
Creamer, flat (Cremax $160.00)	13.00	14.00	77.50	
Coaster, 3¼"	14.00	10.00		
Comport, 9"	775.00	875.00		
*** Cup	12.00	13.00		
Dresser set		1,200.00		
Frog for vase (also crystal $500.00)		675.00		
Ice tub, 3½" high oval	825.00	875.00		
Lamp	250.00	265.00		
Pitcher, 5½", 23 or 24 oz.		495.00		
Pitcher, 8", 32 oz. ftd. cone	32.50	35.00		
Pitcher, 10¼", 48 oz. lemonade	225.00	245.00		
Plate, 6" sherbet	6.00	7.50		
Plate, 8" salad	10.00	12.00		
** Plate, 9" dinner	15.00	17.00	135.00	
Plate, 9" grill		175.00		
Platter, 10¾" oval	16.00	18.00	145.00	
Platter, 11" (like Cherry Blossom)	75.00			
Refrigerator dish and cover, 5" square		65.00		22.00
*** Relish dish, 2-part oval	16.00	18.00	160.00	
**** Salt and pepper, 4" ftd. pair	42.50	50.00		
Salt and pepper, 6" flat	47.50			
*** Saucer	11.00	12.00		
Sherbet	16.00	18.00	85.00	
Sugar (Cremax $160.00)	9.00	11.00	72.50 (open)	
Sugar/candy cover	15.00	17.50		
Tray, 6" square, closed handles	15.00	18.00		
Tray, 9¼", oval for dresser set		185.00		
Tumbler, 3½", 3 oz. ftd.		165.00		
Tumbler, 4", 5 oz. ftd. juice	18.00	21.00		
Tumbler, 4½", 9 oz. flat		175.00		
Tumbler, 4¾", 7 oz. ftd. water	18.00	21.00	185.00	
Tumbler, 5¼", 9 oz. ftd. lemonade	45.00	47.50		
Vase, 3 legged rose bowl		495.00		
Vase, 3 legged flared (also in crystal)		475.00		
Vase, 6⅞" tall (8 sided)		450.00		

* Cremax $125.00
** These have now been found in amber and red.
*** This has been found in yellow.
**** Beware reproductions!

Please refer to Foreword for pricing information

FLORAL AND DIAMOND BAND U.S. GLASS COMPANY, Late 1920's

Colors: Pink, green; some iridescent, black, and crystal.

This pattern was advertised by Sears in the late 1920's and there is not enough of it to accommodate a large number of collectors. Luncheon plates, sugar lids, pitchers, or iced tea tumblers (in both pink and green) are difficult to unearth. Many Floral and Diamond butter bottoms have been "borrowed" to be used on other U.S. Glass patterns such as Strawberry and Cherryberry. This has transpired because all U.S. Glass butter bottoms are plain and, thus, interchangeable since the patterns are found on the top only. Floral and Diamond butter dishes used to be cheaply priced in contrast to Strawberry and Cherryberry; so, collectors bought the inexpensive Floral and Diamond butter dishes to use the bottoms for those more costly patterns. These past collecting practices have now created a shortage of butter bottoms in Floral and Diamond.

Another collecting problem with U.S. Glass patterns is the varying shades of green. Some of the green is blue tinted. It is up to you to decide how serious you are about color matching. An additional fact that new collectors need to be aware of is mould roughness along the seams of pieces in U. S. Glass patterns. This is **normal** for Floral and Diamond and not considered an impairment by long time collectors who have come to disregard **some** roughness.

Only the small creamer and sugar have been found in black. These sugars and creamers are often found with a cut flower over the top of the customarily found moulded flower design. You can find this cut flower on other colors also.

Crystal pitchers and butter dishes are rare in Floral and Diamond! Notice the crystal pitcher on the right in the bottom photograph. It is yellow in appearance and that is a problem in collecting crystal if you find any crystal to collect.

Floral and Diamond pitchers with excellent iridescent color bring greater prices from Carnival Glass collectors as a pattern called "Mayflower" than they do with Depression Glass collectors. Dealers who sell both Depression and Carnival Glass have been buying these pitchers at Depression Glass shows and reselling them at Carnival Glass conventions and auctions. Sometimes glassware that fits into two different categories, as does Floral and Diamond, receives more respect from one group of collectors than it does the other. It happens all the time. There are many different markets available and each has its own idiosyncrasies.

As you can see by the 1928 ads below, at times this pattern was described as "Floral and Diamond" and sometimes as "Diamond and Floral." Please! You can not order these items shown in the advertisement below! They were the prices for this pattern in 1928! I was flabbergasted to get orders from people who thought they could still order at those prices!

	Pink	Green		Pink	Green
Bowl, 4½" berry	7.50	8.50	Sherbet	6.50	7.50
Bowl, 5¾" handled nappy	11.00	11.00	Sugar, small	9.50	11.00
Bowl, 8" large berry	12.50	13.50	Sugar, 5¼"	14.00	14.00
* Butter dish and cover	130.00	120.00	Sugar lid	50.00	60.00
Butter dish bottom	90.00	90.00	Tumbler, 4" water	20.00	24.00
Butter dish top	40.00	30.00	Tumbler, 5" iced tea	32.00	38.00
Compote, 5½" tall	15.00	16.00			
Creamer, small	10.00	11.00			
Creamer, 4¾"	17.50	19.00			
* Pitcher, 8", 42 oz.	90.00	95.00			
Plate, 8" luncheon	40.00	40.00			

* Iridescent – $275.00; Crystal – $125.00

Seven-Piece Berry Set

You'll really be most satisfied with the purchase of this set. It's very attractive, and affords a fitting and stylish addition to your present pieces. In green pressed glass, with diamond and floral design. Large bowl, 8 inches in diameter, and six sauce dishes to match. 4½ inches in diameter.
35N6838—Weight, packed, 7 pounds. Per set...... **68c**

Seven-Piece   Water Set

Made from green pressed glass, with a floral and diamond design. You'll find that the sparkling scintillating pitcher and glasses are a set you'll be mighty proud to own when serving cold drinks. 3-pint pitcher. Six 8-ounce tumblers.
35N6837—Weight, packed, 12 pounds. Per set. **$1.18**

Please refer to Foreword for pricing information

86

FLORENTINE NO. 1, "OLD FLORENTINE," "POPPY NO. 1"
HAZEL ATLAS GLASS COMPANY, 1932–1935

Colors: Pink, green, crystal, yellow, and cobalt blue.

New collectors tend to confuse Florentine No. 1 and No. 2. Notice the outlines of the pieces standing in the back of the photographs. The serrated edges occur on all flat pieces of Florentine No. 1. All footed pieces (such as tumblers, shakers, or pitchers) have the serrated edge on that foot. In Florentine No. 2 all pieces have a plain edge. Florentine No. 1 was once advertised as hexagonal and Florentine No. 2, was once advertised as round. This should also help you to remember the differences. Both patterns were advertised and sold together. Today, many collectors are following that lead and mixing the two patterns together. It makes sense to expand the boundaries of your collection and give yourself additional pieces to add to your set.

Pink is the hardest color in which to complete a set. The footed tumblers, covered oval vegetable bowl, and ruffled creamer and sugar are almost unavailable at any price to collectors of pink. Sets can be collected in green, crystal, or yellow with work. Serrated edges are readily damaged; that is the first place you should look when you pick up a piece to examine. Be sure to check underneath those edges and not just on the top. You would be surprised how many collectors just run their hand around the edge and expect to find damage with that cursory feel. Tactile sense comes in to play, but keen eyesight is a must in this day of expensive glass.

The 48 oz. flat-bottomed pitcher was sold with both Florentine No. 1 and No. 2 sets. It was listed as 54 oz. in catalogues, but measures six ounces less. This pitcher is shown in yellow and green on page 91. I lean toward placing this pitcher only with Florentine No. 1 using the handle shape as my sole criteria. However, this pitcher is continually found with flat-bottomed Florentine No. 2 tumblers; so I will list it with both patterns.

Speaking of flat tumblers, many with **paneled** interiors are being found in sets with Florentine No. 1 pitchers. Evidently these paneled tumblers should be considered to be Florentine No. 1 rather than Florentine No. 2. That information is for purists. Paneled flat tumblers are harder to find, but few collectors seem to make this a "must have" style.

There have been a multitude of fired-on colors emerging in luncheon sets, but there is presently little collector demand for these. You can find all sorts of colors and colored bands on crystal if that strikes your fancy. There are even some banded designs found on colors other than crystal.

Many 5½" yellow ash trays have a V.F.W. (Veterans of Foreign Wars) embossed in the bottom. In fact, I have seen more with this embossing than without it.

Florentine No. 1 shakers have been reproduced in pink and cobalt blue. There may be other colors to follow. No cobalt blue Florentine No. 1 shakers have ever been found; so those are no problem.

The pink shaker is more difficult. As I write, I am comparing a reproduction one to several old pairs from my inventory. The old shakers have a major open flower on each side. There is a top circle on this blossom with three smaller circles down each side. The seven circles form the outside of the blossom. The new blossom looks more like a strawberry with no circles forming the outside of the blossom. This repro blossom looks like a poor drawing! Do not use the threading test mentioned under Floral for the Florentine No. 1 shakers, however. It won't work for Florentine although these are made by the same importing company out of Georgia. The threads are correct on this reproduction pattern. The reproductions I have seen have been badly moulded, but that is not to say that it will not be corrected.

	Crystal, Green	Yellow	Pink	Cobalt Blue		Crystal, Green	Yellow	Pink	Cobalt Blue
Ash tray, 5½"	22.00	28.00	28.00		Plate, 8½" salad	7.50	12.00	11.00	
Bowl, 5" berry	11.00	14.00	13.00	18.00	Plate, 10" dinner	16.00	22.00	22.00	
Bowl, 5", cream					Plate, 10" grill	12.00	15.00	18.00	
soup or ruffled nut	20.00		18.00	55.00	Platter, 11½" oval	16.00	22.00	22.00	
Bowl, 6" cereal	22.00	23.00	22.00		* Salt and pepper, ftd.	37.50	55.00	55.00	
Bowl, 8½" large berry	22.00	28.00	28.00		Saucer	3.00	4.00	4.00	17.00
Bowl, 9½" oval vegetable					Sherbet, 3 oz. ftd.	10.00	11.00	10.00	
and cover	50.00	60.00	60.00		Sugar	9.50	12.00	12.00	
Butter dish and cover	125.00	160.00	160.00		Sugar cover	18.00	25.00	25.00	
Butter dish bottom	50.00	85.00	85.00		Sugar, ruffled	35.00		35.00	55.00
Butter dish top	75.00	95.00	75.00		Tumbler, 3¼", 4 oz.				
Coaster/ash tray, 3¾"	18.00	20.00	25.00		ftd.	16.00			
Comport, 3½", ruffled	25.00		15.00	60.00	Tumbler, 3¾", 5 oz.				
Creamer	9.50	18.00	17.00		ftd. juice	16.00	22.00	22.00	
Creamer, ruffled	37.50		37.50	65.00	Tumbler, 4", 9 oz., ribbed	16.00		22.00	
Cup	9.00	10.00	9.00	85.00	Tumbler, 4¾", 10 oz.				
Pitcher, 6½", 36 oz.					ftd. water	22.00	22.00	22.00	
ftd.	40.00	45.00	45.00	850.00	Tumbler, 5¼", 12 oz.				
Pitcher, 7½", 48 oz.					ftd. iced tea	28.00	30.00	30.00	
flat, ice lip or none	70.00	175.00	115.00		Tumbler, 5¼", 9 oz.				
Plate, 6" sherbet	6.00	7.00	6.00		lemonade (like Floral)			110.00	

*Beware reproductions

Please refer to Foreword for pricing information

FLORENTINE NO. 2, "POPPY NO. 2" HAZEL ATLAS GLASS COMPANY 1932–1935

Colors: Pink, green, crystal, some cobalt, amber, and ice blue.

Read about the differences between the two Florentines in the first paragraph on page 88 (under Florentine No.1). Many collectors are mixing the Florentines together. Some pieces of each pattern have been found in boxed sets over the years, so the factory must have mixed them also. I have pictured the ruffled nut or cream soup that seems to be a part of Florentine No. 1 in the bottom photograph in green.

Custard cups or jello molds remain the most elusive piece in Florentine No. 2, although the bulbous 76 oz. pitcher evades many collectors. The custard is similar to a small, flared out bowl and fits a 6¼" indented plate. I recently bought a couple of these plates as saucers. The saucer curves up on the edges while the custard plate is flat.

The 10" relish dish comes divided or plain. There are two styles of divisions; do not be alarmed if yours is different from the "Y" style pictured here. The other style has two curved, separate divisions on each side. There are no price differences on these relish dishes, but the undivided is the most difficult to acquire if you want all three types.

Grill plates with the indent for the cream soup have yet to be found in yellow; not many have surfaced in green or crystal. Considering they were newly discovered, it stands to reason they are not very plentiful. Grill plates are the divided, three sectioned plates commonly used in restaurants and grills during the Depression era.

Green Florentine is more in demand than crystal, but crystal is more rarely found; thus prices for both are about the same. Amber is the rarest Florentine color; but there has never been enough uncovered to collect a set. It may have been a special order or even a trial production. Most sizes of flat tumblers have been found in amber, but still no pitcher has surfaced. You can see amber colored Florentine in earlier editions.

The rarely found 6¼", 24 oz., footed, cone-shaped pitcher is in the middle of the yellow photograph. The more frequently found footed pitcher stands 7½" tall. There is a giant price differential!

Between the two Florentine patterns, the lid to the butter dish and the lid for the oval vegetable are interchangeable. However, if you buy a candy lid thinking you are getting a butter lid, you have a problem since they are not interchangeable. The candy lid measures 4¾" in diameter, but the butter dish lid measures 5" exactly. Those measurements are from outside edge to outside edge!

Fired-on blue shakers in Florentine were shown in an earlier book. Now, **luncheon sets** of red, orange, green, and blue have been reported. The fired-on colors are sprayed over crystal. Once it has been fired-on, (baked, so to speak) the colors will not strip off even with paint removers as some collectors have learned. Fired-on colors are not common.

The 48 oz. flat bottomed pitcher was sold with both Florentine No. 1 and No. 2, sets. It was listed as 54 oz. in catalogues but measures six ounces less. This pitcher is shown in both yellow and green.

Cobalt tumblers seem to go with all the other pieces of cobalt No.1 including the rarely found pitcher. I also suspect that the ruffled comport is not a part of Florentine No. 2. Only a catalogue or a boxed set will help unravel this mystery!

	Crystal, Green	Pink	Yellow	Cobalt Blue		Crystal, Green	Pink	Yellow	Cobalt Blue
Bowl, 4½" berry	12.00	16.00	20.00		Plate, 6" sherbet	4.00		6.00	
Bowl, 4¾" cream soup	14.00	16.00	21.00		Plate, 6¼" with indent	17.50		30.00	
Bowl, 5½"	32.00		40.00		Plate, 8½" salad	8.50	8.50	9.00	
Bowl, 6" cereal	28.00		37.50		Plate, 10" dinner	15.00		14.00	
Bowl, 7½" shallow			85.00		Plate, 10¼" grill	12.00		12.00	
Bowl, 8" large berry	22.00	30.00	32.00		Plate, 10¼", grill				
Bowl, 9" oval vegetable					w/cream soup ring	32.50			
and cover	50.00		65.00		Platter, 11" oval	16.00	16.00	20.00	
Bowl, 9" flat	25.00				Platter, 11½" for				
Butter dish and cover	100.00		140.00		gravy boat			45.00	
Butter dish bottom	25.00		65.00		Relish dish, 10", 3 part				
Butter dish top	75.00		75.00		or plain	19.00	24.00	28.00	
Candlesticks, 2¾" pr.	45.00		60.00		** Salt and pepper, pr.	42.50		50.00	
Candy dish and cover	100.00	120.00	145.00		Saucer (amber 15.00)	4.00		5.00	
Coaster, 3¼"	14.00	16.00	21.00		Sherbet, ftd. (amber 40.00)	10.00		11.00	
Coaster/ash tray, 3¾"	17.50		27.50		Sugar	9.00		11.00	
Coaster/ash tray, 5½"	17.50		35.00		Sugar cover	15.00		23.00	
Comport, 3½", ruffled	25.00	14.00		55.00	Tray, rnd., condiment for				
Creamer	8.00		10.00		shakers, creamer/sugar			60.00	
Cup (amber 50.00)	7.50		9.50		Tumbler, 3⅜", 5 oz. juice	12.00	12.00	21.00	
Custard cup or jello	60.00		80.00		Tumbler, 3⁹⁄₁₆", 6 oz. blown	18.00			
Gravy boat			55.00		*** Tumbler, 4", 9 oz. water	13.00	16.00	21.00	65.00
Pitcher, 6¼", 24 oz.					Tumbler, 5", 12 oz., blown	19.00			
cone-ftd.			145.00		**** Tumbler, 5", 12 oz., tea	33.00		45.00	
* Pitcher, 7½", 28 oz.					Tumbler, 3¼", 5 oz. ftd.	15.00	16.00		
cone-ftd.	32.00		30.00		Tumbler, 4", 5 oz. ftd.	15.00		17.00	
Pitcher, 7½", 48 oz.	70.00	115.00	175.00		Tumbler, 4½", 9 oz. ftd.	26.00		35.00	
Pitcher, 8¼", 76 oz.	90.00	210.00	395.00		Vase or parfait, 6"	30.00		60.00	

* Ice Blue – $500.00   ** Fired-On Red, Orange or Blue, Pr. – $42.50   *** Amber – $75.00   **** Amber – $75.00

FLOWER GARDEN WITH BUTTERFLIES, "BUTTERFLIES AND ROSES"
U.S. GLASS COMPANY, Late 1920's

Colors: Pink, green, blue-green, canary yellow, crystal, amber, and black.

Flower Garden with Butterflies has three different powder jars; that may be why the oval and rectangular trays are so plentiful. Those trays and 8" plates are the only consistently found pieces. Apparently, more powder jars than trays were damaged over the years. There are two different footed powders. The smaller, shown in the top photograph on page 93, stands 6¼" tall; the taller, shown in the lower photograph, stands 7½" high. Lids to the footed powders are interchangeable. The flat powder jar, also shown in green atop page 95, has a 3½" diameter. (We never found a blue flat powder in the eighteen years we collected this pattern.)

Prices have softened for ash trays, but, not as much as indicated under the second column in the eleventh edition. I only noticed that the price was missing a one in front of the eighty-five when I was repricing this edition. If anyone noticed, they did not write, call, or chastise me at shows. Prices do get messed up occasionally; but when you are dealing with thousands of entries, a mistake or two is understandable. That is why disclaimers are usually found at the beginning of most price guides. Ash trays are still troublesome to find in Flower Garden. This is the only pattern in Depression Glass that has a cigarette box holder, match pack holder, and butt snuffer all on the same piece.

I have previously written about the "Shari" perfume or cologne set, but I'm still getting letters about it. It's a semi-circular, footed dresser box that holds five wedge (pie) shaped bottles. It is often confused with Flower Garden. I spotted one at a show recently that still had the original labels intact on the bottles. They touted the New York/Paris affiliation of "Charme Volupte" but nowhere was the word "Shari" mentioned on the labels. One bottle had contained cold cream, another vanishing cream, and three others once held parfumes (sic). There are **dancing girls at either end of the box,** and flowers abound on the semi-circle. This is not Flower Garden, however; neither are the 7" and 10" trivets made by U.S. Glass with flowers all over them. They were mixing bowl covers and they do not have butterflies.

	Amber Crystal	Pink Green Blue-Green	Blue Canary Yellow		Amber Crystal	Pink Green Blue-Green	Blue Canary Yellow
Ash tray, match-pack holders	165.00	185.00	195.00	Mayonnaise, ftd. 4¾" h. x 6¼" w., w/7" plate & spoon	67.50	80.00	125.00
Candlesticks, 4" pr.	42.50	55.00	95.00	Plate, 7"	16.00	21.00	30.00
Candlesticks, 8" pr.	77.50	135.00	130.00	Plate, 8", two styles	15.00	17.50	25.00
Candy w/cover, 6", flat	130.00	155.00		Plate, 10"		42.50	48.00
Candy w/cover, 7½" cone-shaped	80.00	130.00	165.00	Plate, 10", indent for 3" comport	32.00	40.00	45.00
Candy w/cover, heart-shaped		1,250.00	1,300.00	Powder jar, 3½", flat		75.00	
* Cologne bottle w/stopper, 7½"		185.00	275.00	Powder jar, ftd., 6¼"h.	75.00	125.00	165.00
Comport, 2⅞" h.		23.00	28.00	Powder jar, ftd., 7½"h.	80.00	125.00	185.00
Comport, 3" h. fits 10" plate	20.00	23.00	28.00	Sandwich server, center handle	50.00	65.00	95.00
Comport, 4¼" h. x 4¾" w.			50.00	Saucer		27.50	
Comport, 4¾" h. x 10¼" w.	48.00	65.00	85.00	Sugar		65.00	
Comport, 5⅞" h. x 11" w.	55.00		95.00	Tray, 5½" x 10", oval	50.00	55.00	
Comport, 7¼" h. x 8¼" w.	60.00	80.00		Tray, 11¾" x 7¾", rectangular	50.00	65.00	85.00
Creamer		70.00		Tumbler, 7½" oz.	175.00		
Cup		65.00		Vase, 6¼"	70.00	125.00	130.00
				Vase, 10½"		125.00	190.00

* Stopper, if not broken off, ½ price of bottle

Please refer to Foreword for pricing information

PRICE LIST FOR BLACK ITEMS ONLY

Bon bon w/cover, 6⅝" diameter	250.00
Bowl, 7¼", w/cover, "flying saucer"	375.00
Bowl, 8½", console, w/base	150.00
Bowl, 9" rolled edge, w/base	200.00
Bowl, 11" ftd. orange	225.00
Bowl, 12" rolled edge console w/base	200.00
Candlestick 6" w/6½" candle, pr.	350.00
Candlestick, 8", pr.	275.00
Cheese and cracker, ftd., 5⅜" h. x 10" w.	325.00
Comport and cover, 2¾" h. (fits 10" indented plate)	200.00
Cigarette box & cover, 4⅜" long	150.00
Comport, tureen, 4¼" h. x 10" w.	225.00
Comport, ftd., 5⅝" h. x 10" w.	225.00
Comport, ftd., 7" h.	175.00
Plate, 10", indented	100.00
Sandwich server, center-handled	125.00
Vase, 6¼", Dahlia, cupped	135.00
Vase, 8", Dahlia, cupped	200.00
Vase, 9", wall hanging	325.00
Vase, 10", 2-handled	225.00
Vase, 10½", Dahlia, cupped	250.00

FORTUNE HOCKING GLASS COMPANY, 1937–1938

Colors: Pink and crystal.

Mentioning that I had no confirming picture of a crystal Fortune candy dish with a Royal Ruby lid in the eleventh edition was an open door to collectors. Thanks to the seventy-three (at last count) collectors who have shared that photo with me. The lid is not paneled as the normally found candy.

With an investment of time and little money (when contrasted to cost of other patterns) a small pink set can be collected. Tumblers, cups, saucers, and the luncheon plates are not plentiful. Luncheon plates are getting expensive and you generally find them one at a time.

Both tumblers listed below are shown on page 97. A few pitchers are surfacing that are similar to this pattern, and many collectors are buying them for use with their sets. These "go-with" pitchers are selling in the $25.00 range. So far, no actual Fortune pitcher has turned up; but never, say never!

	Pink, Crystal			Pink, Crystal
Bowl, 4" berry	3.50		Cup	4.00
Bowl, 4½" dessert	4.50		Plate, 6" sherbet	3.00
Bowl, 4½" handled	4.50		Plate, 8" luncheon	16.00
Bowl, 5¼" rolled edge	6.00		Saucer	3.00
Bowl, 7¾" salad or large berry	14.00		Tumbler, 3½", 5 oz. juice	8.00
Candy dish and cover, flat	22.50		Tumbler, 4", 9 oz. water	10.00

FRUITS HAZEL ATLAS AND OTHER GLASS COMPANIES, 1931–1935

Colors: Pink, green, some crystal, and iridized.

Fruits collectors have all been searching for the 3½" (5 oz.) juice and 5" (12 oz.) ice tea tumblers. I have never seen either one in pink, yet a few have been reported over the years. Most collectors want green tumblers, since there has never been a pitcher discovered in pink.

Fruits patterned water tumblers (4") in all colors are the pieces usually discovered. Iridized "Pears" tumblers are abundant. These iridescent tumblers were probably made by Federal Glass Company while they were making iridescent Normandie and a few pieces in Madrid. These are not Carnival Glass as they are often represented. These were made over twenty years after the period designated for Carnival Glass. Tumblers with cherries or other fruits are commonly found in pink, but finding **any** green tumblers is more of a dilemma.

Fruits bowls are among the hardest to obtain in Depression Glass. Since this is not one of the major patterns and does not have the thousands of collectors that some other patterns do, the true dearth of both sizes of bowls is only beginning to be determined.

Fruits pitchers in crystal sell for less than half the price of green. Fruits pitchers only have cherries in the pattern. Sometimes these are mistaken for Cherry Blossom flat bottomed pitchers. Notice that the handle is shaped like that of the flat Florentine pitchers (Hazel Atlas Company) and not like Cherry Blossom (Jeannette Glass Company) flat pitchers. Crystal pieces are seldom collected, but tumblers are available if you would like an inexpensive beverage set.

	Green	Pink		Green	Pink
Bowl, 5" berry	25.00	20.00	Sherbet	8.00	6.50
Bowl, 8" berry	60.00	37.00	Tumbler, 3½" juice	25.00	20.00
Cup	8.00	7.00	* Tumbler, 4" (1 fruit)	17.50	15.00
Pitcher, 7" flat bottom	85.00		Tumbler, 4" (combination of fruits)	25.00	20.00
Plate, 8" luncheon	6.50	6.50	Tumbler, 5", 12 oz.	125.00	90.00
Saucer	5.50	4.00			

* Iridized $7.50

Please refer to Foreword for pricing information

GEORGIAN, "LOVEBIRDS" FEDERAL GLASS COMPANY, 1931–1936

Colors: Green and crystal.

Georgian has little "lovebirds" sitting side by side on most pieces except for some dinner plates, tumblers, and hot plates. A reader recently wrote that those birds were not lovebirds but parakeets. I really never gave it much thought since it was being called "lovebirds" before I ever knew what Depression Glass was! In any case, these friendly birds have flown the coop on the tumblers leaving only basket designs on each side. Baskets normally alternate with birds on all other pieces. Sometimes you can find a bargain priced tumbler if the seller does not know about the missing birds.

Both sizes of Georgian tumblers are difficult to find. In a residual effect, prices for iced teas have almost doubled the price of water tumblers. I have owned a dozen waters for every tea to give you an idea of how difficult teas are to find. No pitcher has ever been seen to go with the tumblers.

A few Georgian pieces are regularly found. Berry bowls, cups, saucers, sherbets, sherbet plates, and luncheon plates can be easily gleaned. You may have to search a while for other pieces. There are not as many collectors searching for this pattern, today, as there were in the mid-1970's when a set was donated to the Smithsonian by the Peach State Depression Glass Club in the name of President Jimmy Carter. Those particular pieces were engraved and numbered. The extras were sold or given as prizes. If you run into such a prize, cherish it!

Dinner plates come in two styles. The harder to find style (shown behind the larger creamer in the photo) is the least desired. This style has no "lovebirds," only the center design motif. The more collectible plate (with birds) is pictured to the left of the other plate. This is a case where a less plentiful piece of glass is cheaper because of lack of demand. **Demand** and **not rarity alone** affects prices. Even a rare piece can be impossible to sell if no one wants it!

Georgian lazy susan or cold cuts servers are not found as easily as the Madrid ones that turn up infrequently at best! You can see one pictured on page 99. One walnut tray turned up in Ohio with an original decal label that read "Kalter Auf-schain Cold Cuts Server Schirmer Cincy." That may be why so many have been found in Kentucky and southern Ohio. These lazy susans are made of walnut and are 18½" across with seven 5" openings for holding the so called hot plates. Somehow, I believe these 5" hot plates are misnamed since they are usually found on a cold cuts server! These plates also have only the center motif design.

There is no real mug in Georgian as has been previously reported. Someone found a creamer without a spout and called it a mug. There are many patterns that have creamers or pitchers without a spout; and one other Federal pattern, Sharon, has at least one two-spouted creamer known! (This latter creamer sat in an Ohio flea market for a couple of years before someone paid the $12.00 price tag.) Spouts were applied by hand at most glass factories using a wooden tool. Quality control of this glass was not job one! A creamer or pitcher without a spout or even an extra one is not unexpected!

Those 6" deep berry bowls were heavily utilized; so be wary of pieces that are scratched and worn from usage. You pay a premium for condition! Remember that prices listed in this book are for **mint condition** pieces. Damaged or scratched and worn pieces should fetch less depending upon the extent of damage and wear. If you are collecting the glass to use, some imperfection may not make as much difference as collecting for eventual resale. Mint condition glass will sell more readily and for a much better price if you ever decide to part with your collection.

	Green		Green
Bowl, 4½" berry	8.00	Plate, 6" sherbet	6.00
Bowl, 5¾" cereal	22.50	Plate, 8" luncheon	9.00
Bowl, 6½" deep	62.50	Plate, 9¼" dinner	25.00
Bowl, 7½" large berry	60.00	Plate, 9¼" center design only	20.00
Bowl, 9" oval vegetable	60.00	Platter, 11½" closed-handled	62.50
Butter dish and cover	70.00	Saucer	4.00
Butter dish bottom	40.00	Sherbet	12.00
Butter dish top	30.00	Sugar, 3", ftd.	9.50
Cold cuts server, 18½" wood with		Sugar, 4", ftd.	11.00
seven 5" openings for 5" coasters	800.00	Sugar cover for 3"	35.00
Creamer, 3", ftd.	11.00	Sugar cover for 4"	150.00
Creamer, 4", ftd.	14.00	Tumbler, 4", 9 oz. flat	55.00
Cup	9.00	Tumbler, 5¼", 12 oz. flat	110.00
* Hot Plate, 5" center design	45.00		

* Crystal – $20.00

HEX OPTIC, "HONEYCOMB" JEANNETTE GLASS COMPANY, 1928–1932

Colors: Pink, green, Ultramarine, and iridescent in 1950's.

A new Hex Optic pitcher has been discovered and is pictured twice. What better way to make sure you see the pitcher than to put it in both photographs! Actually, there was a problem with making everything fit because of using the vertical shelf shot for Hobnail on page 102. Another photograph of Hex Optic had to be used from the last photo session and that meant duplicating the pitchers to show colors other than pink. The footed pitcher is seldom seen, but the flat bottomed one is a new discovery. This flat pitcher is 8" tall and holds 96 ozs. Maybe there is a green one hiding out there. Notice that the pitcher is thick! There are other "honeycomb" pretenders out there that are thin. **These thin pitchers are not Jeannette and are not rare!** Most companies made patterns in a "honeycomb" design, but this book only covers Jeannette's Hex Optic!

Kitchenware buyers are more cognizant of Hex Optic than nearly all other patterns of Depression Glass. Sugar shakers, bucket reamers, and butter dishes are passionately searched for in green and pink. Refrigerator dishes, stacking sets, and mixing bowls are also coveted. In fact, were it not for Kitchenware collectors getting hooked on this pattern, Hex Optic might still be unappreciated.

Iridized tumblers, oil lamps, and pitchers were all made during Jeannette's iridized craze of the 1950's. I have never been able to verify when the company made the Ultramarine tumblers. My guess would be in the late 1930's when the company was making Doric and Pansy, but that is only a conjecture.

	Pink, Green		Pink, Green
Bowl, 4¼" ruffled berry	5.50	Plate, 8" luncheon	5.50
Bowl, 7½" large berry	7.50	Platter, 11" round	12.50
Bowl, 7¼" mixing	12.00	Refrigerator dish, 4" x 4"	10.00
Bowl, 8¼" mixing	17.50	Refrigerator stack set, 4 pc.	60.00
Bowl, 9" mixing	22.00	Salt and pepper, pr.	27.50
Bowl, 10" mixing	25.00	Saucer	2.50
Bucket reamer	55.00	Sugar, 2 styles of handles	5.50
Butter dish and cover, rectangular 1 lb. size	75.00	Sugar shaker	165.00
Creamer, 2 style handles	5.50	Sherbet, 5 oz. ftd.	4.50
Cup, 2 style handles	4.50	Tumbler, 3¾", 9 oz.	4.50
Ice bucket, metal handle	18.00	Tumbler, 5", 12 oz.	7.00
Pitcher, 5", 32 oz. sunflower motif in bottom	22.00	Tumbler, 4¾", 7 oz. ftd.	7.50
Pitcher, 9", 48 oz. ftd.	45.00	Tumbler, 5¾" ftd.	10.00
Pitcher, 8", 96 oz. flat	225.00	Tumbler, 7" ftd.	12.00
Plate, 6" sherbet	2.50	Whiskey, 2", 1 oz.	8.00

HOBNAIL HOCKING GLASS COMPANY, 1934–1936

Colors: Crystal, crystal w/red trim, and pink.

As with Hex Optic, Hobnail patterns were made by dozens of other glass companies, but Hocking's Hobnail is more readily recognized because its pieces are identically shaped to those found in Moonstone or even Miss America. After all, the 1940's pattern Moonstone is nothing more than Hobnail with an added white highlight to the hobs. Hobnail serving pieces are difficult to find, but beverage sets are not lacking. Turn to page 102 to see the picture for this pattern.

Red trimmed crystal Hobnail (see photo) has caught the fancy of a few collectors; but this is found mainly on the West Coast. I have had several collectors trying to buy the red trimmed pieces I have pictured. I had a few extra pieces from the purchase of those shown. They sold very fast when we set them out at a glass show!

Footed juice tumblers were sold along with the decanter as a wine set; so, it was also a wine glass. Terminology in glassware catalogues drives me to distraction. I have to decide whether to list what the factory said in catalogues or to list items in today's language. People think water goblets from the Depression era are wine goblets. Dealers need to check with customers when they ask for wines since they may really want water goblets. Three ounces of wine does not seem like much to today's wine connoisseurs! There is a glossary of terms listed in the back of my *Pocket Guide to Depression Glass* for those who have need to refer to it. I try to include explanations of terminology throughout this book, but that means you have to read the whole book to find them!

Only four pieces in pink were made by Hocking, five, if you count the sherbet/saucer plate as two pieces. You can pick another pink Hobnail pattern, such as one made by MacBeth-Evans, to accompany Hocking's; that way, you add a pitcher and tumbler set, something unavailable in this Hocking ware. Most other company's Hobnail patterns are compatible with Hocking's. Crystal Hobnail is not a problem to match, but shades of pink can be.

	Pink	Crystal		Pink	Crystal
Bowl, 5½" cereal		4.00	Plate, 8½" luncheon	3.50	3.50
Bowl, 7" salad		4.50	Saucer/sherbet plate	2.00	2.00
Cup	4.50	4.50	Sherbet	3.50	3.00
Creamer, ftd.		3.50	Sugar, ftd.		4.00
Decanter and stopper, 32 oz.		26.00	Tumbler, 5 oz. juice		4.00
Goblet, 10 oz. water		7.00	Tumbler, 9 oz., 10 oz. water		5.50
Goblet, 13 oz. iced tea		8.00	Tumbler, 15 oz. iced tea		7.00
Pitcher, 18 oz. milk		20.00	Tumbler, 3 oz. ftd. wine/juice		6.50
Pitcher, 67 oz.		25.00	Tumbler, 5 oz. ftd. cordial		6.00
Plate, 6" sherbet	2.00	2.00	Whiskey, 1½ oz.		6.00

HOMESPUN, "FINE RIB" JEANNETTE GLASS COMPANY, 1939–1949

Colors: Pink and crystal.

Hopefully, the tumblers pictured side by side on page 104 will help solve some of the difficulties in identification that have plagued Homespun collectors for years. There are six different flat tumblers and three footed ones. The footed juice is easily recognized, but there are two different 15 oz. footed teas. The taller, 6⅜", is next to the dinner in the top row. Notice that it has a slight stem above the foot. The other iced tea has no stem and stands only 6¼" tall. Over the years, the ⅛" difference has only been noticed by exacting collectors. In the top row are two different styled flat teas. The one pictured on the left has ribs that run to the top edge. This tumbler stands 5⅜" tall and holds 12½ ozs. The other tea has a clear band of glass above the ribs, holds 13½ ozs., and stands 5⅞". Both of these tumblers have a waffle designed bottom. There are four entirely different smaller, flat tumblers. In the second row, next to the sherbet, are the following: 3⅞", 7 oz., ribs to top, straight, concentric ringed bottom; 4⅛", 8 oz., ribs to top, flared, plain bottom; 4⁵⁄₁₆", 9 oz., ribs to top, straight, waffle bottom; and 4¼", 9 oz., band above ribs, waffle bottom. Several of these are harder to find than the others, a fact reflected by the prices below.

The cereal bowl has handles. Those cereals are difficult to find without inner rim chips!

Children's sets of Homespun are still in demand. There is no children's tea pot in crystal and there are no sugar and creamers in this tea set. The tea pot looks like a creamer with a sugar lid. You can see said tea pot in the center of the fourth row.

Homespun is a challenging set to complete; and if you choose to buy only one style of tumbler, then it is even more frustrating finding that one style. I suggest you buy every tumbler you find except for the plentiful footed juice! You will not go broke; there are not that many available.

There is no sugar lid! The lid sometimes found on the Homespun sugar is a Fine Rib pattern powder jar top.

	Pink, Crystal		Pink, Crystal
Bowl, 4½", closed handles	10.00	Saucer	4.00
Bowl, 5" cereal, closed handles	25.00	Sherbet, low flat	16.00
Bowl, 8¼" large berry	20.00	Sugar, ftd.	9.50
Butter dish and cover	55.00	Tumbler, 3⅞", 6 oz. straight	20.00
Coaster/ash tray	6.50	Tumbler, 4", 9 oz. water, flared top	16.00
Creamer, ftd.	10.00	Tumbler, 4¼", 9 oz. band at top	16.00
Cup	10.00	Tumbler, 5¼", 13 oz. iced tea	30.00
Plate, 6" sherbet	6.00	Tumbler, 4", 5 oz. ftd.	7.00
Plate, 9¼" dinner	15.00	Tumbler, 6¼", 15 oz. ftd.	27.50
Platter, 13", closed handles	15.00	Tumbler, 6⅜", 15 oz. ftd.	27.50

HOMESPUN CHILD'S TEA SET

	Pink	Crystal		Pink	Crystal
Cup	30.00	20.00	Tea pot cover	75.00	
Saucer	10.00	8.00	Set: 14-pieces	325.00	
Plate	12.50	9.00	Set: 12-pieces		148.00
Tea pot	45.00				

INDIANA CUSTARD, "FLOWER AND LEAF BAND" INDIANA GLASS COMPANY 1930's; 1950's

Colors: Ivory or custard, early 1930's; white, 1950's.

Indiana Custard entices few new collectors because it was so regionally distributed that many collectors never get a chance to see it in quantity. That is an advantage for those who do seek it. There is not a sufficient supply of this Indiana Custard to maintain immense collecting pressure.

This is the only pattern collected from this era where cups and sherbets are the most troublesome pieces to find. Some collectors consider the sherbet overpriced; but others who have searched for years without acquiring one, would disagree! Cups have been more difficult for me to find than the sherbets, but I seem to find the sherbets in groups of six or eight and the cups one at a time. Both sell quickly; so there is a demand even at the high prices. A minor problem is consistent color. Some pieces acquired a whiter cast than the more normally found beige color.

More Indiana Custard collectors are in the central Indiana area than any place. Of course, it is more plentiful there, making it easier to get hooked on it! This is the region to visit if you are earnestly searching for any Indiana glassware pattern!

I have not been able to ascertain if there is a full set of yellow floral decorated pieces like those pictured on the left below. I have seen a set of Indiana Custard decorated like the saucer standing behind the oval vegetable. A primary problem to collecting this set would be that the decorations flake rather freely. After all these years, gathering a set of a piece or two at a time would become a severe challenge! But, then, some people like the chase! One collector told me that he purposely chose a rarely seen pattern so he could have greater gratification when finding a piece!

	French Ivory		French Ivory
Bowl, 5½" berry	8.00	Plate, 7½" salad	15.00
Bowl, 6½" cereal	20.00	Plate, 8⅞" luncheon	15.00
Bowl, 7½" flat soup	30.00	Plate, 9¾" dinner	25.00
Bowl, 9", 1¾" deep, large berry	30.00	Platter, 11½" oval	30.00
Bowl, 9½" oval vegetable	27.50	Saucer	8.00
Butter dish and cover	60.00	Sherbet	90.00
Cup	37.50	Sugar	11.00
Creamer	16.00	Sugar cover	19.00
Plate, 5¾" bread and butter	6.50		

Please refer to Foreword for pricing information

IRIS, "IRIS AND HERRINGBONE" JEANNETTE GLASS COMPANY, 1928–1932; 1950's; 1970's

Colors: Crystal, iridescent; some pink and green; recently bi-colored red/yellow and blue/green combinations, and white.

Iris was one of the more difficult patterns to place in the division of this book with the *Collectible Glassware from the 40's, 50's, 60's...* since it fits both eras. Crystal production goes back to 1928 for its start. However, some crystal was made in the late 1940's and 1950's and some candy bottoms and vases, as late as the early 1970's. Iridescent belongs entirely within the time structure of my *Collectible Glassware from the 40's, 50's, 60's....* I had remarked that I would not keep putting iridescent prices in this book; but I received enough letters and comments from readers at shows to convince me to carry prices for both colors here!

Prices for crystal Iris have finally slowed from the runaway speed shown two years ago as I wrote the commentary! I was utterly amazed at what collectors were paying for some pieces of Iris! There was already a short supply of several pieces because of the heavy demand from the South, Tennessee in particular, where Iris is the state flower. No dealer can have **enough** inventory of this pattern. Recently, I have noticed that some collectors have decided that prices being asked are more than they are willing to pay. (Collectors always have an option of influencing prices by refusing to buy.)

Had you bought a twelve place setting five years ago, you could double your investment now even if you sold it wholesale to a dealer. I'll bet you wish your stockbroker had known about Depression Glass instead of mutual funds!

Iris **was** a plentiful pattern, but, right now, there is so much in collections that only a few pieces are plentiful. There are plenty of pitchers, water tumblers, and wines to satisfy collectors! Demitasse **cups** are available; saucers are scarce. Many of these cups were originally sold on copper saucers instead of glass, Iris patterned saucers.

Realize iridescent candy bottoms are a product of the 1970's when Jeannette made crystal bottoms and even flashed them with two-tone colors such as red/yellow or blue/green. Many of these were sold as vases; and, over time, the colors have washed or peeled off making them, again, crystal candy bottoms. **These later pieces can be distinguished by the lack of rays on the foot of the dish.** Similarly, white vases were made and sprayed on the outside in green, red, and blue. White vases sell in the area of $10.00–12.50. Yes, the color can be removed, producing a white milk glass vase that should sell in the same price range. **These are not rare!**

The decorated red and gold Iris that keeps turning up was called "Corsage" and "styled by Century" in 1946. This information was on a card attached to a 1946 wedding gift of this ware. You can see a 4" sherbet as an example of this in the bottom photograph on page 107.

The 8 oz. water goblet; 5¾", 4 oz. goblet; 4" sherbet; and the demitasse cup and saucer are the most difficult pieces to find in iridescent. The 5¾", 4 oz. goblet is shown in the *Very Rare Glassware of the Depression Era, 4th Series*. The 4" sherbet is a recent find!

A word about pink vases is in order. Good pink color will bring the price below, but weakly colored pink will not. Find an exceptionally vivid pink vase, and it will fetch even more! That red candlestick in the bottom photograph is flashed red and not truly red glass!

	Crystal	Iridescent	Green/Pink		Crystal	Iridescent	Green/Pink
Bowl, 4½", berry, beaded edge	40.00	9.00		Goblet, 4½", 4 oz., cocktail	25.00		
Bowl, 5", ruffled, sauce	9.00	25.00		Goblet, 4½", 3 oz., wine	16.00		
Bowl, 5", cereal	115.00			Goblet, 5½", 4 oz.	25.00	125.00	
Bowl, 7½", soup	155.00	57.50		Goblet, 5½", 8 oz.	25.00	165.00	
Bowl, 8", berry, beaded edge	80.00	20.00		** Lamp shade, 11½"	85.00		
Bowl, 9½", ruffled, salad	12.50	13.00	100.00	Pitcher, 9½", ftd.	37.50	40.00	
Bowl, 11½", ruffled, fruit	15.00	14.00		Plate, 5½", sherbet	14.00	13.00	
Bowl, 11", fruit, straight edge	55.00			Plate, 8", luncheon	100.00		
Butter dish and cover	47.50	40.00		Plate, 9", dinner	50.00	40.00	
Butter dish bottom	13.50	12.00		Plate, 11¾", sandwich	30.00	30.00	
Butter dish top	34.00	28.50		Saucer	12.00	11.00	
Candlesticks, pr.	40.00	42.50		Sherbet, 2½", ftd.	24.00	14.00	
Candy jar and cover	145.00			Sherbet, 4", ftd.	22.50	150.00	
Coaster	95.00			Sugar	11.00	11.00	110.00
Creamer, ftd.	12.00	12.00	110.00	Sugar cover	12.00	12.00	
Cup	15.00	14.00		Tumbler, 4", flat	130.00		
* Demitasse cup	35.00	125.00		Tumbler, 6", ftd.	18.00	16.00	
* Demitasse saucer	130.00	200.00		Tumbler, 6½", ftd.	34.00		
Fruit or nut set	65.00			Vase, 9"	27.50	24.00	130.00
Goblet, 4", wine		30.00					

* Ruby, Blue, Amethyst priced as Iridescent
** Colors, $65.00

Please refer to Foreword for pricing information

JUBILEE LANCASTER GLASS COMPANY, Early 1930's

Colors: Yellow and pink.

Jubilee is a pattern that keeps surprising collectors with its availability. You search for eons without finding a solitary piece; and when you are about to give up, several pieces are found which get you excited again. A dilemma in collecting Jubilee is eliminating all the look-alike items that dupe collectors who do not study this pattern closely. Some Jubilee collectors exasperate dealers with their preciseness as to what constitutes Jubilee while others are exhilarated in finding similar flower cuttings on Lancaster blanks.

Luncheon sets consisting of cups, saucers, creamer, sugar, footed tumblers, and luncheon plates are readily found. After those pieces, you have a problem getting anything else. I have found more Jubilee in Florida than any place other than Ohio. Of course, Florida is where I have been searching for glass lately!

Several collectors report finding 11½", three-footed, scalloped, flat bowls to go with the curved up 11½" bowl normally called a rose bowl in other elegant patterns. The 3", 8 oz., non-stemmed sherbet has eleven petals as does the three-footed covered candy. You can see that sherbet in the *Very Rare Glassware of the Depression Years, Fourth Series*. Having only eleven petals on the candy and sherbet evidently came from cutting problems experienced when using the standard six inch cutting wheel. The foot of the sherbet and the knob on the candy were in the way when a petal of the design was cut directly up and down. The glass cutter had to move over to the side in order to cut a petal. Because of this placement, only an eleven petal flower resulted on these pieces. Those two eleven petal pieces **are** Jubilee! Yes, most pieces do have twelve petals!

The 12" vases are 4" in diameter with a base that is only 3½" in diameter. The bulbous middle is 6".

I have not been able to find any more information on that auction held near Columbus, Ohio, where the widow of a glass cutter for Lancaster sold some sets of Jubilee. Several of the newly listed pieces came from that auction. Somewhere in Ohio, there are crystal Jubilee items that have never previously been reported. Have you seen any of them?

According to the catalogue number, the liner plate to the mayonnaise is the same piece as the 8¾" plate. There is no indented plate for the mayonnaise shown in the catalogues. However, the plate under the mayonnaise in the top photograph has an indent. This mayonnaise has sixteen petals! As I have mentioned before, true Jubilee should have twelve petals and an open-centered flower, but there are exceptions! The catalogue sheets that show the mayonnaise picture one with sixteen petals! There are other Lancaster look-alike patterns that have sixteen petals or twelve petals with a smaller petal in between the larger ones. Many collectors are willing to settle for these at a lesser price; however, purist collectors will accept nothing but the twelve petal, open center pieces. Most of my customers delight in buying look-alike pieces for less than prices paid for the real thing.

I have eliminated the terminology of goblets and have properly listed footed tumblers and stemware.

	Pink	Yellow
Bowl, 8", 3-ftd., 5⅛" high	250.00	200.00
Bowl, 9" handled fruit		125.00
Bowl, 11½", flat fruit	195.00	160.00
Bowl, 11½", 3-ftd.	250.00	250.00
Bowl, 11½", 3-ftd., curved in		225.00
Bowl, 13", 3-ftd.	250.00	225.00
Candlestick, pr.	185.00	185.00
Candy jar, w/lid, 3-ftd.	325.00	325.00
Cheese & cracker set	255.00	250.00
Creamer	35.00	20.00
Cup	40.00	14.00
Mayonnaise & plate	295.00	250.00
w/original ladle	310.00	265.00
Plate, 7" salad	22.50	14.00
Plate, 8¾" luncheon	27.50	15.00
Plate, 13½" sandwich	85.00	50.00
Plate, 14", 3-ftd.		200.00
Saucer, two styles	12.00	6.00
Sherbet, 3", 8 oz.		70.00
Stem, 4", 1 oz., cordial		235.00
Stem, 4⅞", 3 oz.		135.00
Stem, 5½", 7 oz., sherbet/champagne		85.00
Stem, 7½", 11 oz.		145.00
Sugar	35.00	20.00
Tray, 11", 2-handled cake	65.00	45.00
Tumbler, 5", 6 oz., ftd. juice		95.00
Tumbler, 6⅛", 12½", iced tea		125.00
Tumbler, 6", 10 oz., water	75.00	35.00

	Pink	Yellow
Tray, 11", center-handled sandwich	195.00	200.00
Vase, 12"		350.00

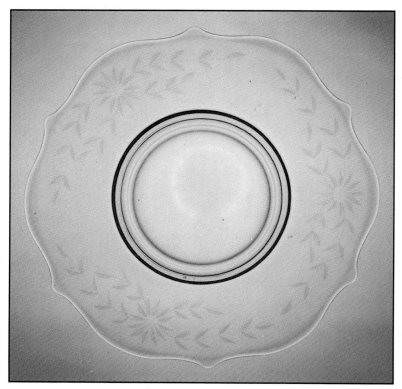

LACED EDGE, "KATY BLUE" IMPERIAL GLASS COMPANY, Early 1930's

Colors: Blue w/opalescent edge and green w/opalescent edge.

Laced Edge, as this pattern was christened by Imperial, is frequently called "Katy Blue" by its long time collectors. Unfortunately, not all pieces are blue; displays labeled that way when green opalescent is shown can give you a chuckle. Shown below are three cups and saucers that are not opalescent. Although the plain blue, cobalt blue, and crystal are shown to illustrate that this pattern can be found in other colors, only opalescent green and blue are being considered in this book. Blue and green pieces without the white sell for about half of the prices listed if you can find a buyer. Crystal pieces do not seem to be selling at any price. I have never seen crystal pieces with white edging in this pattern; if you have a piece, I would appreciate knowing what you have.

Some collectors do not accept the 12" cake plate (luncheon plate in Imperial catalogue) or the 9" vegetable (salad in ad) bowl as Laced Edge because the edges are more open than those of the other items. Thanks to a Laced Edge collector from Illinois, you can observe an ad on page 111 which shows an inflated retail price along with the cost in coupons for Laced Edge pieces. The handwritten note below says the coupons came from a margarine product. If anyone knows of "Oak Grove" oleomargine, drop me a line. You could get six tumblers for five fewer coupons than the platter or divided oval bowl!

I know that the large accumulation I bought several years ago came from the family of a butter and eggs salesman who stopped that occupation in 1941. The pieces I bought were left over premiums he was to give out to his customers.

Notice the oval vegetable bowl is missing on this ad. Evidently, the divided bowl was thought to be more practical. You will have a difficult time finding the regular oval vegetable today.

Creamers have several different styles of lips because they were individually made using wooden tools. Cereal bowls vary from 4⅞" to 5⅝"; soup bowls vary from 6⅞" to 7¼" and berry bowls from 4⅜" to 4¾". Size differences are due to the turning out of the edge of the bowl. Some edges go straight up while others are flattened. Many collectors are willing to accept these variances to have enough bowls.

There are major differences in the edge coloration. Some white barely covers the edge and other pieces have a bold white opalescent edge up to ½" down the side. To get all your pieces to match exactly in coloration would be a major task!

The white edging technique was called "Sea Foam" by Imperial and was put on many other Imperial colors and patterns besides Laced Edge.

	Opalescent		Opalescent
Bowl, 4⅜"–4¾" fruit	30.00	Mayonnaise, 3-piece	135.00
Bowl, 5"	37.50	Plate, 6½" bread & butter	18.00
Bowl, 5½"	37.50	Plate, 8" salad	32.00
Bowl, 5⅞""	37.50	Plate, 10" dinner	85.00
Bowl, 7" soup	80.00	Plate, 12" luncheon (per catalogue description)	80.00
Bowl, 9" vegetable	95.00	Platter, 13"	155.00
Bowl, 11" divided oval	115.00	Saucer	15.00
Bowl, 11" oval	140.00	Sugar	40.00
Candlestick, double, pr.	150.00	Tidbit, 2-tiered, 8" & 10" plates	100.00
Cup	35.00	Tumbler, 9 oz.	60.00
Creamer	40.00		

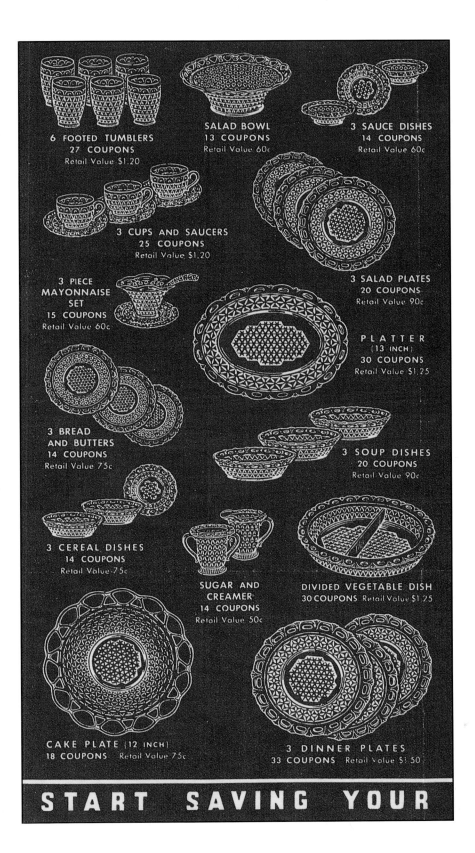

LACED EDGE

LAKE COMO HOCKING GLASS COMPANY, 1934–1937

Color: White with blue scene.

Lake Como is one pattern that many collectors say that they never see when they are out looking for glass. I find Lake Como occasionally, but it is usually very faded. Either the blue design wore off the Vitrock easily or this pattern was heavily used. Pieces usually found include shakers, sugars, and creamers. Rarely do any other items make their presence known. When exhibited, "like new" Lake Como sells very quickly!

The prices below are for **mint** condition glass with little wear on the design. You should be able to find worn Lake Como at 50% to 80% of the prices listed depending upon the amount of wear. Some pieces of all collections I have acquired have been worn. One collector told me that he had decided to buy less than mint glass in order to have some of the harder to find pieces.

Notice the flat soup in the foreground. The floral decoration on the edge is embossed instead of painted in blue. This is the same design found regularly on Vitrock pieces. You will find platters and vegetable bowls are almost as difficult to find as soup bowls; but most collectors are looking for multiple soups, which makes for a greater problem than finding only one platter. Finding either style cup will be a headache. Most settle for only one type.

	White		White
Bowl, 6" cereal	22.00	Plate, 9¼" dinner	30.00
Bowl, 9¾" vegetable	60.00	Platter, 11"	65.00
Bowl, flat soup	95.00	Salt & pepper, pr.	42.50
Creamer, ftd.	30.00	Saucer	11.00
Cup, regular	30.00	Saucer, St. Denis	12.00
Cup, St. Denis	27.50	Sugar, ftd.	30.00
Plate, 7¼" salad	18.00		

LAUREL McKEE GLASS COMPANY, 1930's

Colors: French Ivory, Jade Green, White Opal, and Poudre Blue.

Poudre Blue is the Laurel color most desired by collectors, but it is the color least often found. Unfortunately, not all items were made in blue. That could be a positive aspect since you will not have to locate as many pieces to complete a set. Some collectors are changing to Jade Green for diversity. French Ivory entices few collectors; so prices there have remained rather steadfast.

Serving pieces in all colors are scarce. I will mention that some collectors of Depression Glass are sending photos showing how they have combined several colors of one pattern to achieve extensive serving capabilities. Dearth of pieces in a single color is giving birth to some truly creative settings!

Children's Laurel tea sets are avidly sought. The Scotty Dog decorated sets are the most desired children's sets in Depression Glass! Both Jade Green and French Ivory Scotty Dog sets are coveted! When have you seen a set or even one piece for sale?

Red, green, or orange rimmed children's sets are found in Laurel in a limited supply with orange being the most difficult color to locate. The orange and red trimmed pieces in the bottom photograph did not photograph as distinctively different as they really are. That orange trimmed Jade plate shows the color more accurately than on the French Ivory. Watch for wear on these colored trims; it appears many children may have played with these dishes if wear is any indication of handling.

Several people are beginning to buy the dinner sized trimmed ivory. Red trimmed is the most often found, but sets can also be built with green trim. As with the children's pieces, wear on the trim is a detriment. Both of these trims are illustrated in the top photograph.

Shakers are hard to find with strong patterns. Many Laurel designs are weak or obscure. Definitely, it's better to own a patterned Laurel shaker than one that has only the right shape! Doric and Pansy shakers are the only other Depression pattern where this is problem! Jade shakers are quite rare, but there are not enough collectors buying them to expose their true scarcity.

	White Opal, Jade Green	French Ivory	Poudre Blue		White Opal, Jade Green	French Ivory	Poudre Blue
Bowl, 4¾" berry	6.50	7.50	13.00	Plate, 6" sherbet	5.00	5.00	10.00
Bowl, 6" cereal	7.50	9.00	20.00	Plate, 7½" salad	10.00	9.00	14.00
Bowl, 6", three legs	12.50	15.00		Plate, 9⅛" dinner	14.00	12.00	22.00
Bowl, 7⅞" soup	32.00	32.00		Plate, 9⅛" grill, round or scalloped	12.00	12.00	
Bowl, 9" large berry	18.00	20.00	45.00	Platter, 10¾" oval	22.00	25.00	37.00
Bowl, 9¾" oval vegetable	20.00	20.00	45.00	Salt and pepper	60.00	45.00	
Bowl, 10½", three legs	28.00	33.00	65.00	Saucer	3.50	3.00	7.50
Bowl, 11"	30.00	35.00	65.00	Sherbet	10.00	11.00	
Candlestick, 4" pr.	35.00	30.00		Sherbet/champagne, 5"	40.00	35.00	
Cheese dish and cover	52.50	55.00		Sugar, short	8.50	9.00	
Creamer, short	10.00	10.00		Sugar, tall	11.00	11.00	30.00
Creamer, tall	12.00	12.00	30.00	Tumbler, 4½", 9 oz. flat	42.50	30.00	
Cup	7.50	7.00	20.00	Tumbler, 5", 12 oz. flat		45.00	

CHILDREN'S LAUREL TEA SET

	Plain	Green or Decorated Rims	Scotty Dog Green	Scotty Dog Ivory
Creamer	25.00	40.00	115.00	87.50
Cup	20.00	30.00	65.00	42.50
Plate	10.00	16.00	55.00	35.00
Saucer	8.00	10.00	55.00	25.00
Sugar	25.00	40.00	115.00	87.50
14-piece set	205.00	305.00	930.00	590.00

Please refer to Foreword for pricing information

LINCOLN INN FENTON GLASS COMPANY, Late 1920's

Colors: Red, cobalt, light blue, amethyst, black, green, green opalescent, pink, crystal, amber, and jade (opaque).

A Lincoln Inn 11" center-handled server has been discovered in both red and cobalt blue! One can be seen in *Very Rare Glassware of the Depression Years, Fourth Series*. A rainbow of colors found in Lincoln Inn gives searchers a wide selection for collecting, but red and several shades of blue remain the most desirable colors. The good news is that those are the colors that are also the most often found!

Champagne/sherbets are copious in all colors. If you desire to collect tall sherbets, then this pattern may add quite a few to your set. Fenton manufactured a high sherbet in every color made in this pattern. You can also find tumblers and stems easily, but obtaining serving pieces in **any** color is a chore.

Pitchers are rarely seen; but keep in mind that Fenton remade an iridized, dark carnival colored pitcher a few years ago! All light blue pitchers have been found in Florida; so watch for them there!

Lincoln Inn plates could also be found with a fruit design in the center according to a 1930's catalogue. I can finally show you one in the bottom photo. I spoke with a collector at a recent show who had found several pink 8" plates with fruits in the center. It was the first report of colored, fruit designed plates. I recently spotted a 9" crystal bowl with fruit designs at an antique mall in Florida, but the bowl's owner apparently thought it was Lalique — or better!

Lincoln Inn shakers continue to be difficult to find in all colors. There are some collectors who only search for shakers. Although these are not the highest priced shakers in Depression Glass, they are among the toughest to find. Red and black shakers are the most desired colors; but don't pass by **any** color in your travels. I found a red pair sitting with Royal Ruby in a corner of a shop a few years ago! They were very reasonably priced! You need to look in every nook and cranny in shops that do not specialize in Depression Glass.

Many red pieces are amberina in color. Amberina is red glass that has a yellow tint to it. Older red glass was made by reheating glass that first came from the furnace as yellow glass. When the glass was reheated, to turn it red; uneven heating caused some of it to remain yellow. Some dealers have told collectors this is a rare color in order to sell it. In a certain sense, that may have an element of truth. Actually, it was a mistake; and the amounts of yellow on each piece make it difficult to match pieces — and many knowledgeable glass collectors spurn amberina pieces.

	Cobalt Blue, Red	All Other Colors		Cobalt Blue, Red	All Other Colors
Ash tray	17.50	12.00	Tumbler, 9 oz. flat water		19.50
Bon bon, handled square	15.00	12.00	Tumbler, 5 oz. ftd.	25.00	11.00
Bon bon, handled oval	16.00	12.00	Tumbler, 9 oz. ftd.	26.00	14.00
Bowl, 5" fruit	11.50	8.50	Tumbler, 12 oz. ftd.	40.00	19.00
Bowl, 6" cereal	13.00	9.00	Vase, 9¾"	125.00	75.00
Bowl, 6" crimped	13.00	8.50	Vase, 12" ftd.	145.00	95.00
Bowl, handled olive	15.00	9.50			
Bowl, finger	20.00	12.50			
Bowl, 9", shallow		23.00			
Bowl, 9¼" ftd.	40.00	19.00			
Bowl, 10½" ftd.	50.00	30.00			
Candy dish, ftd. oval	22.50	13.00			
Comport	25.00	14.50			
Creamer	22.50	14.50			
Cup	16.50	9.00			
Goblet, water	24.00	15.50			
Goblet, wine	27.00	16.50			
Nut dish, ftd.	20.00	12.00			
Pitcher, 7¼", 46 oz.	800.00	700.00			
Plate, 6"	7.50	4.50			
Plate, 8"	12.50	7.50			
Plate, 9¼"	26.00	11.50			
Plate, 12"	32.00	15.50			
* Salt/pepper, pr.	250.00	150.00			
Sandwich server, center hdld.	95.00	75.00			
Saucer	4.50	3.50			
Sherbet, 4½", cone shape	17.00	11.50			
Sherbet, 4¾"	19.00	12.50			
Sugar	20.00	14.00			
Tumbler, 4 oz. flat juice	26.00	9.50			

*Black $300.00

Please refer to Foreword for pricing information

LORAIN, "BASKET," No. 615 INDIANA GLASS COMPANY, 1929–1932

Colors: Green, yellow, and some crystal.

Lorain experiences that persistent problem of mould roughness that plagues much of Indiana's glassware; if you are a fanatic about **mint** condition glassware, then you had better focus on some other pattern. Otherwise, you can find collecting this challenging pattern a stimulating experience that will reward you with beautiful arrays of glass.

After selling several collections of Lorain, and corresponding with numerous collectors who have hunted for Lorain for years, I have arrived at several conclusions that will help you in your pursuit of this pattern. Buy any cereal bowls you can find, but check out the inner rims closely; they damage easily. The 8" deep berry is the next hardest piece to locate; most collectors only need one of these, so that is not as big a problem as finding six or eight cereals. Dinner plates are almost as scarce as cereals. Oval vegetable bowls are infrequently found in both colors. Saucers are harder to locate than cups because of mould roughness and wear and tear on them over the years. It is amazing how collecting has changed. Dealers used to refuse to buy saucers unless there were cups with them. Today, many of these once scorned saucers are eagerly bought whether there are cups or not! There are at least a dozen patterns in Depression Glass where saucers are more difficult to locate than cups.

Prices for all harder to find pieces continue to rise. More new collectors are starting green Lorain than yellow because of price and availability. Green is less expensive and more easily found. There are a few pieces found in crystal, but I would not suggest you try to complete a set. It would be extremely difficult. A few pieces could accompany your colored sets. Notice that we have used a few pieces in the photograph of the green on page 119.

Some crystal is found with colored borders of red, yellow, green, and blue. For those who have written to ask about the snack tray, one with yellow trim is pictured in the bottom photograph. It was made from the platter mould that had an indent added for a cup rest. Crystal cups are sometimes trimmed in the four colors to match the snack tray, but often they are only crystal. To date, these snack trays have only been found in crystal or crystal trimmed. A true green or yellow snack tray would be a find!

New collectors, please note that the white and green avocado colored sherbets (which have an open lace border) are a 1950's and later issue and should be treated as such. They were used regularly by florists for small floral arrangements and many are found with a tacky, clay-like substance in the bottom that was used to hold flowers. They have always been assumed to be an Indiana product; but several have been found with Anchor Hocking stickers. I have not been able to find these in catalogues, but Anchor-Hocking did affix labels in the late 1950's and early 1960's. If any one out there has more information on these, please give us benefit of your knowledge!

	Crystal, Green	Yellow
Bowl, 6" cereal	40.00	60.00
Bowl, 7¼" salad	40.00	60.00
Bowl, 8" deep berry	85.00	140.00
Bowl, 9¾" oval vegetable	40.00	50.00
Creamer, ftd.	16.00	22.00
Cup	11.00	15.00
Plate, 5½" sherbet	7.50	11.00
Plate, 7¾" salad	10.00	15.00
Plate, 8⅜" luncheon	16.00	26.00
Plate, 10¼" dinner	40.00	55.00
Platter, 11½"	25.00	42.00
Relish, 8", 4-part	16.50	35.00
Saucer	4.50	6.00
Sherbet, ftd.	20.00	30.00
Snack tray, crystal/trim	21.00	
Sugar, ftd.	16.00	22.00
Tumbler, 4¾", 9 oz. ftd.	20.00	30.00

Please refer to Foreword for pricing information

MADRID FEDERAL GLASS COMPANY, 1932–1939; INDIANA GLASS COMPANY, 1980's

Colors: Green, pink, amber, crystal, and "Madonna" blue. (*See Reproduction Section.*)

Madrid has been a genuine headache since 1976 when the Federal Glass Company reissued this pattern for the Bicentennial under the name "Recollection" glassware. Each piece was dated 1976; but it was issued in amber color instead of some other. This newer amber was a slightly darker shade of amber than the first issues. Collectors were informed and many assumed it would someday be collectible and bought sets. Unfortunately, Indiana Glass bought the moulds for Madrid when Federal became insolvent and there have been headaches for collectors ever since. First Indiana removed the 1976 date and made crystal. The old crystal butter was selling for several hundred dollars and the new one sold for $2.99. Prices plummeted!

Shortly afterwards, Indiana made pink; and even though it was a lighter pink than the original, prices nose-dived on the old pink Madrid. Then, Indiana made blue; and although it is a brighter, harsher blue than the beautiful, soft blue of the original Madrid, it had a devastating effect on the prices of the 1930's blue. You can see the new pink in the Reproduction Section in the back. All pieces made in pink have now been made in blue. The latest color, teal, is a very greenish blue and is the first color made that was not previously made in the 1930's.

Only the items priced below were originally made in blue. Yet, some of those original items have been remade; so, buyer, know your dealer if collecting Madrid! If a piece is found in blue that is not priced below, rest assured it is new!

Madrid gravy boats and platters have almost always been found in Iowa. Someday, someone will remember how these were attained. I am betting it was a premium for some item used by rural folks! I just spoke to a lady from Iowa who attended a recent auction where a gravy boat and platter were sold. You can see one in the foreground of the top photograph. More platters for this boat are found than the gravy itself. These platters are selling in the $250 range by themselves.

Mint condition sugar lids in any color are a treasure. Footed tumblers are harder to find than flat ones. That is also true for shakers. Footed shakers are the only style you can find in blue. Look at the shakers in the bottom photograph. Any heavy, flat ones you spot are new!

Collectors of green Madrid have turned out to be almost as scarce as the pattern! Green is almost as rare as blue, but more pieces are available in green. You also do not have to worry about reproductions in green — yet!

The wooden lazy susans are being found in eastern Kentucky and southern Ohio. A label found on one of these says "Kalter Aufschain Cold Cuts Server Schirmer Cincy." You can see one of these pictured in *Very Rare Glassware of the Depression Years, Second Series.*

	Amber	Pink	Green	Blue		Amber	Pink	Green	Blue
Ash tray, 6" square	200.00		150.00		Pitcher, 8½", 80 oz.	60.00		200.00	
Bowl, 4¾" cream					Pitcher, 8½",				
soup	15.00				80 oz. ice lip	60.00		225.00	
Bowl, 5" sauce	6.00	6.50	6.50		Plate, 6" sherbet	4.00	3.50	4.00	8.00
Bowl, 7" soup	15.00		16.00	30.00	Plate, 7½" salad	11.00	9.00	9.00	20.00
Bowl, 8" salad	14.00		17.50		Plate, 8⅞" luncheon	8.00	7.00	9.00	18.00
Bowl, 9⅜" lg. berry	18.50	19.00			Plate, 10½" dinner	37.50		35.00	65.00
Bowl, 9½" deep					Plate, 10½" grill	9.50		15.00	
salad	30.00				Plate, 10¼" relish	15.00	12.50	16.00	
Bowl, 10" oval veg.	15.00	15.00	17.00	38.00	Plate, 11¼" rd. cake	14.00	10.00		
*Bowl, 11" low console	15.00	11.00			Platter, 11½" oval	15.00	14.00	16.00	24.00
Butter dish w/lid	70.00		80.00		Salt/pepper, 3½"				
Butter dish bottom	27.50		37.50		ftd., pr.	90.00		90.00	135.00
Butter dish top	37.50		42.50		Salt/pepper, 3½"				
*Candlesticks, pr., 2¼".	22.00	20.00			flat, pr.	45.00		64.00	
Cookie jar w/lid	45.00	30.00			Saucer	4.00	5.00	5.00	10.00
Creamer, ftd.	8.50		11.00	20.00	Sherbet, two styles	7.50		11.00	15.00
Cup	6.50	7.50	8.50	16.00	Sugar	7.50		8.50	15.00
Gravy boat and					Sugar cover	40.00		45.00	160.00
platter	1,100.00				Tumbler, 3⅞", 5 oz.	14.00		32.00	38.00
Hot dish coaster	40.00		37.50		Tumbler, 4¼", 9 oz.	15.00	15.00	20.00	25.00
Hot dish coaster					Tumbler, 5½",				
w/Indent	37.50		37.50		12 oz. 2 styles	20.00		30.00	38.00
Jam dish, 7"	21.00		18.50	35.00	Tumbler, 4", 5 oz. ftd.	25.00		37.50	
Jello mold, 2⅛" T	13.00				Tumbler, 5½",				
Pitcher, 5½"					10 oz. ftd.	25.00		38.00	
36 oz. juice	40.00				Wooden lazy susan,				
**Pitcher, 8", sq. 60 oz.	45.00	35.00	135.00	160.00	cold cuts coasters	750.00			

* Iridescent priced slightly higher
** Crystal – $150.00

Please refer to Foreword for pricing information

MANHATTAN, "HORIZONTAL RIBBED" ANCHOR HOCKING GLASS COMPANY, 1938–1943

Colors: Crystal, pink; some green, ruby, and iridized.

If you find a piece of Manhattan that does not fit the measurements in the list below, then you may have a piece of Anchor Hocking's newer line PARK AVENUE. For new readers, I will repeat what I said for those who do not update your books regularly.

PARK AVENUE was a new pattern line introduced by Anchor Hocking in 1987 to "re-create the Glamour Era of 1938 when Anchor Hocking first introduced a classic" according to the Inspiration '87 catalogue issued by the company. Anchor Hocking went to the trouble to preserve the integrity of their older glassware, however! None of the pieces in this line are exactly like the old Manhattan! They are only similar and Manhattan was never made in blue as this line has been. Many collectors of Manhattan have bought this new pattern to use as everyday dishes. Thus, everyone remains happy, company and collector alike. Manhattan's collectability has not been affected by the making of PARK AVENUE; however, it has caused some confusion with the older Manhattan cereal bowls. These 5¼" cereals are rarely seen, particularly in **mint** condition; you need to be aware of the differences in these pieces. PARK AVENUE lists a small bowl at 6". All the original Manhattan bowls measure 1¹⁵⁄₁₆" **high.** If the bowl you have measures more than that, then you have a piece of PARK AVENUE! Be very suspicious if the bowl is mint! I hope this clears up the measuring problems that people ordering through the mail have had in buying the cereal bowls. You can see an original on the right in front of the creamer (top photograph).

All metal accessories were made outside the factory. Anchor Hocking sold their wares to other companies who made these accoutrements with tongs or spoons hanging or otherwise attached to them. There is a remote possibility that metal pieces were sold to Hocking; but years ago workers told me that they never assembled anything but glass at the factory. Of course, I have found that workers memories are not always totally reliable!

The price rise and scarcity of Manhattan comports can be attributed to Margarita or Martini drinkers!

Pink Manhattan cups, saucers, and dinner plates do exist, but are rarely seen. You can detect a cup in the bottom photograph, but I have never found a saucer to go with it. The saucer/sherbet plates of Manhattan are like many of Hocking's saucers; they have no cup ring. The pink dinner plate displayed at a Houston show years ago has been in someone's collection for some time now. Another Manhattan Royal Ruby juice pitcher was found last year in a northern Kentucky antique show. I will picture it in a future edition.

The handled berry measures 5⅜". Cereals do not have handles! I mention the measurements because there is a vast price difference. In fact, the reason the 5⅜" handled berry has increased in price so much has come from dealers marketing these as cereals!

The sherbet in Manhattan has a beaded bottom, but the center insert to the relish tray does not have these beads. Relish tray inserts can be found in crystal, pink, and Royal Ruby. The center insert is always crystal on these relish trays although I see a pink sherbet was placed in the center of the pink relish in the bottom picture by some helpful gremlin at the photo session!

Manhattan is one pattern where collectors do not seem to mind look-alike pieces. Many collectors buy Hazel Atlas shakers to use with Manhattan since they are round and look better to them than the original squared ones that Hocking made. I have intentionally left out all the Manhattan look-alikes in the photographs! Too many new collectors are being confused by showing pieces that are not Manhattan.

		Crystal	Pink			Crystal	Pink
*	Ashtray, 4" round	11.00			Relish tray, 14", 4-part	18.00	
	Ashtray, 4½" square	18.00			Relish tray, 14" with inserts	50.00	50.00
	Bowl, 4½" sauce, handles	9.00		***	Relish tray insert	5.50	6.00
	Bowl, 5⅜" berry w/handles	17.50	18.00		Pitcher, 24 oz.	32.00	
	Bowl, 5¼" cereal, no handles	30.00			Pitcher, 80 oz. tilted	42.00	60.00
	Bowl, 7½" large berry	14.00			Plate, 6" sherbet or saucer	7.00	50.00
	Bowl, 8", closed handles	20.00	22.00		Plate, 8½ salad	15.00	
	Bowl, 9" salad	19.00			Plate, 10¼" dinner	20.00	125.00
	Bowl, 9½" fruit open handle	35.00	32.00		Plate, 14" sandwich	22.00	
	Candlesticks, 4½" (square) pr.	15.00			Salt & pepper, 2" pr. (square)	27.50	45.00
	Candy dish, 3 legs		12.00		Saucer/sherbet plate	7.00	50.00
**	Candy dish and cover	37.50			Sherbet	9.00	15.00
	Coaster, 3½"	15.00			Sugar, oval	10.00	11.00
	Comport, 5¾"	32.00	32.00	****	Tumbler, 10 oz. ftd.	17.00	17.00
	Creamer, oval	10.00	11.00		Vase, 8"	18.00	
	Cup	17.50	150.00	**	Wine, 3½"	5.50	

    * Ad for Hocking $15.00; ad for others $12.50
   ** Look-Alike
  *** Ruby – $3.50
 **** Green or iridized – $15.00

Please refer to Foreword for pricing information

MAYFAIR FEDERAL GLASS COMPANY, 1934

Colors: Crystal, amber, and green.

Federal had to redesign their own "Mayfair" glass moulds into what finally became known as the "Rosemary" pattern because Hocking had patented the name **Mayfair** first. The green and amber pieces pictured in the bottom photograph represent a "transitional period" of glassware made between the old Federal "Mayfair" pattern and what was to become known as the "Rosemary" pattern. Observe that these transitional pieces have arching in the bottom of each piece rather than the waffle design, and there is no waffling between the top arches. If you turn to the Rosemary (188–189) for reference, you will see that the design under the arches is entirely plain. Most collectors consider these transitional pieces a part of Federal Mayfair rather than Rosemary and that is why they are placed here. I suspect that after examining the reworking of the Mayfair moulds, someone decided that the changes made were not different enough, and they were again redesigned into the final pattern, Rosemary. That's only speculation, but it seems logical.

Federal's Mayfair was a very limited production, possibly because of pattern name difficulties. Amber and crystal are the colors that can be collected (in the true pattern form), but not all pieces appear in amber. So far, amber cream soups can only be found in the transitional pattern. That may mean that cream soups were only designed after the change from Mayfair. They appear only in the transitional pattern and again in the Rosemary pattern. No cream soup in crystal has been found since no crystal Rosemary or transitional pieces have been discovered. Crystal Mayfair can be collected as a set. Green can only be bought in transitional form, but amber is found in both, or so I believe. Feel free to prove me wrong!

I prefer the scalloped lines of Mayfair to those of the plainer Rosemary. This is a challenging set to collect. Once you gather it, you will not be sorry. Mix the transitional with the regular pattern in amber. They go well together and only an expert collector will spot the difference.

There are no sherbets in this pattern. The Mayfair sugar, like Rosemary, looks like a large sherbet since it does not have handles. I once bought six sugar bowls from a flea market dealer who sold them as sherbets. Both the Mayfair and the transitional pattern differences can be seen in the amber sugar.

Often you will find several pieces of Mayfair together, rather than a piece here and there. You can get a rapid start on a collection that way. Start a set! You'll like it!

	Amber	Crystal	Green		Amber	Crystal	Green
Bowl, 5" sauce	8.50	6.50	12.00	Plate, 9½" dinner	14.00	10.00	14.00
Bowl, 5" cream soup	18.00	11.00	18.00	Plate, 9½" grill	13.50	8.50	13.50
Bowl, 6" cereal	17.50	9.50	20.00	Platter, 12" oval	27.50	20.00	30.00
Bowl, 10" oval vegetable	30.00	18.00	30.00	Saucer	4.50	2.50	4.50
Creamer, ftd.	13.00	10.50	16.00	Sugar, ftd.	13.00	11.00	13.00
Cup	8.50	5.00	8.50	Tumbler, 4½", 9 oz.	27.50	15.00	30.00
Plate, 6¾" salad	7.00	4.50	9.00				

Please refer to Foreword for pricing information

MAYFAIR, "OPEN ROSE" HOCKING GLASS COMPANY, 1931–1937

Colors: Ice blue, pink; some green, yellow, and crystal. *(See Reproduction Section.)*

Mayfair is one of the most collected patterns of Depression Glass. I spend hours answering questions and calls about reproductions and rare pieces in Mayfair. I have updated the Reproduction Section in the back to take care of the odd colors of cookie jars and shakers now being found.

Another question that I am continually asked concerns the value of frosted pieces in Mayfair. Originally, glass companies dipped glass items in camphoric acid to "satinize" them. Often, these frosted pieces were hand painted and sold by special order only. As you can see on page 127, there is an extensive line of satin-finished Mayfair. These pieces are rarer than the unfrosted pieces, but there are only a few collectors searching for them; so the prices are **usually** lower.

Pink Mayfair collectors have a dilemma when picking out the tumbler size and stems to collect. Most collectors buy flat waters, footed teas, and water goblets to start. After they finish these, additional stems are added.

The 10" celery measures 11¼" handle to handle and the 9" one measures 10¼" handle to handle. The measurements in this book normally do not include handles!

The crystal items shown in the top photograph are also rarely seen, but I have never met a collector of crystal Mayfair. Most commonly seen are the pitcher, shakers, and the divided platter. A reader writes that the divided platter was given as a premium with the purchase of coffee or spices in late 1930's. The crystal footed vase is the only one known thus far, and I have had a report of a covered sugar. Collectors of pink Mayfair and collectors of sugar and creamers have not been too excited over that report. Usually, the comment made had to do with asking if there were any way to dye crystal glass some other color!

Two large Texas collections of rarely found Mayfair recently were sold (What other size collection would be in Texas?) and have now been assimilated into other collections. The only known footed shaker reportedly changed hands for a price of five digits. That would make it the most expensive piece of Depression Glass known! Numerous rare pieces that had not been on the open market for years are now in new collections. You may see a price advertised or displayed at shows for more than my listed price. It is difficult to list a price for an item that both buyer and seller have sworn to keep secret! You must ultimately decide the worth of an item to you!

Seven three-legged Mayfair console bowls on the market in the last three years have saturated that market for a while. Notice the covered, three-footed Mayfair console bowl on 129. At least two of the known pink footed bowls were found this way. The lid is the same one that fits the 10" two-handled vegetable bowl shown in the bottom photograph on that page. Observe the two different styles of cups on page 130. It is the round one that is rarely found!

There are some secondary details about this pattern that need to be pointed out. Some Mayfair stems have a plain foot while others are rayed. All stems and tumblers shown in yellow and green are rayed, but the footed water in pink has a plain foot. Footed iced teas vary in height. Some teas have a short stem above the foot and others have practically none. This stem causes the heights to vary to some extent. It is just a mould variation, but may account for capacity differences. Note under measurements on page 4 the listings of tumblers that I have taken from old Hocking catalogues. In two catalogues from 1935, these were listed as 13 oz.; but in 1936, both catalogues listed the tumbler as 15 oz. I have never found a 13 oz. tumbler over the years! (Catalogue mistake?)

Yellow and green Mayfair **can be collected,** but it takes both time and money to do so! Of course, that holds true for pink or blue! Even a setting for four with all the pieces in easily found colors is expensive! However, if you try not to buy **everything** made, you can put a small set together for about the same money as most other patterns.

I used to have time to get out and find rare glass. After twelve weeks of self-imposed prison at my computer, believe me, I would prefer to be out among all the flea markets and shows! (I have been able to squeeze in a few hours fishing early in the mornings when the cold fronts, rain, and wind will let me.) I wish you luck in finding rare and unusual glassware! It is generally found by those who work at it!

After writing four books last spring, I decided to go shopping since I had heard how difficult it was to find glass to resell. After five weeks, over six thousand miles driven in seven states, and visiting 563 shops and antique malls, I can honestly say that there is still glass that can be bought to be sold at a profit. Admittedly, it does take more work than it used to, but if you are willing to put in the time (waiting for a shop to open, and helping close one down late that evening), you can find good buys and even a few bargains.

	*Pink	Blue	Green	Yellow		*Pink	Blue	Green	Yellow
Bowl, 5" cream soup	42.50				Butter dish and cover or 7" covered vegetable	65.00	285.00	1,250.00	1,250.00
Bowl, 5½" cereal	24.00	47.50	75.00	75.00	Butter bottom with indent				265.00
Bowl, 7" vegetable	25.00	50.00	125.00	125.00					
Bowl, 9", 3⅛ high, 3 leg console	5,000.00		5,000.00		Butter dish top	40.00	235.00	1,125.00	1,125.00
Bowl, 9½" oval vegetable	27.50	67.50	115.00	120.00	Cake plate, 10" ftd.	30.00	70.00	100.00	
Bowl, 10" vegetable	26.00	67.50		120.00	Candy dish and cover	52.50	285.00	575.00	475.00
Bowl, 10" same covered	115.00	120.00		950.00	Celery dish, 9" divided			150.00	150.00
Bowl, 11¾" low flat	55.00	70.00	40.00	185.00	Celery dish, 10"	40.00	60.00	110.00	110.00
Bowl, 12" deep scalloped fruit	55.00	90.00	40.00	215.00	Celery dish, 10" divided	200.00	60.00		

*Frosted or satin finish items slightly lower

Please refer to Foreword for pricing information

MAYFAIR, "OPEN ROSE" (Cont.)

	*Pink	Blue	Green	Yellow
Cookie jar and lid	50.00	285.00	575.00	850.00
Creamer, ftd.	27.50	80.00	205.00	200.00
Cup	18.00	52.00	145.00	145.00
Cup, round	325.00			
Decanter and stopper, 32 oz.	160.00			
Goblet, 3¾", 1 oz. cordial	1,100.00		900.00	
Goblet, 4⅛", 2½ oz.	900.00		900.00	
Goblet, 4", 3 oz. cocktail	72.50		375.00	
Goblet, 4½", 3 oz. wine	72.50		425.00	
Goblet, 5¼", 4½ oz. claret	900.00		900.00	
Goblet, 5¾", 9 oz. water	57.50		450.00	
Goblet, 7¼", 9 oz. thin	215.00	175.00		
** Pitcher, 6", 37 oz.	52.50	147.50	525.00	500.00
Pitcher, 8", 60 oz.	52.50	165.00	475.00	420.00
Pitcher, 8½", 80 oz.	100.00	190.00	550.00	550.00
Plate, 5¾" (often substituted as saucer)	13.00	25.00	87.50	87.50
Plate, 6½" round sherbet	12.50			
Plate, 6½" round, off-center indent	25.00	27.50	115.00	
Plate, 8½" luncheon	25.00	52.50	80.00	80.00
Plate, 9½" dinner	50.00	77.50	140.00	140.00
Plate, 9½" grill	40.00	52.50	77.50	77.50
Plate, 11½" handled grill				100.00
Plate, 12" cake w/handles	40.00	67.50	37.50	
*** Platter, 12" oval, open handles	27.50	67.50	165.00	115.00
Platter, 12½" oval, 8" wide, closed handles			225.00	225.00
Relish, 8⅜", 4-part	30.00	62.50	165.00	165.00
Relish, 8⅜" non-partitioned	210.00		275.00	275.00
**** Salt and pepper, flat pr.	60.00	285.00	1,050.00	800.00
Salt and pepper, ftd.	8,500.00			
Sandwich server, center handle	45.00	75.00	37.50	125.00
Saucer (cup ring)	32.50			145.00
Saucer (see 5¾"plate)				
Sherbet, 2¼" flat	160.00	115.00		
Sherbet, 3" ftd.	16.00			
Sherbet, 4¾" ftd.	77.50	77.50	150.00	150.00
Sugar, ftd.	28.00	80.00	195.00	195.00
Sugar lid	1,500.00		1,100.00	1,100.00
Tumbler, 3½", 5 oz. juice	42.00	115.00		
Tumbler, 4¼", 9 oz. water	28.00	100.00		
Tumbler, 4¾", 11 oz. water	175.00	125.00	200.00	200.00
Tumbler, 5¼", 13½ oz. iced tea	45.00	210.00		
Tumbler, 3¼", 3 oz. ftd. juice	80.00			
Tumbler, 5¼", 10 oz. ftd.	35.00	120.00		180.00
Tumbler, 6½", 15 oz. ftd. iced tea	35.00	225.00	220.00	
Vase (sweet pea)	135.00	110.00	285.00	
Whiskey, 2¼", 1½ oz.	65.00			

* Frosted or satin finish items slightly lower
** Crystal – $15.00
*** Divided Crystal – $12.50
**** Crystal – $17.50 pr. – Beware reproductions.

Please refer to Foreword for pricing information

MISS AMERICA (DIAMOND PATTERN) HOCKING GLASS COMPANY, 1935–1938

Colors: Crystal, pink; some green, ice blue, Jad-ite, and Royal Ruby. *(See Reproduction Section.)*

Enjoy the rarely seen Royal Ruby Miss America pictured on page 133. This set was bought from the grandson of a former employee who retired in 1962, and is now in a collection in Arkansas. The fifty pieces contained some surprises! I discovered that there were two styles of water goblets, footed juices, and sherbets! Notice how one of the water goblets and one of the footed juices flare out at the top. The sherbets do the same; but only one style was photographed. This set contained the first Miss America cups, sherbets, footed and flat juices I had seen in Royal Ruby. It was originally a basic set for eight with cups, saucers, and luncheon plates; but it had a few other pieces. Even though this was obviously a trial color, pieces turn up occasionally. Butter dishes were reproduced in red in the late 1970's; but they were an amberina red. No original red butter has been seen!

Reproductions have been a problem for the Miss America pattern since the early 1970's. Please refer to page 236 for a complete run down on Miss America reproductions. Lately, there are many reports of cobalt creamers and sugars; this pattern was **not made in cobalt** originally. That means that other colors may follow.

Reproduction shakers have been troublesome! There are few green shakers available that are old. In fact, I haven't seen an older pair since the early 1970's. Rarely, have I had as many questions about Miss America shakers as in the last few years because there have been reproductions of the reproductions and even those have now been duplicated by another importer. There are at least four or five generations of reproduction Miss America shakers; it depends upon which one you find as to what to look for on them. Interestingly enough, there originally were two different moulds used for old shakers. The shakers that are fatter toward the foot are the best ones to buy, since that style has not been reproduced — **yet**. The shakers that get thin (as shown in the photograph) are the style that has been reproduced. Both styles were made originally, but only the thin style has been copied and copied! Buy shakers from a **reputable dealer**.

Any time a glass pattern was made for several years, it will be possible to find pieces that deviate in design. There was more than one mould made for each piece; so each item can vary as often as any mould was changed, remade, or simply became worn.

The pink, five-part divided relish is on the wish list of many Miss America collectors. Most of the ones that surfaced over the years were found in the central Ohio region.

There are a few odd-colored or flashed pieces of Miss America that surface occasionally. Flashed-on red, green, or amethyst make interesting conversation pieces, but are not plentiful enough to collect a set. You can see an amethyst flashed-on goblet and a Jad-ite luncheon plate on the bottom of page 133.

	Crystal	Pink	Green	Royal Ruby			Crystal	Pink	Green	Royal Ruby
Bowl, 4½" berry			12.00			Goblet, 5½", 10 oz.				
Bowl, 6¼" cereal	10.00	22.00	18.00			water	21.00	42.50		250.00
Bowl, 8" curved in at						Pitcher, 8", 65 oz.	46.00	120.00		
top	40.00	72.50		425.00		Pitcher, 8½", 65 oz.				
Bowl, 8¾" straight						w/ice lip	65.00	135.00		
deep fruit	35.00	60.00			**	Plate, 5¾" sherbet	6.00	10.00	7.00	45.00
Bowl, 10" oval						Plate, 6¾"			7.50	
vegetable	15.00	28.00				Plate, 8½" salad	7.50	22.00	9.50	140.00
Bowl, 11", shallow				800.00	***	Plate, 10¼" dinner	15.00	27.50		
* Butter dish and						Plate, 10¼" grill	11.00	24.00		
cover	210.00	575.00				Platter, 12¼" oval	14.00	26.00		
Butter dish bottom	10.00	22.00				Relish, 8¾", 4 part	11.00	24.00		
Butter dish top	200.50	553.00				Relish, 11¾" round				
Cake plate, 12" ftd.	26.00	42.00				divided	25.00	1,100.00		
Candy jar and						Salt and pepper, pr.	29.00	58.00	290.00	
cover, 11½"	57.50	145.00				Saucer	4.00	7.00		65.00
*** Celery dish, 10½"					**	Sherbet	800	14.00		125.00
oblong	15.00	30.00				Sugar	8.00	16.00		175.00
Coaster, 5¾"	15.00	27.50			***	Tumbler, 4", 5 oz.				
Comport, 5"	14.00	25.00				juice	16.50	45.00		200.00
Creamer, ftd.	9.50	18.00		175.00		Tumbler, 4½",				
Cup	10.00	22.50	12.00	225.00		10 oz. water	15.00	30.00	18.00	
Goblet, 3¾", 3 oz.						Tumbler, 5¾", 14 oz.				
wine	22.00	75.00		250.00		iced tea	25.00	77.50		
Goblet, 4¾", 5 oz.										
juice	27.00	82.50		250.00						

*Absolute mint price   **Also in Ice Blue $50.00   ***Also in Ice Blue $150.00

Please refer to Foreword for pricing information

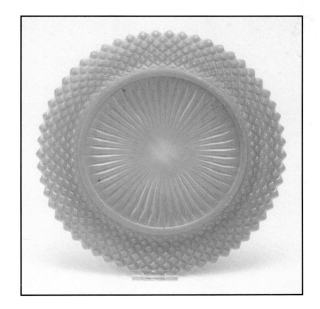

MODERNTONE HAZEL ATLAS GLASS COMPANY, 1934–1942; Late 1940's–Early 1950's

Colors: Amethyst, cobalt blue; some crystal, pink, and Platonite fired-on colors.

Cobalt blue glass is highly collectible which makes Moderntone quite desirable. Cobalt colored glassware is often displayed in windows. Sometimes the color and not the pattern attracts buyers. The sun really makes an exhibit of the color itself.

Realize that there is no Moderntone tumbler. Tumblers sold as Moderntone were advertised along with this pattern, but they were never sold as a part of the set. There are even two different style tumblers that have been "adopted" for this set. The juice and water shown here are paneled and have a rayed bottom. Other cobalt tumblers are not paneled and have a plain bottom that is often marked **H** over **A** which is the Hazel Atlas trademark. Either tumbler is acceptable, but the paneled is preferred by most collectors. All these tumblers are hard to find except for the water. Green, pink, or crystal tumblers are also found, but there is little market for these except the shot or whiskey glass which is sought by those enthusiasts. I am frequently asked just which lid is the real lid for the Moderntone butter or sugar. There is no **true** sugar or butter lid. Evidently, the butter bottom and sugar were sold to some other company who made the tops. No one knows whether the lids are supposed to have black, red, or blue knobs, but I have seen all those colors on Moderntone! Red seems to be the predominate color.

By adding a lid, mustards were made from the handle-less custard. There is also a punch set being sold as Moderntone which uses a Hazel Atlas mixing bowl and the same roly poly cups found with the Royal Lace toddy set. This was assembled by someone else; but some collectors accept it to go-with Moderntone. I think It is merely a blue punch set.

A similar punch set uses a Hazel Atlas cobalt blue mixing bowl in a metal holder with Moderntone custard cups sitting on the metal rim. That **is** being accepted as a Moderntone punch set by many collectors.

The boxed set with the crystal shot glasses in the metal holder came with a Colonial Block creamer. The box was marked "Little Deb" Lemonade Server Set. You can see the set in the bottom photograph. It's a shame the shot glasses and pitcher were not cobalt! That pitcher has turned up in cobalt and several have turned up with Shirley Temple's picture! These boxed crystal children's sets sell in the $40.00 range.

Where have all the ruffled cream soups and sandwich plates gone? Sandwich plates can be found, but most are heavily scratched causing collectors to avoid them. The cheese dish lid has been moved to the side to show the wooden cheese plate that fits inside the metal lid. There have been some big prices paid for these recently. This cheese dish is a salad plate with a metal cover and wooden cutting board.

Both green and pink ash trays are found sporadically, but there is little demand for them now. Blue ash trays still command a hefty price for an ash tray. Crystal Moderntone is found occasionally; and there are a few collectors for it. Price it about one-third the amethyst. It's a shame some of the crystal flat soups could not be changed into some other color. Finding any Moderntone bowls without inner rim damage is a problem for collectors. Prices below are for **mint** condition pieces. That is why bowls are so highly priced. Used, nicked, and bruised bowls are the norm; mint condition bowls are rare.

Platonite Moderntone has been moved into the *Collectible Glassware from the 40's, 50's, 60's...* since it better fits the era covered in that book.

	Cobalt	Amethyst		Cobalt	Amethyst
* Ash tray, 7¾", match holder in center	160.00		Plate, 7¾" luncheon	12.50	9.00
Bowl, 4¾" cream soup	20.00	17.00	Plate, 8⅞" dinner	17.50	12.00
Bowl, 5" berry	25.00	22.50	Plate, 10½" sandwich	55.00	40.00
Bowl, 5" cream soup, ruffled	50.00	30.00	Platter, 11" oval	45.00	37.50
Bowl, 6½" cereal	70.00	70.00	Platter, 12" oval	75.00	50.00
Bowl, 7½" soup	140.00	90.00	Salt and pepper, pr.	40.00	35.00
Bowl, 8¾" large berry	50.00	40.00	Saucer	5.00	4.00
Butter dish with metal cover	98.00		Sherbet	13.00	12.00
Cheese dish, 7" with metal lid	450.00		Sugar	11.00	10.00
Creamer	11.00	10.00	Sugar lid in metal	37.50	
Cup	11.00	11.00	Tumbler, 5 oz.	50.00	30.00
Cup (handle-less) or custard	18.00	14.00	Tumbler, 9 oz.	33.00	25.00
Plate, 5⅞" sherbet	6.50	5.00	Tumbler, 12 oz.	100.00	85.00
Plate, 6¾" salad	11.00	9.00	** Whiskey, 1½ oz.	40.00	

* Pink $75.00; green $95.00
** Pink or green $17.50

MOONDROPS NEW MARTINSVILLE GLASS COMPANY, 1932–1940

Colors: Amber, pink, green, cobalt, ice blue, red, amethyst, crystal, dark green, light green, jadite, smoke, and black.

Moondrops collectors are merciless in their pursuit of red and cobalt blue! There are few collectors for other colors. Amber is the least desired color; if you like that color, you can probably find a bargain awaiting you! In Moondrops there are a variety of pieces not found in other patterns in this book! Perfume bottles, powder jars, mugs, gravy boats, and triple candlesticks are indications that this glassware is more elegant than most of its contemporaries. Bud vases, decanters, and rocket-style stems add a range of unusual pieces from which to choose. The rocket style can be seen by the dark green bud vase on the left side of the picture at the top of page 137. The base looks ready to launch! I just bought a crystal rocket decanter at a Chicago show. I had never seen one in crystal. Not much crystal Moondrops is available!

The butter has to have a matching glass top to obtain the price listed below. The metal top with a bird finial found on butter bottoms is better than none; that top only sells for about $25.00. However, the metal top **with the fan finial** sells for approximately $55.00! Still, collectors prefer glass tops on their butter dishes!

	Blue, Red	Other Colors		Blue, Red	Other Colors
Ash tray	32.00	17.00	Goblet, 5⅛", 3 oz. metal stem wine	16.00	11.00
Bowl, 4¼", cream soup	95.00	35.00	Goblet, 5½", 4 oz. metal stem wine	20.00	11.00
Bowl, 5¼" berry	18.00	10.00	Goblet, 6¼", 9 oz. metal stem water	23.00	16.00
Bowl, 6¾" soup	85.00		Gravy boat	120.00	90.00
Bowl, 7½" pickle	22.00	14.00	Mayonnaise, 5¼"	55.00	32.00
Bowl, 8⅜" ftd., concave top	45.00	25.00	Mug, 5⅛", 12 oz.	40.00	23.00
Bowl, 8½" 3-ftd. divided relish	29.00	18.00	Perfume bottle, "rocket"	210.00	150.00
Bowl, 9½" 3-legged ruffled	65.00		Pitcher, 6⅞", 22 oz. small	165.00	90.00
Bowl, 9¾" oval vegetable	45.00	23.00	Pitcher, 8⅛", 32 oz. medium	185.00	115.00
Bowl, 9¾" covered casserole	185.00	97.50	Pitcher, 8", 50 oz. large, with lip	195.00	115.00
Bowl, 9¾" handled oval	52.50	36.00	Pitcher, 8⅛", 53 oz. large, no lip	185.00	125.00
Bowl, 11" boat-shaped celery	32.00	23.00	Plate, 5⅞"	11.00	8.00
Bowl, 12" round 3-ftd. console	85.00	32.00	Plate, 6⅛" sherbet	8.00	5.00
Bowl, 13" console with "wings"	120.00	42.00	Plate, 6" round, off-center sherbet indent	12.00	9.00
Butter dish and cover	430.00	255.00	Plate, 7⅛" salad	14.00	10.00
Butter dish bottom	62.50	47.50	Plate, 8½" luncheon	15.00	12.00
Butter dish top (glass)	367.50	207.50	Plate, 9½" dinner	25.00	16.00
Candles, 2" ruffled pr.	40.00	24.00	Plate, 14" round sandwich	38.00	18.00
Candles, 4½" sherbet style pr.	27.00	20.00	Plate, 14" 2-handled sandwich	43.00	23.00
Candlesticks, 5" ruffled, pr.	35.00	21.00	Platter, 12" oval	35.00	22.00
Candlesticks, 5" "wings" pr.	95.00	50.00	Powder jar, 3 ftd.	175.00	110.00
Candlesticks, 5¼" triple light pr.	110.00	60.00	Saucer	6.00	5.00
Candlesticks, 8½" metal stem pr.	40.00	30.00	Sherbet, 2⅝"	16.00	11.00
Candy dish, 8" ruffled	37.50	20.00	Sherbet, 4½"	26.00	16.00
Cocktail shaker with or without hdl.,			Sugar, 2¾"	15.00	10.00
metal top	60.00	35.00	Sugar, 3½"	16.00	11.00
Comport, 4"	27.50	18.00	Tumbler, 2¾", 2 oz. shot	16.00	10.00
Comport, 11½"	65.00	35.00	Tumbler, 2¾", 2 oz. handled shot	16.00	11.00
Creamer, 2¾" miniature	18.00	11.00	Tumbler, 3¼", 3 oz. ftd. juice	16.00	11.00
Creamer, 3¾" regular	16.00	10.00	Tumbler, 3⅝", 5 oz.	15.00	10.00
Cup	16.00	10.00	Tumbler, 4⅜", 7 oz.	16.00	10.00
Decanter, 7¾" small	67.50	38.00	Tumbler, 4⅜", 8 oz.	16.00	11.00
Decanter, 8½" medium	70.00	42.00	Tumbler, 4⅞", 9 oz. handled	30.00	16.00
Decanter, 11¼" large	98.00	50.00	Tumbler, 4⅞", 9 oz.	19.00	15.00
Decanter, 10¼" "rocket"	425.00	375.00	Tumbler, 5⅛", 12 oz.	30.00	14.00
Goblet, 2⅞", ¾ oz. cordial	38.00	26.00	Tray, 7½", for mini sugar/creamer	37.50	19.00
Goblet, 4", 4 oz. wine	22.00	13.00	Vase, 7¾" flat, ruffled top	60.00	57.00
Goblet, 4¾", "rocket" wine	60.00	30.00	Vase, 8½" "rocket" bud	250.00	175.00
Goblet, 4¾", 5 oz.	24.00	15.00	Vase, 9¼" "rocket" style	235.00	135.00
Goblet, 5¾" 8 oz.	33.00	19.00			

Please refer to Foreword for pricing information

MT. PLEASANT, "DOUBLE SHIELD" L. E. SMITH GLASS COMPANY, 1920's–1934

Colors: Black amethyst, amethyst, cobalt blue, crystal, pink, green, white.

Collectors for cobalt blue and black glass often buy Mt. Pleasant unawares. Many times someone has brought a piece of this pattern in for me to identify and was excited to know that it was even in a book! The cobalt blue leaf-shaped dishes attract non collectors also. One lady wrote, after seeing her cobalt leaf in a friend's book, that she had received a set of one large and six smaller ones as a wedding gift in 1931. The larger leaf measures 11¼" and is being found infrequently. Sets such as the lady above described may mean that the larger plate is six times rarer! Maybe that is why I never knew it existed until a few years ago.

I do have a warning for collectors of black. You need to watch out for leaping plates that commit suicide without provocation. At Houston, one of the black decaled plates pictured at the top of 139 jumped off our table as a lady with a big purse brushed by our table. She didn't touch it you understand; it just jumped off all by itself.

A few undecorated white pieces were reported as were several pieces of striped decorated crystal. Decaled and enameled pieces are not often found. I have had only sporadic reports of pink and green pieces.

More cobalt blue is found in the Midwest and northern New York than any other place. Mt. Pleasant was promoted heavily at hardware stores in those areas; black predominates in most other areas of the country. Many pieces are found with a platinum (silver) band around them. This decorated band eroded with use. Price is often less for decorated pieces as they are harder to match and therefore, harder to sell.

	Pink, Green	Amethyst, Black, Cobalt		Pink, Green	Amethyst, Black, Cobalt
Bonbon, 7", rolled-up, handled	16.00	23.00	Leaf, 11¼"		28.00
Bowl, 4" opening, rose	18.00	26.00	Mayonnaise, 5½", 3-ftd.	18.00	28.00
Bowl, 4⅞", square ftd. fruit	13.00	20.00	Mint, 6", center handle	16.00	22.00
Bowl, 6", 2-handled, square	13.00	18.00	Plate, 7", 2-handled, scalloped	9.00	15.00
Bowl, 7", 3 ftd., rolled out edge	16.00	25.00	Plate, 8", scalloped or square	10.00	15.00
Bowl, 8", scalloped, 2-handled	19.00	30.00	Plate, 8", 2-handled	11.00	18.00
Bowl, 8", square, 2-handled	19.00	30.00	Plate 8¼, square w/indent for cup		16.00
Bowl, 9", scalloped, 1¾" deep, ftd.		28.00	Plate, 9" grill		12.00
Bowl, 9¼", square ftd. fruit	19.00	30.00	Plate, 10½", cake, 2-handled	16.00	28.00
Bowl, 10", scalloped fruit		40.00	Plate, 10½", 1¼" high, cake		37.50
Bowl, 10", 2-handled, turned-up edge		30.00	Plate, 12", 2-handled	20.00	33.00
Cake plate, 10½", ftd., 1¼" high		36.00	Salt and pepper, 2 styles	24.00	42.00
Candlestick, single, pr.	20.00	28.00	Sandwich server, center-handled		38.00
Candlestick, double, pr.	26.00	45.00	Saucer	2.50	5.00
Creamer	18.00	19.00	Sherbet, 2 styles	10.00	16.00
Cup (waffle-like crystal)	4..50		Sugar	18.00	18.00
Cup	9.50	12.00	Tumbler, ftd.		22.00
Leaf, 8"		16.00	Vase, 7¼"		30.00

NEW CENTURY, and incorrectly, "LYDIA RAY" HAZEL ATLAS GLASS COMPANY, 1930–1935

Colors: Green; some crystal, pink, amethyst, and cobalt.

New Century is the **official** name for this pattern made by Hazel Atlas. "Lydia Ray" was the name used by collectors until an **official** name was found. I mention this for new collectors since the name "New Century" was also used (incorrectly) by another author to identify the **Ovide**. This has caused confusion in the past.

New Century is one of those designs that a few collectors just love. Green is the most desired color; sets can only be acquired in green. I have been told that it is impossible to collect a set in crystal by several who tried to do so. Crystal is so scarce that prices are on the same level as green. Years ago, I ran into several crystal powder jars. They were made with a sugar lid on the top of a sherbet. The knob of the sherbet had glass marbles or beads attached by a wire. I have not seen these for a while. You can make a footed powder jar in many patterns by putting a sugar lid on a sherbet. It will not work for all patterns, but it will for many.

So far, pink, cobalt blue, and amethyst have only been found in water sets and an occasional cup or saucer. Only flat tumblers have been seen in these colors.

Bowls are harder to find than for most patterns. I haven't had a berry bowl to sell for years. Cream soups, casseroles, wines, and cocktails are rarely seen. As with Adam, the casserole bottom is harder to find than the top.

There are seven different tumblers if you count the whiskey, but only the nine and ten ounce flat tumblers are found regularly. Four of the five sizes of flat tumblers can be seen in amethyst. I seem to be missing a shot glass in all colors! Maybe they are harder to find than I realized!

	Green, Crystal	Pink, Cobalt Amethyst		Green, Crystal	Pink, Cobalt Amethyst
Ash tray/coaster, 5⅜"	28.00		Plate, 8½" salad	10.00	
Bowl, 4½" berry	18.00		Plate, 10" dinner	18.00	
Bowl, 4¾" cream soup	20.00		Plate, 10" grill	12.00	
Bowl, 8" large berry	22.00		Platter, 11" oval	18.00	
Bowl, 9" covered casserole	60.00		Salt and pepper, pr.	35.00	
Butter dish and cover	55.00		Saucer	3.00	7.50
Cup	6.50	19.00	Sherbet, 3"	9.00	
Creamer	8.50		Sugar	8.00	
Decanter and stopper	55.00		Sugar cover	15.00	
Goblet, 2½ oz. wine	25.00		Tumbler, 3½", 5 oz.	12.00	12.00
Goblet, 3¼ oz. cocktail	22.00		Tumbler, 3½", 8 oz.	20.00	
Pitcher, 7¾", 60 oz. with or			Tumbler, 4¼", 9 oz.	15.00	14.00
without ice lip	35.00	35.00	Tumbler, 5", 10 oz.	17.00	16.00
Pitcher, 8", 80 oz. with or			Tumbler, 5¼", 12 oz.	25.00	25.00
without ice lip	40.00	42.00	Tumbler, 4", 5 oz. ftd.	18.00	
Plate, 6" sherbet	3.50		Tumbler, 4⅞", 9 oz. ftd.	20.00	
Plate, 7⅛" breakfast	9.00		Whiskey, 2½", 1½ oz.	18.00	

NEWPORT, "HAIRPIN" HAZEL ATLAS GLASS COMPANY, 1936–1940

Colors: Cobalt blue, amethyst; some pink, "Platonite" white, and fired-on colors.

Newport collectors wrote me several scorching letters after I mentioned that there was a difference of ⁵⁄₁₆" between a dinner and a luncheon plate. Several were upset because they had another piece to find and others had been trying to buy the dinners for luncheon plate prices. The dinner plate measures 8¹³⁄₁₆" while the luncheon plate measures 8½". I only brought the matter up because of problems that dealers who mail order were having! The only official listing I have states plates of 6", 8½", and 11½". However, after obtaining these two plates, I found actual measurements quite different as you can see by the size listings in the price guide below. One of the problems with catalogue measurements is that they are not always accurate and sometimes not even very close!

Amethyst Newport makes a great table setting! I personally like the shapes of this pattern more than Moderntone which is about the only other choice you have in accumulating a set of amethyst glassware from this era. Moroccan Amethyst came much later!

Sets of pink Newport were given away as premiums for buying seeds from a catalogue in the 1930's. A few of these sets are entering the market but are not presently selling very well.

Cereal bowls and tumblers are practically non-existent in the market in any color. I finally found a large amethyst berry bowl; but I am having trouble replacing the large cobalt berry bowl that was "crunched" before our photography session a few years ago. It is bad enough to lose pieces of glass, but losing them before they are pictured upsets me even more. Worse, they were so "crunched" (hundreds and hundreds of pieces) that they could not be salvaged with glue for future use.

Platonite Newport can now be found in my book *Collectible Glassware from the 40's, 50's, 60's....*

	Cobalt	Amethyst		Cobalt	Amethyst
Bowl, 4¾" berry	18.00	14.00	Plate, 8¹³⁄₁₆", dinner	30.00	30.00
Bowl, 4¾" cream soup	18.00	18.00	Plate, 11¾" sandwich	40.00	32.00
Bowl, 5¼" cereal	35.00	30.00	Platter, 11¾" oval	42.00	35.00
Bowl, 8¼" large berry	40.00	35.00	Salt and pepper	47.50	40.00
Cup	12.00	10.00	Saucer	5.00	5.00
Creamer	16.00	13.00	Sherbet	15.00	13.00
Plate, 5⅞" sherbet	7.00	6.00	Sugar	16.00	14.00
Plate, 8½" luncheon	14.00	12.00	Tumbler, 4½", 9 oz.	37.50	32.00

"NORA BIRD" PADEN CITY GLASS COMPANY, LINE #300, 1929–1930's

Colors: Pink, green, crystal, amber.

"Nora Bird" is a name given to this Paden City pattern by collectors. It was a numbered etching on Paden City's popular #300 line blank. The bird on each piece can be found in flight or getting ready to fly. Some collectors have suggested this bird is a pheasant which is probably true since several pheasant patterns made by other glass companies were available during this time. I believe there's an Eastern symbol of health and happiness associated with this bird which would also fit the time when we were fascinated with influences from the Orient.

The #300 line is usually seen in several colors that have not been found with "Nora Bird" etch. As late as the last edition, it was believed that pink, green, and crystal were the only colors on which "Nora Bird" etching could been found. Amber has now shown itself. See the candlestick in the bottom picture on page 145. This candlestick is a different style than the ones previously found.

Note the pink octagonal lid on the flat candy dish in the top photograph. This is not a part of the #300 line as are the other two candy dishes pictured. The 5¼" footed, pink candy dish, and the flat, open handled, green candy are both shaped like the candy dishes in "Cupid" pattern. The lids to these two candy dishes are interchangeable. Finding a candy in "Nora Bird" should be easier now with three from which to choose! Sadly, finding even one is not an easy accomplishment. Some of these are in the hands of candy dish collectors rather than "Nora Bird" collectors.

There are two styles of creamers and sugars in pink. These two types are also found with "Cupid" etch. So far, we have only found the round handled set in green in "Nora Bird." The tray shown below may have been for the sugar and creamer; but since it has only recently been discovered, I am not positive of its intended purpose. Additionally, a collector in Texas has found two green tumblers that are different from those listed. They are 2¼", 3 ounces; and 5¼", 10 ounces.

There may be more pieces in this pattern than I have listed; please let me know if you find something else. A pitcher to go with the five different tumblers discovered would be enchanting!

	Pink, Green		Pink, Green
* Candlestick, pr.	80.00	Saucer	15.00
Candy dish w/cover, 6½", 3 part	125.00	Sugar, 4½", round handle	42.50
Candy with lid, ftd., 5¼" high	125.00	Sugar, 5", pointed handle	42.50
Creamer, 4½", round handle	45.00	Tumbler, 2¼", 3 oz.	35.00
Creamer, 5", pointed handle	45.00	Tumbler, 3"	40.00
Cup	55.00	Tumbler, 4"	50.00
Ice tub, 6"	110.00	Tumbler, 4¾", ftd.	60.00
Mayonnaise and liner	87.50	Tumbler, 5¼", 10 oz.	60.00
Plate, 8"	25.00		

* Amber 100.00

NORMANDIE, "BOUQUET AND LATTICE" FEDERAL GLASS COMPANY 1933–1940

Colors: Iridescent, amber, pink, crystal.

If you are one of those who like amber colored glassware, then Normandie would be an ideal pattern to start. It has most basic items, and it is economical enough that you will not have to take out an equity loan to collect a setting for six, eight, or even twelve. Buy those hard to find items first or when you see them! That is great information for collecting any pattern. Rarer, harder to find items increase in price much faster than commonly found items.

I have noticed there have been some fashion color shifts recently. Autumn colors are coming into vogue again. If some magazine were to feature amber glassware on the cover, we would probably experience a run on amber like has never been seen before.

Pink Normandie has been elusive for years for those collectors searching for it. Amber has been available in most items, but tumblers, sugar lids, and dinner plates have become scarce even in this color. Those items mentioned above have never been easily found in pink, even in the good old days of collecting! You will notice some skyrocketing prices on these pieces in pink. Tumblers are rare enough to approach prices of American Sweetheart with Normandie collectors being vastly outnumbered by those of American Sweetheart. Pink Normandie pitchers can be bought at a reasonable price unlike American Sweetheart; so it all balances out in the end.

The console bowl and candlesticks sometimes found with sets of iridized Normandie are Madrid. These were sold about the same time. Several collectors have reported finding this console set with Normandie sets. That does not make it Normandie; it is still Madrid! The pattern on the glass determines what it is, not the color. See Madrid for pricing these console sets.

Some iridescent Normandie is now being found at Depression Glass shows. That means that people are asking for it, and dealers are listening to those requests. For years, this color sat on shelves unwanted at **any** price. Recently, however, a rumor circulated that it was getting hard to find and collectors started buying this iridescent color of Normandie. There were enough buyers to raise the prices a little. Iridescent is still reasonably priced in comparison to the pink and amber.

	Amber	Pink	Iridescent
Bowl, 5" berry	6.00	7.50	5.00
* Bowl, 6½" cereal	25.00	30.00	8.50
Bowl, 8½" large berry	18.00	22.00	14.00
Bowl, 10" oval veg.	18.00	35.00	17.00
Creamer, ftd.	8.50	11.00	8.00
Cup	7.50	8.50	6.00
Pitcher, 8", 80 oz.	75.00	150.00	
Plate, 6" sherbet	4.50	4.00	3.00
Plate, 7¾" salad	8.50	11.00	52.50
Plate, 9¼" luncheon	8.50	13.00	15.00
Plate, 11" dinner	30.00	100.00	11.50
Plate, 11" grill	14.00	17.00	9.00
Platter, 11¾"	18.00	25.00	12.00
Salt and pepper, pr.	50.00	75.00	
Saucer	4.00	4.00	3.00
Sherbet	6.50	8.50	7.00
Sugar	8.00	9.00	6.00
Sugar lid	90.00	175.00	
Tumbler, 4", 5 oz. juice	30.00	85.00	
Tumbler, 4¼", 9 oz. water	20.00	50.00	
Tumbler, 5", 12 oz. iced tea	35.00	100.00	

* Mistaken by many as butter bottom.

No. 610, "PYRAMID" INDIANA GLASS COMPANY, 1926–1932

Colors: Green, pink, yellow, white, crystal, blue, or black in 1974–1975 by Tiara.

"Pyramid" is a collectors' name for Indiana's pattern No. 610. Indiana gave most of their patterns a number and not a name. Collectors do not seem to indulge in calling patterns by numbers however; so most of Indiana's patterns are known by an unofficial moniker.

Something new to report is a green water set with satinized panels which was sold at the Houston Depression Glass show this year! Although the satinization was carelessly done, it was an eye catching set from a distance! It was probably an early designed piece with a different base than the squared one normally seen.

Hopefully, you are reading this paragraph about the crystal shaker shown in the bottom photograph. This shaker was made by Indiana, but it is not "Pyramid." It is often represented to be "Pyramid," but it is not. If you see one, look at it closely. The design is upside down from that of all No. 610 pieces and slightly different in make-up. It would serve as a great go-with item since there are no shakers in this older Indiana pattern.

Crystal pitchers and tumblers in "Pyramid" are harder to find than colored counterparts, although there are fewer collectors searching for them. Prices on crystal pitchers are higher than all but the yellow. Yellow pitchers are found most frequently; but there are so many collectors of yellow No. 610 that the price continues an upward trend! Ice buckets turn up often, even in yellow. However, the yellow **lid** to the ice bucket is nearly impossible to find!

Oval bowls and pickle dishes are both 9½". The oval bowl has pointed edges as can be seen in bowls of white, green, and yellow. The pickle dish is shown only on the left side in pink. The edges of that pickle dish are rounded instead of pointed.

Eight ounce tumblers come in two styles. One style has a 2¼" square foot while the other has a 2½" square foot. That variance most people would not notice unless these two tumblers were placed side by side.

Blue and black pieces of "Pyramid" were made by Indiana for Tiara during the 1970's. You will see two sizes of black tumblers, blue berry bowls, and the 4-part center-handled relish in either color. If you like these colors, it is fine to buy them! Just realize that they are **not** old and do not pay antique glass prices for them. That handled 4-part relish is sometimes mistaken for Tea Room, but it is not.

This art deco style pattern has received accolades in realms outside Depression Glass and prices have risen with increased exposure for this glassware.

No. 610 was and still is easily damaged. Be sure to examine all the ridged panels and all the corners on each piece. You will be amazed how often a chipped or cracked piece of "Pyramid" is sold as mint!

	Crystal	Pink	Green	Yellow
Bowl, 4¾" berry	11.00	20.00	22.00	35.00
Bowl, 8½" master berry	16.00	30.00	32.00	55.00
Bowl, 9½" oval	27.00	30.00	30.00	50.00
Bowl, 9½" pickle, 5¾" wide	19.00	30.00	30.00	55.00
Creamer	16.00	25.00	25.00	35.00
Ice tub	55.00	75.00	90.00	190.00
Ice tub lid				610.00
Pitcher	350.00	215.00	200.00	450.00
Relish tray, 4-part handled	23.00	40.00	45.00	60.00
Sugar	16.00	25.00	25.00	35.00
Tray for creamer and sugar	20.00	22.00	25.00	50.00
Tumbler, 8 oz. ftd., 2 styles	55.00	35.00	40.00	65.00
Tumbler, 11 oz. ftd.	65.00	45.00	55.00	75.00

No. 612, "HORSESHOE" INDIANA GLASS COMPANY, 1930–1933

Colors: Green, yellow, pink, crystal.

The official name for this Indiana pattern is No. 612, but collectors dubbed it "Horseshoe." Honestly, does that design look like any horseshoe you ever saw? In today's world, perhaps you have never seen a horseshoe.

Green "Horseshoe" butter dishes are the piece most often missing from collections, although the footed iced tea tumblers, both flat tumblers, grill plates, and pitchers are becoming scarce! Yellow pitchers, grill plates, and the footed iced teas create problems for collectors of that color. I have never pictured the yellow grill plate, but I will make it a point to do that in the next edition.

The butter dish has always been highly priced. If you can find a first edition of my book, the butter dish was $90.00 back in 1972. That was one of the most expensive butters in those days.

New collectors have avoided "Horseshoe" for years because it was so expensive. Other pattern's prices have caught up now and it does not seem all that expensive. Prices have risen for the first time in several years because new collectors have stimulated prices recently with their determined exploring for all the hard to find pieces. As always, prices for the rarer pieces are rising the fastest.

Be apprised that there are two styles of plates and platters. Some plates and platters are plain in the center, while others have a pattern. See the difference on the standing plates on either side of the pitcher in the photo.

Candy dishes only have the pattern on the top. The bottom is plain. A few **pink** candy dishes have been found, but that is the only piece ever seen in pink. No yellow butter dish, candy dish, or flat tumblers have ever yet been discovered! Please let me know if you spot the first of these!

	Green	Yellow		Green	Yellow
Bowl, 4½" berry	25.00	20.00	Plate, 6" sherbet	8.00	9.00
Bowl, 6½" cereal	25.00	25.00	Plate, 8⅜" salad	10.00	10.00
Bowl, 7½" salad	23.00	23.00	Plate, 9⅜" luncheon	12.50	13.50
Bowl, 8½" vegetable	30.00	30.00	Plate, 10⅜" grill	85.00	85.00
Bowl, 9½" large berry	37.50	40.00	Plate, 11½" sandwich	20.00	20.00
Bowl, 10½" oval vegetable	22.50	27.50	Platter, 10¾" oval	25.00	25.00
Butter dish and cover	750.00		Relish, 3 part ftd.	20.00	37.50
Butter dish bottom	175.00		Saucer	5.00	5.00
Butter dish top	575.00		Sherbet	14.00	15.00
Candy in metal holder motif			Sugar, open	14.50	15.00
on lid	175.00		Tumbler, 4¼", 9 oz.	150.00	
also, pink	160.00		Tumbler, 4¾", 12 oz.	150.00	
Creamer, ftd.	17.00	18.00	Tumbler, 9 oz. ftd.	22.00	22.00
Cup	10.00	11.00	Tumbler, 12 oz. ftd.	140.00	150.00
Pitcher, 8½", 64 oz.	250.00	300.00			

No. 616, "VERNON" INDIANA GLASS COMPANY, 1930–1932

Colors: Green, crystal, yellow.

There is something appealing about No. 616, another of Indiana's numbered patterns, which is not readily accumulated. It was given the name "Vernon" by another author. Our family once used crystal No. 616 as "every day" dishes when I first started buying Depression Glass in the early 1970's. I warn you there are rough mould lines protruding from the tumblers.

As I mentioned earlier, mould roughness on Indiana patterns is something you will have to learn to live with or pick some pattern made by another company. Many crystal "Vernon" pieces are found trimmed in platinum (silver). Few of these decorated pieces have worn platinum. Evidently, Indiana's process for applying this trim was better than many of the other glass companies! Those 11½" sandwich plates make great dinner plates! If you use this pattern, it is either those or the little 8" luncheon. For hearty appetites, there is no contest!

Getting the pattern to show is our biggest problem! The pattern is very delicate and light passes through without picking up the design well. My copy this time looks great; I hope we have solved that problem!

You will find that both yellow and green sets are difficult to complete, but there is even less green than yellow available. I have had difficulty locating a green tumbler and creamer.

	Green	Crystal	Yellow		Green	Crystal	Yellow
Creamer, ftd.	25.00	12.00	25.00	Saucer	5.50	3.50	5.50
Cup	15.00	8.00	15.00	Sugar, ftd.	25.00	11.00	25.00
Plate, 8" luncheon	9.50	6.00	9.50	Tumbler, 5" ftd.	35.00	14.00	35.00
Plate, 11½" sandwich	25.00	12.00	25.00				

Please refer to Foreword for pricing information

No. 612

No. 616

No. 618, "PINEAPPLE & FLORAL" INDIANA GLASS COMPANY, 1932–1937

Colors: Crystal, amber; some fired-on red, green; late 1960's, avocado; 1980's pink, cobalt blue, etc.

Indiana has reissued No. 618 diamond shaped comports and 7" salad bowls in a multitude of colors. Many of these have sprayed-on colors, although the light pink is an excellent transparent color. Prices on these two older crystal pieces have diminished because of these remakes. Amber and fired-on red are safe colors to collect to avoid reproductions. In crystal, you just have to be careful of those two items.

The two-tiered tid bit with a metal handle is not priced in my listings. These sell in the $25.00 range. Tid bits were sometimes made by the glass companies, but were often made elsewhere. They can easily be made today if you can find the metal hardware. Many tid bits are a product of the early 1970's when a dealer in St. Louis would make up any pattern for $10.00 if you furnished the plates.

Although a crystal set is not easily put together, it is not impossible either. You will find that tumblers, cream soups, and sherbets are the most perplexing pieces to find. As with many of Indiana's patterns, mould roughness on the seams is a detriment to some collectors. This is true on all sizes of tumblers! If this roughness does not bother you, then search for the harder to find pieces as soon as you can!

There are two different plates that have an indented center ring. No one has discovered exactly what these pieces were intended to be, but a cheese dish is the idea most often proposed.

Amber No. 618 is not collected as often as the crystal because there is so little of it available.

The fired-on red pitcher that has been found with sets of "Pineapple and Floral" has also been found with a set of fired-on red Daisy. The color is of poor quality, as is most fired-on red. There is a cross hatching design on the base similar to that of No. 618, but that is where the resemblance to "Pineapple and Floral" ends.

	Crystal	Amber, Red		Crystal	Amber, Red
Ash tray, 4½"	17.50	19.00	Plate, 11½" w/indentation	25.00	
Bowl, 4¾" berry	25.00	20.00	Plate, 11½" sandwich	17.50	16.00
Bowl, 6" cereal	25.00	20.00	Platter, 11" closed handles	17.50	18.00
* Bowl, 7" salad	2.00	10.00	Platter, relish, 11½" divided	19.00	
Bowl, 10" oval vegetable	25.00	20.00	Saucer	5.00	5.00
* Comport, diamond-shaped	1.00	8.00	Sherbet, ftd.	20.00	18.00
Creamer, diamond-shaped	7.50	10.00	Sugar, diamond-shaped	7.50	10.00
Cream soup	20.00	20.00	Tumbler, 4¼", 8 oz.	35.00	25.00
Cup	10.00	9.00	Tumbler, 5", 12 oz.	45.00	
Plate, 6" sherbet	5.00	6.00	Vase, cone-shaped	40.00	
Plate, 8⅜" salad	8.50	8.50	Vase holder (27.50)		
** Plate, 9⅜" dinner	17.50	15.00			

* Reproduced in several colors
** Green $35.00

OLD CAFE HOCKING GLASS COMPANY, 1936–1940

Colors: Pink, crystal, and Royal Ruby.

Dinner plates are the hardest pieces of Old Cafe to find save the pitchers. All other items are available with searching. This is a pattern that you will have to ask dealers to bring to shows. Bowls have been confusing. The 5" bowl has an open handle while the 4½" bowl has two closed handles as does the 3¾" berry. The sherbet is footed, but also measures 3¾". It is pictured to the left of the cup and saucer.

Old Cafe pitchers are rarely seen. They are expensive when compared to the other pieces of Old Cafe. One collector wrote to thank me for finally showing him that the pitchers did exist. He had the go-with pitcher (with evenly spaced panels and not alternating large with two small panels) that many collectors are using with this set. Those go-with pitchers can even be spotted in green, a color never found in Old Cafe. That pitcher was made by Hocking also; and several collectors have told me they are happy with it for their sets even if it is not the **real** thing.

The juice pitcher seems to be Old Cafe even though it is not shown in Hocking's catalogues (neither was the larger one). Notice that it is shaped similarly to the Mayfair juice pitcher.

That Royal Ruby Old Cafe cup was found on crystal saucers just as in Coronation pattern. No Old Cafe Royal Ruby saucers have been found. A 5½" crystal candy with a Royal Ruby lid has also been reported. Watch for it! Few lamps have been seen. Lamps were made by drilling through the bottom of a vase, turning it upside down and wiring it.

The low candy is 8⅜" including handles and 6½" without. It was not considered to be a plate. You can see pink and crystal ones in the photograph.

Hocking made a cookie jar (a numbered line) which is an excellent go-with piece. It is ribbed up the sides similar to Old Cafe but has a cross-hatched lid that is not even close to this pattern. Only the bottom is similar to this pattern!

	Crystal, Pink	Royal Ruby		Crystal, Pink	Royal Ruby
Bowl, 3¾" berry	3.00	5.50	Pitcher, 6", 36 oz.	70.00	
Bowl, 4½", tab handle			Pitcher, 80 oz.	90.00	
Bowl, 5"	5.00		Plate, 6" sherbet	2.50	
Bowl, 5½" cereal	6.50	10.00	Plate, 10" dinner	35.00	
Bowl, 9", closed handles	10.00	14.00	Saucer	3.00	
Candy dish, 8" low	11.00	11.00	Sherbet, ¾" low ftd.	6.00	10.00
Candy jar, 5½", crystal with ruby cover		15.00	Tumbler, 3" juice	11.00	10.00
Cup	5.00	8.00	Tumbler, 4" water	11.00	18.00
Lamp	20.00	30.00	Vase, 7¼"	15.00	20.00
Olive dish, 6" oblong	5.00				

OLD COLONY "LACE EDGE," "OPEN LACE" HOCKING GLASS COMPANY, 1935–1938

Colors: Pink and some crystal.

Old Colony name (instead of Lace Edge) has taken some time to get used to, but more and more collectors are converting. I have moved Old Colony to its proper alphabetical placement in this book. I have received numerous gratifying comments at shows on the store window photographs in this pattern. Don't you wish that our ancestors had stocked up on those dime sherbets and underliners? These underliners appear to be salad plates! No sherbet plate has ever surfaced.

In December of 1990 I spent a day at Anchor Hocking going through files and catalogues. I spotted these old store display photographs which proclaimed the name of the glass as Old Colony. I was excited to find the *real* name of this pattern! Originally, this trip was for my *Collectible Glassware from the 40's, 50's, 60's...* book, but that trip aided this book also.

A major problem to collecting Old Colony (besides finding it) concerns the damaged lace on the outside of the pieces. It chipped and cracked very easily and still does. Plates and bowls have to be stacked cautiously because of that. Candlesticks, console bowls, and vases are also hard to find in mint condition. You will notice some hefty price increases in the rarely found pieces of Old Colony.

I have separated items in the photographs in order to discuss them. The flower bowl with crystal frog in the top photograph on page 158 becomes the candy jar with a cover shown in the bottom photograph. The 7" comport pictured behind the sherbet in the top photo is the covered comport in the bottom photo. This piece was listed as a covered comport; but today, many collectors call it a footed candy jar. The top photograph shows the ribbed and plain 7¾" bowls. The plain is the same piece as the butter bottom although Hocking called this a covered bon bon, and not a butter. The bottom photograph shows both styles of 9½" bowls. Prices for the ribbed bowls are beginning to rise above that of the plainer one.

Ribs on the footed tumbler extend approximately half way up the side as they do on the cup. This tumbler is often confused with the Coronation tumbler that has a similar shape and design. To compare, refer to the Coronation photograph. Notice the fine ribbed effect from the middle up on the Coronation tumbler. This upper ribbing is missing on the Old Colony tumbler.

Satinized or frosted pieces presently sell for a fraction of the cost of their unfrosted counterparts. Lack of demand is the main reason. So far, only a few collectors think frosted Old Colony is beautiful!

The true 9" comport in Old Colony has a **rayed base**. There is a similar comport that measures 9". This "pretender" has a plain foot and was probably made by Standard or Lancaster Glass. It has been shown in earlier editions. Hocking may have gotten the idea for Old Colony from one of these other companies' designs when they bought them. Both Lancaster and Standard had very similar designs, but their glass was better quality and rings when **gently** flipped on the edge with your finger. Hocking's Old Colony makes a clunk sound. The pink color of other companies' glass is usually a brighter shade of pink. If the piece is not shown in my listing or is in any color other than pink or crystal, the likelihood of your having an Old Colony piece is slim at best.

That picture of the 9" comport was bumped from the book by the photograph on the bottom of page 157. I obtained a vase and a flat juice tumbler, both of which I have never pictured before, at least unfrosted! To put these in the book it was necessary to duplicate some pieces shown elsewhere. You might be able to see the ribs on the footed tumbler better than in the photo on page 158.

		*Pink		*Pink
**	Bowl, 6⅜" cereal	22.00	Flower bowl, crystal frog	25.00
	Bowl, 7¾" ribbed salad	45.00	Plate, 7¼" salad	22.50
	Bowl, 8¼" (crystal)	12.00	Plate, 8¼" luncheon	20.00
	Bowl, 9½", plain	24.00	Plate, 10½" dinner	27.50
	Bowl, 9½", ribbed	30.00	Plate, 10½" grill	20.00
***	Bowl, 10½", 3 legs, (frosted, $30.00)	200.00	Plate, 10½", 3-part relish	25.00
	Butter dish or bon bon with cover	65.00	Plate, 13", solid lace	32.00
	Butter dish bottom, 7¾"	25.00	Plate, 13", 4-part solid lace	32.00
	Butter dish top	40.00	Platter, 12¾"	32.50
***	Candlesticks, pr. (frosted $40.00)	235.00	Platter, 12¾", 5-part	30.00
	Candy jar and cover, ribbed	45.00	Relish dish, 7½", 3-part deep	65.00
	Comport, 7"	24.00	Saucer	11.00
	Comport, 7" and cover, ftd.	47.50	*** Sherbet, ftd.	95.00
	Comport, 9"	750.00	Sugar	22.50
	Cookie jar and cover	65.00	Tumbler, 3½", 5 oz. flat	90.00
	Creamer	22.50	Tumbler, 4½", 9 oz. flat	18.00
	Cup	24.00	Tumbler, 5", 10½ oz. ftd.	65.00
	Fish bowl, 1 gal. 8 oz. (crystal only)	30.00	Vase, 7", (frosted $50.00)	350.00

* Satin or frosted items 50% lower in price or less

** Officially listed as cereal or cream soup; green – $75.00

*** Price is for absolute mint condition

Please refer to Foreword for pricing information

OLD ENGLISH, "THREADING" INDIANA GLASS COMPANY, Late 1920's

Colors: Green, amber, pink, crystal, and forest green.

Old English is usually found in green. All pieces are found in that color. Amber Old English has a very strong color that some collectors find more alluring than the paler amber colors of most Depression patterns. A complete set in amber may not be attainable since some pieces have never been seen. That doesn't mean that they were never made; but the possibility at this time is looking disheartening at best. This Indiana pattern has amber color more reminiscent of Cambridge or New Martinsville.

Pink is the most elusive color with only the center handled server, cheese and cracker, and sherbets being found regularly. You will find other pieces in pink, but not easily. You can see a pink pitcher and both sizes of tumblers in *Very Rare Glassware of the Depression Years, Fourth Series*. Speaking of pitchers, did you see the pitcher and tumblers below with flashed-on black and red decorations? I have seen a couple of these sets. They must have been made for a special order or promotion.

The center-handled sandwich server is rarely seen. I have one pictured in pink, but it has been over ten years since I have seen a green one.

Footed pieces are easier to find than flat items. Both large and small berry bowls and the flat candy dish are obscure. You will find several footed candies and lids before you see a flat one. Sugar and candy jar lids have the same cloverleaf-type knob as the pitcher. The flat candy lid is similar in size to the pitcher lid which is notched on the bottom rim to allow for pouring. You can not mix the two lids since the candy lid is not notched.

Egg cups have only been found in crystal. The darker green fan vase behind the covered sugar on the bottom of page 160 is the only piece I have found in this color. Have you seen any other pieces?

	Pink, Green, Amber			Pink, Green, Amber
Bowl, 4" flat	17.50	Pitcher		65.00
Bowl, 9" ftd. fruit	28.00	Pitcher and cover		120.00
Bowl, 9½" flat	35.00	Plate, indent for compote		20.00
Candlesticks, 4" pr.	32.50	Sandwich server, center handle		55.00
Candy dish & cover, flat	50.00	Sherbet, 2 styles		20.00
Candy jar with lid	50.00	Sugar		17.50
Compote, 3½" tall, 6⅜" across, 2 handled	22.50	Sugar cover		35.00
Compote, 3½" tall, 7" across	22.00	Tumbler, 4½" ftd.		22.50
Compote, 3½" cheese for plate	16.00	Tumbler, 5½" ftd.		33.00
Creamer	17.50	Vase, 5⅜", fan type, 7" wide		47.50
Egg cup (crystal only)	8.00	Vase, 8" ftd., 4½" wide		45.00
Fruit stand, 11" ftd.	40.00	Vase, 8¼" ftd., 4¼" wide		45.00
Goblet, 5¾", 8 oz.	30.00	Vase, 12" ftd.		57.50

"ORCHID" PADEN CITY GLASS COMPANY, Early 1930's

Colors: Yellow, cobalt blue, green, amber, pink, red, and black.

It was believed that "Orchid" etched pieces turned up only on the #412 Line, square, Crow's Foot blanks made by Paden City, not on the rounded style which is #890 Line. Well, there are two pieces pictured here that are not on either style! The red 8" vase in top photograph and the 6⅜" tall comport in cobalt blue. That red vase reminds me that Cathy and I spotted a black one at a flea market in Florida. It will be pictured in my next book on rare glass.

There are two and maybe even three different "Orchid" designs found on Paden City blanks. Collectors do not mind mixing different "Orchid" varieties together because so little of any variety is found.

Limited availability of all Paden City patterns is a definite collector concern. I suspect the small amount of glass made (when compared to the output of other companies) will keep driving up prices with each purchase. "Orchid" prices have not yet gone out of sight like those of "Cupid," even though there are fewer pieces of "Orchid" being found.

Lately, I've met some growers of orchids who are seeking this colored glassware. The already small supply is rapidly dwindling!

	All Other Colors	Red Black Cobalt Blue		All Other Colors	Red Black Cobalt Blue
Bowl, 4⅞" square	20.00	37.50	Comport, 6⅝" tall, 7" wide	40.00	85.00
Bowl, 8½", 2-handled	57.50	87.50	Creamer	30.00	55.00
Bowl, 8¾" square	50.00	72.50	Ice bucket, 6"	77.50	135.00
Bowl, 10", ftd.	55.00	110.00	Mayonnaise, 3 piece	65.00	110.00
Bowl, 11", square	57.50	100.00	Plate, 8½", square		50.00
Candlesticks, 5¾" pr.	75.00	125.00	Sandwich server, center handled	42.50	77.50
Candy with lid, 6½", square, three part	65.00	125.00	Sugar	30.00	55.00
Comport, 3¼" tall, 6¼" wide	22.00	40.00	Vase, 8"	60.00	135.00
			Vase, 10"	65.00	135.00

"ORCHID"

OVIDE, incorrectly dubbed "NEW CENTURY" HAZEL ATLAS GLASS COMPANY, 1930–1935

Colors: Green, black, white Platonite trimmed with fired-on colors in 1950's.

I have chosen one of the decorated sets of Ovide to feature in this book. Just call this one "Windmills" for lack of an actual name. Hazel Atlas used a multitude of decorations on this popular Platonite. One of the more popular is the black floral design with red and yellow edge trim. That set encompassed kitchenware items (stacking sets and mixing bowls) as well as a dinnerware line. Evidently, various people found these patterns acceptable judging from the profusion of pieces now being found.

The "Flying Ducks" (geese) set is priced as "Decorated White" and not as "Art Deco." The egg cup in the "Flying Ducks" pattern is selling in the $12.00 range. It is strange that no other patterns have had egg cups reported.

Very little black, transparent green, or yellow Ovide are being found. A luncheon set in black or yellow can be assembled, but it would be easier to put together the same set in black or yellow Cloverleaf. Cloverleaf would cost three or four times as much. Depression Glass dealers are inclined to bring the Cloverleaf pattern to shows, but few handle undecorated Ovide.

It has been conjectured by some that Ovide pieces were probably intended to be Cloverleaf but had weak patterns. It is a point to consider since Cloverleaf pieces are found with very inadequate patterns, deficient enough that Cloverleaf collectors ignore them.

You will find the latter Platonite Ovide in *Collectible Glassware from the 40's, 50's, 60's….*

	Black	Green	Decorated White	Art Deco		Black	Green	Decorated White	Art Deco
Bowl, 4¾" berry			7.00		Plate, 8" luncheon		3.00	14.00	45.00
Bowl, 5½" cereal			13.00		Plate, 9" dinner			20.00	
Bowl, 8" large berry			22.50		Platter, 11"			22.50	
Candy dish and cover	45.00	22.00	35.00		Salt and pepper, pr.	27.50	27.50	24.00	
Cocktail, ftd. fruit	5.00	4.00			Saucer	3.50	2.50	6.00	18.00
Creamer	6.50	4.50	17.50	80.00	Sherbet	6.50	3.00	14.00	45.00
Cup	6.50	3.50	12.50	50.00	Sugar, open	6.50	4.00	17.50	80.00
Plate, 6" sherbet		2.50	6.00		Tumbler			16.50	80.00

Please refer to Foreword for pricing information

OYSTER AND PEARL ANCHOR HOCKING GLASS CORPORATION, 1938–1940

Colors: Pink, crystal, Royal Ruby, white with fired-on pink or green.

Royal Ruby Oyster and Pearl can be seen under the Royal Ruby pattern shown on page 196, but prices are included here. Oyster and Pearl is often used as supplementary pieces for other patterns. Both the relish dish and candlesticks sell well since they are reasonably priced in comparison to other patterns. These pieces make wonderful gifts because they have an attractive design. Be forewarned that giving presents of glass can create new collectors!

The Oyster and Pearl relish dish is 11½" including the handles. I mention that because it is listed as 10¼". All measurements in this book are calculated without handles unless otherwise mentioned. Glass companies rarely measured the handles. I have made a point to talk about measurements with handles in my commentary since I have been getting so many letters about measurements on pieces that I have already listed. There is no divided bowl in Oyster and Pearl; it was listed as a relish!

I have a report of a lamp made from several candlesticks, but I have not received a picture yet. Many patterns had lamps made out of candle holders or other pieces. Sometimes these were factory made; more often, these were assembled by some other company. Lamps do add interest to your collection; if you would like one, then buy it!

Red decorated crystal pieces are rarely found, but they sell faster than undecorated crystal. The 10½" fruit bowl is a great salad bowl and the 13½" plate makes a wonderful server, but several collectors have told me they also make an ideal small punch bowl and liner.

The pink color fired-on over white was named Dusty Rose; the fired-on green was designated Springtime Green by Hocking. Collectors do not seem to have a middle ground on these fired-on colors. They either love them or hate them. The undecorated white is more scarce, but not as desirable. I have a letter from a collector who has found this pattern with opaque blue instead of pink or green. Alas, there was no photo to confirm it!

The pink, 6½", deep, bowl with the metal attached to the handle was another of the marketing ploys of that time. With tongs it could serve as a small ice bowl or serving dish. It was another way to sell this bowl!

The spouted, 5¼" bowl is often referred to as heart shaped. It might serve as a gravy or sauce boat although most people use them for candy dishes. The same bowl is found without the spout. Although pictured in Dusty Rose and Springtime Green, this bowl has never been found without a spout in those colors.

	Crystal, Pink	Royal Ruby	White and Fired-On Green Or Pink
Bowl, 5¼" heart-shaped, 1-handled	8.00	13.00	10.00
Bowl, 5½", 1-handled	8.00	13.00	
Bowl, 6½" deep-handled	11.00	20.00	
Bowl, 10½" deep fruit	22.00	50.00	14.00
Candle holder, 3½" pr.	22.00	50.00	15.00
Plate, 13½" sandwich	18.00	45.00	
Relish dish, 10¼" oblong, divided	10.00		

"PARROT," SYLVAN FEDERAL GLASS COMPANY, 1931–1932

Colors: Green, amber; some crystal and blue.

The elevator ride of green "Parrot" prices has stopped near the top floor for now. "Parrot" pitchers finally leveled off after more than doubling in price over a two year period. From the tenth edition price of $1,300 to today's $2,700 is quite an increase; and several have sold for that price. After years of pitchers selling in the same price range, suddenly everyone wanted one and there were few to be found! Now, those that wanted them have them; so, the price has leveled momentarily! Originally, there were 37 pitchers found in the basement of an old hardware store in central Ohio. Today, there are over 30 still in existence. Doubling in price in so short a time is the phenomenal part. I suspect we could see more of that happening in the Depression Glass market in the future.

Both styles of hot plates are pictured in the bottom photograph! One is shaped like the Madrid hot plate with the pointed edges. The other is round, and more like the one in Georgian pattern. It seems the round hot plate may be the harder to find; but presently, **any** hot plate is bothersome to find and perhaps even more troublesome to pay the price! Prices for the hot plates have also leveled for now! A collector in Tennessee has found an **amber hot plate with pointed edges**. That is the only one known! I have seen it, but have been unable to obtain a printable photograph.

The high sherbets are remaining in hiding. Less than a dozen of the sherbets are known. The one pictured is the only one I have ever owned.

Yes, I know that shaker is cracked! That is my way of preserving the old glass by giving it a function. Many dealers have offered me hard to find, but damaged pieces at reasonable prices so I can photograph them for my books. It seems better than having them thrown away or my having a good pair stored that some collector could really be enjoying!

Prices for amber "Parrot" have increased little, even though it is more rare. The amber butter dish, creamer, and sugar lid are all harder to find than green. Since there are fewer collectors of amber, prices are not as adversely influenced by demand as are the prices of green.

Most collectors identify the "Parrot" shapes as those found on Madrid. Observe that most "Parrot" tumblers are found on Madrid mould shapes except for the heavy footed tumbler. Apparently, the thin, moulded, footed tumbler did not receive the "Parrot" design very well and a heavier style tumbler was used. This thin, 10 oz. footed tumbler has only been found in amber. When you see one of these, you will understand what I mean when I say it does not accept the design well! The supply of heavy, footed tumblers in both colors, green water tumblers and thin, flat iced teas in amber have more than met the demand of collectors. Prices for those latter two tumblers have remained steady during the other "Parrot" price increases.

There has been only one **mint** condition butter dish top found in amber. The butter bottom has an indented ledge for the top. The jam dish is the same as the butter bottom without the ledge, but it has never been found in green. Additionally, very few **mint** amber sugar lids have been discovered.

There are quantities of sugar and butter lids found. The major concern is finding **mint** condition lids. The pointed edges and ridges on "Parrot" chipped! You should carefully check these points when buying "Parrot." Damaged or **repaired** glassware should not bring **mint** prices. I emphasize that here because many sugar and butter lids have been repaired. If it has been reworked, it should be sold as repaired and priced accordingly!

	Green	Amber		Green	Amber
Bowl, 5" berry	24.00	17.50	Plate, 9" dinner	50.00	38.00
Bowl, 7" soup	42.00	32.00	Plate, 10½" round grill	32.00	
Bowl, 8" large berry	80.00	75.00	Plate, 10½" square grill		30.00
Bowl, 10" oval vegetable	55.00	65.00	Plate, 10¼" square (crystal only)	26.00	
Butter dish and cover	350.00	1,200.00	Platter, 11¼" oblong	52.00	70.00
Butter dish bottom	60.00	200.00	Salt and pepper, pr.	235.00	
Butter dish top	290.00	1,000.00	Saucer	15.00	15.00
Creamer, ftd.	50.00	60.00	*Sherbet, ftd. cone	24.00	22.00
Cup	40.00	40.00	Sherbet, 4¼" high	1,050.00	
Hot Plate, 5", pointed	825.00	875.00	Sugar	35.00	40.00
Hot plate, 5", round	950.00		Sugar cover	140.00	410.00
Jam dish, 7"		35.00	Tumbler, 4¼", 10 oz.	135.00	100.00
Pitcher, 8½", 80 oz.	2,700.00		Tumbler, 5½", 12 oz.	160.00	115.00
Plate, 5¾" sherbet	35.00	22.00	Tumbler, 5¾" ftd. heavy	125.00	105.00
Plate, 7½" salad	35.00		Tumbler, 5½", 10 oz. ftd. (Madrid mould)		145.00

*Blue – $150.00

PATRICIAN, "SPOKE" FEDERAL GLASS COMPANY, 1933–1937

Colors: Pink, green, crystal, and amber ("Golden Glo").

Patrician is a Depression Glass pattern in which amber is the most collected color! Distributed nationally, Amber is easily found; and the large 10½" dinner plates were given away in twenty pound sacks of flour as cake plates. I know that when I started buying Depression Glass in the early 1970's, Patrician was the one pattern in my area that I saw more often than any others. My mom had stacks of Patrician plates and sent food home on one most Friday nights with the lady who helped in her day care center. When I found out about Depression Glass, that ritual stopped quickly.

Cereal bowls are sometimes confused with jam dishes. If you find what appears to be a butter dish bottom, which has no indented ledge for the top to rest upon, then you have found the jam. The jam is 6¾" wide and stands 1¼" high. Cereal bowls are 6" in diameter and 1¾" deep.

Green Patrician is more easily found and collected than pink or crystal. Green dinner plates are infrequently seen. After seeing so many in amber, you'd think other colors would also be plentiful. Evidently, only amber dinners were given away as cake plates. To complete a set in pink is difficult, but not yet impossible. I think it might be in crystal. Not all pieces have been uncovered in crystal; so you definitely would have to settle for a smaller set — if you could find enough!

Two styles of pitchers were made. The one pictured has a moulded handle and is easier to find in amber than the one with an applied handle. In crystal, the applied handle pitcher is the easiest to find!

Only the amber applied-handled pitcher can be considered rare in that color; but mint condition sugar lids, cookie or butter bottoms, and footed tumblers are harder to find than other pieces. Check sugar lids for signs of repair. That cookie bottom is rare in green. There are several lids found for each bottom. Most people think that all tops are harder to find than bottoms. This does not hold true for butter dishes and cookie jars in Patrician. Saucers are also harder to find than cups. This situation occurs in few patterns, but Patrician is one of them.

There is a green vase that was made from stretching a cookie bottom. It was probably a worker's experiment, but it can be seen in *Very Rare Glassware of the Depression Years, Fourth Series*.

	Amber, Crystal	Pink	Green		Amber, Crystal	Pink	Green
Bowl, 4¾" cream soup	16.00	18.00	20.00	Plate, 6" sherbet	10.00	8.00	8.00
Bowl, 5" berry	12.00	12.00	12.00	Plate, 7½" salad	15.00	15.00	14.00
Bowl, 6" cereal	24.00	24.00	25.00	Plate, 9" luncheon	12.00	10.00	11.00
Bowl, 8½" large berry	45.00	25.00	35.00	Plate, 10½" dinner	6.50	35.00	40.00
Bowl, 10" oval vegetable	30.00	25.00	35.00	Plate, 10½" grill	13.50	15.00	15.00
Butter dish and cover	90.00	225.00	110.00	Platter, 11½" oval	30.00	25.00	25.00
Butter dish bottom	60.00	175.00	60.00	Salt and pepper, pr.	55.00	85.00	60.00
Butter dish top	30.00	50.00	50.00	Saucer	9.50	9.50	9.50
Cookie jar and cover	85.00		525.00	Sherbet	13.00	14.00	14.00
Creamer, footed	10.00	12.00	12.00	Sugar	9.00	9.00	9.00
Cup	8.00	11.00	11.00	Sugar cover	55.00	60.00	55.00
Jam dish	30.00	30.00	35.00	Tumbler, 4", 5 oz.	30.00	30.00	30.00
Pitcher, 8", 75 oz. moulded				Tumbler, 4¼", 9 oz.	28.00	26.00	25.00
handle	110.00	110.00	125.00	Tumbler, 5½", 14 oz.	42.00	30.00	42.00
Pitcher, 8¼", 75 oz., applied				Tumbler, 5¼", 8 oz. ftd.	47.50		55.00
handle	150.00	135.00	150.00				

"PATRICK" LANCASTER GLASS COMPANY, EARLY 1930's

Colors: Yellow and pink.

Yellow "Patrick" luncheon sets can be found occasionally, but other pieces are harder to find than the proverbial hen's tooth. Finding a pink "Patrick" luncheon set would be like finding wisdom teeth in that chicken! I have only been able to add a pink champagne and a yellow cocktail to my photo since the last book. Recently, I did find a pink, two-handled bowl which gives me a start for the next time.

Yes! Pink "Patrick" sugar or creamers are really selling for $75.00 each! The "Patrick" three-footed candy is shaped just like the one shown in Jubilee. I have never seen one except in a catalogue. The already infinitesimal supply of "Patrick" is dwindling rapidly and prices are ascending! Jubilee was distributed heavily in the Northwest and Florida, but "Patrick" is scarcely found anywhere.

As in Jubilee, serving dishes are rare in "Patrick." There are additional floral patterns made by Lancaster with the mould shapes of "Patrick" and Jubilee that can be combined with these sets if you get frustrated in finding serving pieces.

	Pink	Yellow		Pink	Yellow
Bowl, 9", handled fruit	175.00	125.00	Mayonnaise, 3-piece	195.00	135.00
Bowl, 11", console	140.00	125.00	Plate, 7" sherbet	20.00	12.00
Candlesticks, pr.	150.00	150.00	Plate, 7½" salad	25.00	20.00
Candy dish, 3-ftd	150.00	150.00	Plate, 8" luncheon	45.00	27.50
Cheese & cracker set	150.00	125.00	Saucer	20.00	12.00
Creamer	75.00	37.50	Sherbet, 4¾"	60.00	50.00
Cup	65.00	37.50	Sugar	75.00	37.50
Goblet, 4" cocktail	90.00	80.00	Tray, 11", 2-handled	75.00	60.00
Goblet, 4¾", 6 oz. juice	90.00	75.00	Tray, 11", center-handled	145.00	95.00
Goblet, 6", 10 oz. water	100.00	70.00			

"PEACOCK REVERSE" PADEN CITY GLASS COMPANY, LINE #412, 1930's

Colors: Cobalt blue, red, amber, yellow, green, pink, black, and crystal.

Paden City's Line #412 (commonly called "Crow's Foot" by collectors) and Line #991 (which is known as "Penny Line") make up the mould blanks on which "Peacock Reverse" has been seen. Paden City lines were used for many different designs; so it is not unusual to spot a blank only to find that it does not have the etched pattern you want.

The eight sided plate previously reported is pictured in pink. Note that we have found two colored sugars, but have yet to spot a creamer. The newly discovered, lipped, footed comport measures 4¼" tall and 7⅜" wide. There are two styles of candy dishes. Notice that both have patterns only on the lids. The plain bottoms can be found with lids of some other etch or even without an etch. That should make bottoms easier to find; but does it?

All colors are desirable, but most collectors seek cobalt blue and red. Thankfully, those are the colors that usually turn up. Prices for "Peacock Reverse" are not determined by color as much as other patterns. Collectors embrace any piece in any color they can acquire!

Almost any piece listed under "Crow's Foot" (squared) or "Orchid" could be found with the "Peacock Reverse" design. Let me know what unlisted pieces or colors you spot!

	All Colors		All Colors
Bowl, 4⅞" square	35.00	Plate, 5¾" sherbet	22.50
Bowl, 8¾" square	85.00	Plate, 8½" luncheon	40.00
Bowl, 8¾" square with handles	90.00	Plate 10⅜", 2-handled	55.00
Bowl, 11¾" console	85.00	Saucer	20.00
Candlesticks, 5¾" square base, pr.	125.00	Sherbet, 4⅝" tall, 3⅜" diameter	50.00
Candy dish, 6½" square	150.00	Sherbet, 4⅞" tall, 3⅝" diameter	50.00
Comport, 3¼" high, 6¼" wide	60.00	Server, center-handled	75.00
Comport, 4¼" high, 7⅜" wide	75.00	Sugar, 2¾" flat	77.50
Creamer, 2¾" flat	77.50	Tumbler, 4", 10 oz. flat	65.00
Cup	75.00	Vase, 10"	100.00

"PEACOCK & WILD ROSE" PADEN CITY GLASS COMPANY, LINE #1300, 1930's

Colors: Pink, green, amber, cobalt blue, black, light blue, crystal, and red.

Notice that Paden City's "Peacock and Wild Rose" is found on Line #1300 which is the same line on which most "Cupid" etched pieces occur. Although there are several bird designs in Paden City patterns, there is more recognition for the peacock patterns than for any other.

It's a shame that the abundant serving pieces found here can not be transferred to other patterns! "Peacock and Wild Rose" appears to have only serving pieces and vases. No cups, saucers, creamers, sugars, or luncheon plates have ever been reported. Maybe a mixture of these two Paden City peacock patterns is called for; but then a problem would exist in color matching. There is very little red or cobalt blue found.

I spotted an elliptical vase at a market not long ago. It was several rows across from me, but I can really move when motivated by what I thought was a "Cupid" vase. It turned out to be "Peacock and Wild Rose." I was disappointed that it was not "Cupid," and more so when I checked out the price for this badly damaged piece! I have only seen elliptical vases in pink, but surely they can be found in green. The bulbous base of the 12" vase shows faint signs of being paneled. Vases are the commonly found pieces in this Paden City line. There are two styles of 10" vases.

A light blue (like that found in "Cupid") 11" console bowl has been found. You can see it pictured in *Very Rare Glassware of the Depression Years, Fourth Series.* The bowls and plates with handles in the middle were candy or pastry trays. They probably do not work well for serving most vegetables.

	All Colors		All Colors
Bowl, 8½", flat	75.00	Candy dish w/cover, 7"	150.00
Bowl, 8½", fruit, oval, ftd.	90.00	Cheese and cracker set	110.00
Bowl, 8¾", ftd.	80.00	Comport, 3¼" tall, 6¼" wide	55.00
Bowl, 9½", center-handled	75.00	Ice bucket, 6"	145.00
Bowl, 9½", ftd.	85.00	Ice tub, 4¾"	135.00
Bowl, 10½", center-handled	80.00	Pitcher, 5" high	150.00
Bowl, 10½", ftd.	95.00	Plate, cake, low foot	85.00
Bowl, 10½", fruit	95.00	Relish, 3-part	65.00
Bowl, 11", console	75.00	Vase, 8¼" elliptical	195.00
Bowl, 14", console	85.00	Vase, 10", two styles	110.00
Candlestick, 5", pr.	125.00	Vase, 12"	140.00

"PEACOCK & WILD ROSE"

PETALWARE MacBETH-EVANS GLASS COMPANY, 1930–1940

Colors: Monax, Cremax, pink, crystal, cobalt and fired-on red, blue, green, and yellow.

The appearance of red trimmed Petalware on the cover of my eighth edition book and my sixth edition *Pocket Guide to Depression Glass* has created an avalanche of collectors searching for that decoration. While scouring the trail of this elusive red trimmed set, many have become enamored of other decorated Petalware patterns. More collectors are now seeking Florette which is the pointed petal, red flower decoration (sans red trim) pictured on the bottom two shelves on page 173. Observe the flat soup on the bottom row. These are rarely seen in Monax, let alone decorated Florette. Too, all series of fruit- and bird-decorated Petalware are now fair game.

Monax and Cremax are names given the colors by MacBeth-Evans. Cremax refers to the opaque beige colored Petalware and Monax is the whiter color shown in all the pictures except at the bottom of 174. Cremax will glow green under a black light, but Monax does not. A large number of Petalware devotees are beginning to collect pastel decorated Cremax shown on the bottom of page 174. I have been asked for it at several different shows recently. Since little of it is found, prices are rising on that! Notice the crystal tumbler with matching pastel bands in that photo. These are found in three sizes which all sell in the $6.00 to $8.00 range to collectors seeking additional pieces to go-with their sets.

Red trimmed Petalware has three sizes of decorated tumblers, a pitcher, and sherbets to match it. I have listed the two sizes of tumblers pictured. You can find these tumblers both frosted or unfrosted. The pitcher to match is a frosted Federal Star juice pitcher, but decorated with the matching red florals. A pitcher was brought for me to see at the Peach State Depression Glass Show last year. Somebody send the measurements on the water tumbler, please!

I have tried to show as wide a variety of decorated Petalware as possible. On page 173 and the bottom of page 175 are plates from different series of fruits, birds, and flowers. The fruit-decorated Petalware with the names of fruit printed on the plate is found in sets of eight. One such set consists of plates showing cherry, apple, orange, plum, strawberry, blueberry, pear, and grape. You may find other sets with different fruits. Some plates have stickers (bottom of page 175 in row with bluebird plates) which read "Rainbow Hand Painted." Some sets have colored bands and others have 22K gold trim.

Pink Petalware has caught the eye of some new collectors. I suggested previously that pink was inexpensive and an excellent pattern for new collectors to start. Pink Petalware is still less expensive than most other pink patterns.

The cobalt mustard (foreground at top of 175) has a metal lid and it is Petalware! A few additional pieces of cobalt blue Petalware turned up in the mid-1970's, but they all disappeared into collections and have not been seen since! The 9" berry bowl varies from 8¾" at times. You will find other quarter inch variances on many pieces in this pattern. It was made for a long time and replacing worn out moulds caused some size discrepancies. Very few 4" Monax sherbets have been seen in recent years. The last one I owned was a casualty of my concrete basement floor in 1976. That is a long time between seeing a piece again!

PETALWARE MacBETH-EVANS GLASS COMPANY, 1930–1940 (Cont.)

	Crystal	Pink	Monax Plain	Cremax, Monax Florette, Fired-On Decorations	Red Trim Floral
Bowl, 4½" cream soup	4.50	12.00	12.00	14.00	
Bowl, 5¾" cereal	4.00	10.00	8.00	14.00	35.00
Bowl, 7" soup			57.50	70.00	
*Bowl, 9" large berry	8.50	18.00	18.00	33.00	125.00
Cup	3.00	7.00	5.00	10.00	25.00
**Creamer, ftd.	3.00	8.00	6.00	12.50	32.50
Lamp shade (many sizes) $8.00 to $15.00					
Mustard with metal cover in cobalt blue only, $10.00					
Pitcher, 80 oz. (crystal decorated bands)	25.00				
Plate, 6" sherbet	2.00	2.50	2.50	6.00	18.00
Plate, 8" salad	2.00	5.00	4.00	10.00	25.00
Plate, 9" dinner	4.00	12.00	9.00	16.00	35.00
Plate, 11" salver	4.50	14.00	10.00	18.00	
Plate, 12" salver		11.00	18.00		37.50
Platter, 13" oval	8.50	17.50	15.00	25.00	
Saucer	1.50	2.00	2.00	3.50	10.00
Saucer, cream soup liner			18.00		
Sherbet, 4" low ftd.			30.00		
**Sherbet, 4½" low ftd.	3.50	8.00	8.00	12.00	35.00
**Sugar, ftd.	3.00	7.50	6.00	10.00	32.50
Tidbit servers or lazy susans, several styles 12.00 to 17.50					
Tumbler, 3⅝", 6 oz.	35.00				
Tumbler, 4⅝", 12 oz.	37.50				
***Tumblers (crystal decorated pastel bands) 7.50 to 10.00					

*Also in cobalt at $45.00   **Also in cobalt at $30.00   ***Several sizes

PRIMO, "PANELED ASTER" U.S. GLASS COMPANY, EARLY 1930's

Colors: Green and yellow.

Primo is another Depression Glass pattern where little catalogue information has been discovered. A collector asked me to watch for this pattern and for over a year, I have hunted Primo. Some conclusions I reached in that year are both sizes of bowls, dinner, grill, and cake plates will take some searching. I still have not found a green berry bowl to photograph.

A major detriment to collecting Primo is mould roughness and inner rim damage on pieces that have rims. I saw several sets in antique malls in Mississippi and Alabama, but most of the pieces were very rough or chipped. Prices asked were for mint pieces; I wonder if anyone buys damaged Primo that way? Since the pieces were still sitting on the shelves, I believe not.

The coaster/ash tray combinations do not have the Primo pattern on them. Evidently, they were made by U.S. Glass to go with other patterns besides Primo, since no pieces of Primo have been found in the pink or black to go with those colored coasters. Notice how exactly the tumbler fits the coaster! These coasters have been found in boxed Primo sets that were advertised as "Bridge Sets."

I continue to add new pieces to the listing as they are found. There have been no new reports of center-handled servers, but it is possible these do exist!

The report of a three-footed, round console bowl in Primo turned out to be another U.S. Glass pattern known as "Thorn" which is found in pink, green, iridescent, and black.

	Yellow, Green		Yellow, Green
Bowl, 4½"	15.00	Plate, 10" dinner	20.00
Bowl, 7¾"	25.00	Plate, 10" grill	12.50
Cake plate, 10", 3-footed	25.00	Saucer	3.00
Coaster/ash tray	8.00	Sherbet	12.00
Creamer	12.00	Sugar	12.00
Cup	12.00	Tumbler, 5¾", 9 oz.	20.00
Plate, 7½"	10.00		

PRINCESS HOCKING GLASS COMPANY, 1931–1935

Colors: Green, Topaz yellow, apricot yellow, pink, and blue.

Today, Princess iced tea tumblers and bowls are hard to find in all colors. Besides the aforementioned items, green Princess collectors have to search long and hard for the undivided relish and the elusive squared foot pitcher with tumblers to match. Collectors of pink Princess have problems finding coasters, ash trays, and the squared foot pitchers with matching tumblers. The hardest to find yellow pieces include the butter dish, juice pitcher, undivided relish, 10¼" handled sandwich plate, coasters, and ash trays.

Finding mint condition bowls presents a problem due to inner rim roughness. Some of this damage was caused by stacking the bowls together over the years; but some loss was caused by the very sharply defined inner rim itself. The undivided relish is touted as a soup bowl by some dealers. To me, it seems very shallow for a soup bowl.

Pink Princess prices have made some dramatic increases in the last year. At this rate, a pink set will soon be as costly as green. A pink, three-footed bowl has been found in Texas. It is 8¾" square and stands only 1½" high. You can see a photograph in *Very Rare Glassware of the Depression Years, Fourth Series*.

There is some color variation in yellow Princess. Topaz is the official color listed by Hocking, and it is a bright, attractive shade of yellow. However, some yellow turned out close to amber and has been termed "apricot" by collectors. Most favor the Topaz which makes the darker, amber shade difficult to sell. The colors are so different that it is almost as if Hocking meant to have two different colors. For some reason (probably distribution) yellow Princess abounds in the metropolitan area of Detroit. Incidentally, almost all yellow Princess juice pitchers have been found in north and central Kentucky.

The handled sandwich plate actually measures 10¼" (or 11¼" if measured including handles). These are rarely found in yellow and have been fetching high prices when they do occasionally turn up. This plate is just like the handled grill plate without the dividers. You can see one in the background of the photograph at the bottom of page 178. These plates are common in pink and green. The grill plate without handles and dinner plate have been corrected to read 9½" in the listing instead of 9" listed in Hocking catalogues.

Pieces of blue Princess are discovered on rare occasions. Only the cookie jar and cup and saucer are desired by collectors of those items. Blue Princess suffers the fate of many seldom-found patterns or colors of Depression Glass. It is too rare to collect a set; and therefore, only a few collectors covet a piece.

Please refer to Foreword for pricing information

PRINCESS HOCKING GLASS COMPANY, 1931–1935 (Cont.)

	Green	Pink	Topaz, Apricot		Green	Pink	Topaz, Apricot
Ash tray, 4½"	70.00	85.00	90.00	**Plate, 9½" grill	14.00	14.00	5.50
Bowl, 4½" berry	25.00	25.00	45.00	Plate, 10¼" handled sandwich	14.00	25.00	160.00
Bowl, 5" cereal or oatmeal	30.00	25.00	30.00	Plate, 10½" grill, closed			
Bowl, 9" octagonal salad	38.00	35.00	120.00	handles	10.00	12.00	5.50
Bowl, 9½" hat-shaped	45.00	40.00	120.00	Platter, 12" closed handles	24.00	24.00	60.00
Bowl, 10" oval vegetable	28.00	25.00	60.00	Relish, 7½" divided	26.00	28.00	100.00
Butter dish and cover	90.00	90.00	650.00	Relish, 7½" plain	110.00	170.00	150.00
Butter dish bottom	30.00	30.00	225.00	Salt and pepper, 4½" pr.	55.00	55.00	70.00
Butter dish top	60.00	60.00	425.00	Spice shakers, 5½" pr.	40.00		
Cake stand, 10"	25.00	30.00		***Saucer (same as sherbet			
Candy dish and cover	60.00	65.00		plate)	10.00	10.00	3.50
Coaster	35.00	65.00	90.00	Sherbet, ftd.	22.00	22.00	35.00
*Cookie jar and cover	55.00	65.00		Sugar	10.00	12.00	8.50
Creamer, oval	14.00	15.00	14.00	Sugar cover	22.00	22.00	17.50
**Cup	12.00	12.00	8.00	Tumbler, 3", 5 oz. juice	28.00	28.00	28.00
Pitcher 6", 37 oz.	50.00	60.00	550.00	Tumbler, 4", 9 oz. water	26.00	25.00	24.00
Pitcher, 7⅜", 24 oz. ftd.	525.00	475.00		Tumbler, 5¼", 13 oz. iced tea	38.00	28.00	28.00
Pitcher, 8", 60 oz.	55.00	55.00	90.00	Tumbler, 4¾", 9 oz. sq. ftd	65.00	60.00	
***Plate, 5½" sherbet	10.00	10.00	3.50	Tumbler, 5¼", 10 oz. ftd.	30.00	28.00	21.00
Plate, 8" salad	14.00	14.00	10.00	Tumbler, 6½", 12½ oz. ftd.	85.00	85.00	150.00
Plate, 9½" dinner	26.00	25.00	15.00	Vase, 8"	35.00	40.00	

*Blue $850.00
**Blue $110.00
***Blue $60.00

QUEEN MARY (PRISMATIC LINE), "VERTICAL RIBBED"
HOCKING GLASS COMPANY, 1936–1949

Colors: Pink, crystal, and some Royal Ruby.

Crystal Queen Mary is attracting as many new collectors as pink. Price is one of the reasons, but the main reason may be that it is available. Recently, some crystal pieces have become harder to find; still, nothing can come close to being as difficult to acquire as the pink dinner plates and footed tumblers. Prices for those crystal items will have a long way to go to catch up to the pink that just keeps soaring! A crystal set can be completed at reasonable prices if you start rounding it up before more people discover it.

Queen Mary collectors are asking about the pink footed creamer and sugar that I showed in earlier editions. I still have not found any confirmation on them at Anchor Hocking and they have not been seen in crystal. They certainly appear to be Queen Mary.

The 6" cereal bowl has the same shape as the butter bottom. Butter dishes were also called preserve dishes. There are two sizes of cups. The smaller cup sits on the saucer with cup ring. The larger cup rests on the combination saucer/sherbet plate. Lately, the smaller cup and saucer have outdistanced the larger cup in price in some areas of the country.

The butter dish shown has been frosted and a metal band added to it. These look somewhat like a crown. I was told long ago that these were made about the time of the English Coronation in the late 1930's. That makes a good story; whether it is true or not, I do not know. You may also see Manhattan frosted vases with the same decoration.

In the 1950's, the 3½" ash tray in the Queen Mary pattern was made in forest green and Royal Ruby.

The 2" x 3¾" ash tray and 2" x 3¾" oval cigarette jar have been found together labeled "Ace Hi Bridge Smoking Set."

A pair of lamp shades were found in this pattern. They had been made from frosted candy lids (also with similar metal decorations as the butter); they were not the most beautiful pieces I have seen, but definitely interesting!

	Pink	Crystal		Pink	Crystal
Ash tray, 2" x 3¾" oval	5.00	3.00	Creamer, ftd.	37.50	
*Ash tray, 3½" round		3.00	Creamer, oval	7.50	5.50
Bowl, 4" one handle or none	5.00	3.50	Cup, large	7.00	5.50
Bowl, 4½", berry	6.00	4.00	Cup, small	10.00	8.00
Bowl, 5" berry	10.00	6.00	Plate, 6" and 6⅝"	5.00	4.00
Bowl, 5½", two handles	6.00	5.50	Plate, 8¾" salad		5.50
Bowl, 6" cereal	23.00	6.50	Plate, 9¾" dinner	50.00	15.00
Bowl, 7" small	12.00	7.00	Plate, 12" sandwich	14.00	9.00
Bowl, 8¾" large berry	16.00	10.00	Plate, 14" serving tray	20.00	12.00
Butter dish or preserve and cover	120.00	25.00	Relish tray, 12", 3-part	14.00	9.00
Butter dish bottom	30.00	6.50	Relish tray, 14", 4-part	16.00	12.00
Butter dish top	90.00	18.50	Salt and pepper, pr.		19.00
Candy dish and cover	35.00	20.00	Saucer/cup ring	5.00	2.50
**Candlesticks, 4½" double branch, pr.		14.50	Sherbet, ftd.	9.00	5.00
Celery or pickle dish, 5" x 10"	21.00	9.00	Sugar, ftd.	37.50	
Cigarette jar, 2" x 3" oval	7.50	5.50	Sugar, oval	7.50	4.50
Coaster, 3½"	4.00	2.50	Tumbler, 3½", 5 oz. juice	9.00	4.00
Coaster/ash tray, 4¼" square	6.00	5.00	Tumbler, 4", 9 oz. water	11.00	5.50
Comport, 5¾"	12.50	6.50	Tumbler, 5", 10 oz. ftd.	60.00	25.00

*Royal Ruby $5.00;   Forest Green $3.00;   ** Royal Ruby $65.00

RADIANCE NEW MARTINSVILLE GLASS COMPANY, 1936–1939

Colors: Red, cobalt and ice blue, amber, crystal, pink, and emerald green.

A few collectors have strongly insinuated that Radiance is too elegant a glassware to be included in this book, that it was more superior glassware than those mass-produced wares of the Depression era and belongs in my *Elegant Glassware of the Depression Era*. That argument could be made for many other patterns. Radiance had already been accepted as Depression Glassware before I wrote my first book; so I inherited acceptable standards long before the idea of an elegant glassware book was conceived!

Radiance punch, cordial, and condiment sets remain evasive. You can see a red punch set below. The punch ladle is the Achilles heel of this set. This ladle is a punch cup that has had a long handle attached. Evidently, many of these did not survive the test of time. An amber cordial set is pictured on the bottom of page 181.

The crystal punch bowl sets being found on emerald green plates were made by Viking after they bought out New Martinsville. One such set was pictured in the last edition. These are found frequently — unlike their older counterparts!

Red and the ice blue are the most sought colors. There is no way a set could be collected in cobalt since only a few items were made in this beautiful color. All known pieces are asterisked in the price listing below.

A few pieces are being found in pink including creamer, sugar, tray, cup, saucer, and shakers. These are selling in the same range as the red since they are scarce at this time. You can see a pink cup and saucer on the bottom of page 181.

The most troublesome pieces to find in red and ice blue include the butter dish, pitcher, handled decanter, and the five-piece condiment set. Vases have been found made into lamps. I question this being a factory project, but it could have been.

There are several dissimilar gold and platinum decorated designs on crystal. The major problem with these decorated pieces is finding identical ones. Many collectors have shied away from buying decorated pieces; if not worn, they could make an interesting addition to your crystal collection.

Price crystal about fifty percent of amber. Only the crystal pieces that item collectors seek sell very well. These include pitchers, butter dishes, shakers, sugars, creamers, and cordials.

	Ice Blue, Red	Amber
Bowl, 5", nut 2-handled	20.00	10.00
Bowl, 6", bonbon	30.00	15.00
Bowl, 6", bonbon, footed	32.00	17.50
Bowl, 6", bonbon w/cover	95.00	45.00
Bowl, 7", relish, 2-part	30.00	18.00
Bowl, 7", pickle	25.00	15.00
Bowl, 8", relish, 3-part	35.00	25.00
* Bowl, 9", punch	190.00	100.00
Bowl, 10", celery	30.00	18.00
Bowl, 10", crimped	45.00	25.00
Bowl, 10", flared	42.00	22.00
Bowl, 12", crimped	50.00	30.00
Bowl, 12", flared	47.50	27.50
Butter dish	450.00	200.00
Candlestick 6" ruffled pr.	160.00	80.00
Candlestick 8" pr.	100.00	60.00
Candlestick 2-lite, pr.	110.00	70.00
Cheese/cracker, (11" plate) set	50.00	30.00
Comport, 5"	30.00	18.00
Comport, 6"	35.00	22.00
Condiment set, 4-piece w/tray	285.00	150.00
Creamer	25.00	15.00
Cruet, indiv.	75.00	36.00
Cup, ftd.	18.00	12.00
Cup, punch	15.00	7.00

	Ice Blue, Red	Amber
** Decanter w/stopper, handled	165.00	90.00
Goblet, 1 oz., cordial	40.00	27.50
Ladle for punch bowl	130.00	95.00
Lamp, 12"	110.00	56.00
Mayonnaise, 3 piece, set	75.00	35.00
*** Pitcher, 64 oz.	225.00	150.00
Plate, 8", luncheon	16.00	10.00
**** Plate, 14", punch bowl liner	85.00	45.00
Salt & pepper, pr.	90.00	50.00
Saucer	8.50	5.50
Sugar	25.00	15.00
Tray, oval	30.00	24.00
***** Tumbler, 9 oz.	30.00	20.00
****** Vase, 10", flared or crimped	65.00	45.00
Vase, 12", flared or crimped	85.00	55.00

* Emerald Green $125.00
** Cobalt blue $185.00
*** Cobalt blue $350.00
**** Emerald green $25.00
***** Cobalt blue $28.00
****** Cobalt blue $75.00

Please refer to Foreword for pricing information

RAINDROPS, "OPTIC DESIGN" FEDERAL GLASS COMPANY, 1929–1933

Colors: Green and crystal.

The Raindrops design has rounded bumps and not elongated ones. Almost all Raindrops pieces are signed with Federal's trademark of an **F** in a shield.

Shakers have overtaken the sugar bowl lid as the most desirable pieces to own in this pattern. In fact, Raindrops sugar lids have turned out to be common in comparison to shakers. Subsequently, the price of shakers has soared over the last few years. A couple of shaker collectors have told me that these are harder to find than yellow and green Mayfair! That is quite a statement, but both collectors had at least one of those colors in Mayfair. I asked!

Raindrops makes a great little luncheon or bridge set. It even has a few accessory pieces that other smaller sets do not. You can find three sizes of serving bowls in Raindrops. The 7½" bowl will be the one you will probably find last. Few have come to light!

Raindrops has two styles of cups. One is flat bottomed and the other has a slight foot. The flat bottomed is 2⁵⁄₁₆" high and the footed is 2¹¹⁄₁₆" (reported by a Raindrops collector). An additional tumbler has been added to the price list. It has a capacity of 14 oz. and is 5⅜" tall.

	Green		Green
Bowl, 4½" fruit	6.00	Sugar	7.50
Bowl, 6" cereal	8.00	Sugar cover	40.00
Bowl, 7½" berry	40.00	Tumbler, 3", 4 oz.	5.00
Cup	5.50	Tumbler, 2⅛", 2 oz.	5.00
Creamer	7.50	Tumbler, 3⅞", 5 oz.	6.50
Plate, 6" sherbet	2.50	Tumbler, 4⅛", 9½ oz.	9.00
Plate, 8" luncheon	5.50	Tumbler, 5", 10 oz.	9.00
Salt and pepper, pr.	295.00	Tumbler, 5⅜", 14 oz.	12.00
Saucer	2.00	Whiskey, 1⅞", 1 oz.	7.00
Sherbet	6.50		

"RIBBON" HAZEL ATLAS GLASS COMPANY, Early 1930's

Colors: Green; some black, crystal, and pink.

Prices for "Ribbon" bowls are rapidly increasing. If you do not have these in your set, latch on to whatever you can find! My artistic photographer placed the cereal and berry on an angle so that they could be better seen. What do you think?

The black bowl was turned over to show the pattern that is on the outside. Most black glass has to be turned over to see the pattern. I see very little "Ribbon" for sale at shows. "Ribbon" is one of the patterns that is not found on the West Coast or so I have been informed by several would be collectors.

Tumblers, sugars, and creamers are not yet as difficult to find as bowls, but even they are starting to be in shorter supply.

The candy dish remains the most commonly seen piece of "Ribbon." Easily found and economically priced make it a perfect gift for non-collectors. It is also serviceable!

Maybe one of the reasons that "Ribbon" bowls are so elusive is that there were two designs made. The normally found smaller bowls have evenly spaced small panels on them while the panels on larger bowls expand in size as it approaches the top of the bowl. This makes the larger bowl flare at the top while the smaller bowls are more straight sided. This is evident on both the large green and black bowls pictured when compared to the cereal and berry. It is also evident on the tumbler, creamer, and sugar which are all larger at the top than the bottom! I have reports of larger bowls with sides straight up like the cereal. This bowl was comparable to a Cloverleaf bowl. I have only seen pictures of these bowls, but they measure 8" according to reports. You may notice that other "Ribbon" shapes are the same as Cloverleaf and Ovide, two other Hazel Atlas patterns.

Shakers are the only pieces in pink that have been reported to me. If you have any other pieces, I would like to hear from you.

	Green	Black		Green	Black
Bowl, 4" berry	20.00		Plate, 8" luncheon	5.00	14.00
Bowl, 5" cereal	25.00		* Salt and pepper, pr.	30.00	45.00
Bowl, 8" large berry	30.00	35.00	Saucer	2.50	
Candy dish and cover	35.00		Sherbet, ftd.	5.50	
Creamer, ftd.	15.00		Sugar, ftd.	14.00	
Cup	5.00		Tumbler, 6", 10 oz.	27.50	
Plate, 6¼" sherbet	2.50				

* pink — $35.00

Please refer to Foreword for pricing information

RING, "BANDED RINGS" HOCKING GLASS COMPANY, 1927–1933

Colors: Crystal, crystal w/pink, red, blue, orange, yellow, black, silver, etc. bands; green, some pink, "Mayfair" blue, and red.

Decorated crystal Ring is the most collected form of this pattern. Although crystal or crystal trimmed in platinum are more readily found, it is those colored bands that seem to catch collectors' eyes. You could put a set of green together over a period of time — say ten to twenty years unless you get very lucky! A reader informed me that obtaining a subscription to *Country Gentleman* in the 1930's got you a green Ring berry bowl set consisting of an 8" berry and six 5" berry bowls. That must not have enticed too many subscribers since I have seen few green bowls over the years. There is a green flat tumbler behind the sherbet on the right. It is the first decorated piece of green Ring I have seen; unfortunately, it doesn't appear very green in the photograph.

Pitcher and tumbler sets seem to be the only pieces found in pink. Wisconsin collectors report that the pink pitcher sets are very plentiful in that part of the country. Pink pitchers do not seem to be commonly found anywhere else.

Ring enthusiasts usually start by collecting one particular color scheme. There is a predominant scheme involving black, yellow, red, and orange colored rings in that order. I have tried to show you that arrangement here. Those other varieties drive the perfectionists crazy! Of course, some people consider perfectionists crazy already!

Crystal with platinum (silver) bands is the second most collected Ring. Worn trims plague collectors of this decoration. The colored rings do not seem to have that problem. It may be because the rings do not decorate the rims — or that painted trims proved more durable.

	Crystal	Decor., Green		Crystal	Decor., Green
Bowl, 5" berry	3.50	6.00	Plate, 11¾", sandwich	7.00	14.00
Bowl, 7" soup	10.00	14.00	*** Salt and pepper, pr., 3"	20.00	40.00
Bowl, 5¼", divided	12.00		Sandwich server, center handle	16.00	27.50
Bowl, 8" large berry	7.00	12.00	Saucer	1.50	2.00
Butter tub or ice tub	22.00	35.00	Sherbet, low (for 6½" plate)	8.00	15.00
Cocktail shaker	20.00	27.50	Sherbet, 4¾" ftd.	5.00	9.00
** Cup	4.50	5.00	Sugar, ftd.	4.50	5.50
Creamer, ftd.	4.50	6.00	Tumbler, 3", 4 oz.	4.00	6.00
Decanter and stopper	25.00	40.00	Tumbler, 3½", 5 oz.	5.00	6.50
Goblet, 7¼", 9 oz.	7.50	15.00	Tumbler, 4", 8 oz., old fashion	14.00	17.50
Goblet, 3¾", 3½ oz. cocktail	11.00	18.00	Tumbler, 4¼", 9 oz.	4.50	10.00
Goblet, 4½", 3½ oz., wine	13.00	20.00	* Tumbler, 4¾", 10 oz	7.50	
Ice bucket	20.00	35.00	Tumbler, 5⅛", 12 oz.	7.00	10.00
Pitcher, 8", 60 oz.	17.50	25.00	Tumbler, 3½" ftd. juice	6.00	10.00
* Pitcher, 8½", 80 oz.	20.00	33.00	Tumbler, 5½" ftd. water	6.00	10.00
Plate, 6¼" sherbet	2.00	2.50	Tumbler, 6½", ftd. iced tea	8.00	15.00
Plate, 6½", off-center ring	5.00	6.00	Vase, 8"	17.50	35.00
** Plate, 8" luncheon	2.50	4.50	Whiskey, 2", 1½ oz.	6.00	10.00

* Also found in pink. Priced as green.   ** Red $17.50. Blue $27.50   *** Green $55.00

ROCK CRYSTAL, "EARLY AMERICAN ROCK CRYSTAL" McKEE GLASS COMPANY,
1920's and 1930's in colors

Colors: Four shades of green, aquamarine, vaseline, yellow, amber, pink and frosted pink, red slag, dark red, red, amberina red, crystal, frosted crystal, crystal with goofus decoration, crystal with gold decoration, amethyst, milk glass, blue frosted or "Jap" blue, and cobalt blue.

The flat Rock Crystal candy shown in front of the lamp at the bottom of this page was bought years ago from a former employee of McKee. He had many extra candy bottoms and said that they were sold as soup bowls. I assume that may have been a way to get rid of excess stock to employees. A red syrup pitcher has been found! The time period that red was supposedly made and the time period that syrup pitchers were made do not overlap. A red syrup pitcher should not exist; but it does; and that gives hope for red shakers and cruets. You can see this syrup in *Very Rare Glassware of the Depression Years, Fourth Series.*

Remember, we believed there to be two different sizes of punch bowls. The base opening for our bowl is 5" across and stands 6¹⁄₁₆" tall. This base fits a punch bowl that is 4³⁄₁₆" across the bottom. The other style base found has only a 4¹⁄₈" opening but also stands 6¹⁄₁₆" tall. The bowl to fit this base must be around 3½" across the bottom. No one has sent in measurements for that punch bowl yet. Could this piece be a vase that looks like the punch base? The vase theory has been proposed by a long time dealer who has sold many pieces of Rock Crystal over the years! Right now, it is an unsolved mystery.

In the photograph on page 187 are three styles of ice dishes. The one on the left is a combination of the others with a ring and three dividers outside the ring. The one in the center has only dividers and the one on the right has only a ring. The flat juice has been found in some of the ice dishes, but I suspect the liners may have been plain as were Fostoria's. Ice dishes were made to hold shrimp, crab, or juices with surrounding ice keeping the items cold (without diluting the contents or melting on the table). Icers were mostly found in the upper class homes of that day. Few common folks could afford to waste ice and dine that way.

Red, crystal, and amber sets can be completed with diligence. There are so many different pieces available that you need to determine how much you are willing to spend on a set by choosing what items to buy. Instead of buying every tumbler and stem made, you can pick up a couple of each or choose which styles you prefer and buy only them. That way even collectors with limited budgets can start crystal or amber. Red takes a deeper pocket!

Rock Crystal can be collected as a simple luncheon set, a dinner set, or a complete service with many unusual serving and accessory pieces. In fact, Rock Crystal pieces are often bought by collectors of other patterns to use as supplementary items with their own patterns. Vases, cruets, candlesticks, and a multitude of serving pieces are some of the items usually obtained. Serving pieces abound; so grab a few to use!

ROCK CRYSTAL, "EARLY AMERICAN ROCK CRYSTAL" (Cont.)

	Crystal	All Other Colors	Red
* Bon bon, 7½" s.e.	20.00	35.00	55.00
Bowl, 4" s.e.	12.00	22.00	32.00
Bowl, 4½" s.e.	14.00	22.00	32.00
Bowl, 5" s.e.	16.00	24.00	42.00
** Bowl, 5" finger bowl with 7" plate, p.e.	25.00	45.00	65.00
Bowl, 7" pickle or spoon tray	20.00	40.00	65.00
Bowl, 7" salad s.e.	24.00	37.50	65.00
Bowl, 8" salad s.e.	27.50	37.50	75.00
Bowl, 8½" center handle			175.00
Bowl, 9" salad s.e.	25.00	50.00	110.00
Bowl, 10½" salad s.e.	25.00	50.00	90.00
Bowl, 11½" 2-part relish	30.00	50.00	75.00
Bowl, 12" oblong celery	27.50	45.00	85.00
*** Bowl, 12½" ftd. center bowl	75.00	125.00	295.00
Bowl, 12½", 5 part relish	45.00		
Bowl, 13" roll tray	35.00	60.00	125.00
Bowl, 14" 6-part relish	37.50	65.00	
Butter dish and cover	335.00		
Butter dish bottom	200.00		
Butter dish top	135.00		
**** Candelabra, 2-lite pr.	45.00	105.00	250.00
Candelabra, 3-lite pr.	52.50	125.00	325.00
Candlestick, flat, stemmed pr.	40.00	65.00	100.00
Candlestick, 5½" low pr.	40.00	65.00	165.00
Candlestick, 8" tall pr.	95.00	140.00	395.00
Candy and cover, ftd., 9¼"	60.00	90.00	225.00
Candy and cover, round	50.00	75.00	175.00
Cake stand, 11", 2¾" high, ftd.	35.00	52.50	125.00
Comport, 7"	35.00	52.50	95.00
Creamer, flat s.e.	37.50		
Creamer, 9 oz. ftd.	20.00	32.00	67.50
Cruet and stopper, 6 oz. oil	95.00		
Cup, 7 oz.	17.50	27.50	70.00
Goblet, 7½ oz., 8 oz. low ftd.	18.00	27.50	57.50
Goblet, 11 oz. low ftd. iced tea	20.00	30.00	67.50
Ice dish (3 styles)	35.00		
Jelly, 5" ftd. s.e.	18.00	27.50	52.50
Lamp, electric	175.00	300.00	650.00
Parfait, 3½ oz. low ftd.	17.50	37.50	75.00
Pitcher, qt. s.e.	165.00	225.00	
Pitcher, ½ gal., 7½" high	110.00	195.00	
Pitcher, 9" large covered	175.00	300.00	675.00
Pitcher, fancy tankard	195.00	500.00	900.00
Plate, 6" bread and butter s.e.	6.00	9.50	20.00
Plate, 7½" p.e. & s.e.	8.00	12.00	21.00
Plate, 8½" p.e. & s.e.	9.00	12.50	30.00
Plate, 9" s.e.	18.00	22.00	55.00
Plate, 10½" s.e.	25.00	30.00	65.00
Plate, 10½" dinner s.e. (large center design)	47.50	70.00	175.00
Plate, 11½" s.e.	18.00	25.00	57.50
Punch bowl and stand, 14" (2 styles)	550.00		
Punch bowl stand only (2 styles)	175.00		
Salt and pepper (2 styles) pr.	75.00	125.00	
Salt dip	37.50		
Sandwich server, center-handled	30.00	45.00	145.00

   * s.e. McKee designation for scalloped edge
  ** p.e. McKee designation for plain edge
 *** Red Slag – $350.00   Cobalt – $225.00
**** Cobalt – $250.00

ROCK CRYSTAL, "EARLY AMERICAN ROCK CRYSTAL" (Cont.)

	Crystal	All Other Colors	Red
Saucer	7.50	8.50	22.00
Sherbet or egg, 3½ oz. ftd.	17.00	25.00	65.00
Spooner	40.00		
Stemware, 1 oz. ftd. cordial	18.00	40.00	60.00
Stemware, 2 oz. wine	20.00	30.00	52.50
Stemware, 3 oz. wine	20.00	30.00	52.50
Stemware, 3½ oz. ftd. cocktail	15.00	21.00	40.00
Stemware, 6 oz. ftd. champagne	16.00	23.00	35.00
Stemware, 7 oz.	16.00	25.00	52.50
Stemware, 8 oz. large ftd. goblet	18.00	26.00	57.50
Sundae, 6 oz. low ftd.	12.00	18.00	35.00
Sugar, 10 oz. open	15.00	22.00	40.00
Sugar, lid	35.00	45.00	125.00
Syrup with lid	150.00		650.00
Tray, 5⅜" x 7⅜", ⅞" high	65.00		
Tumbler, 2½ oz. whiskey	18.00	25.00	55.00
Tumbler, 5 oz. juice	16.00	25.00	57.50
Tumbler, 5 oz. old fashioned	18.00	27.50	60.00
Tumbler, 9 oz. concave or straight	18.00	26.00	52.50
Tumbler, 12 oz. concave or straight	25.00	35.00	67.50
Vase, cornucopia	65.00	90.00	
Vase, 11" ftd.	60.00	110.00	175.00

Please refer to Foreword for pricing information

ROSE CAMEO BELMONT TUMBLER COMPANY, 1931

Color: Green.

Even though Rose Cameo was patented in 1931 by Belmont Tumbler Company, I still believe that the actual manufacturing was done by Hazel Atlas. Rarely have glass shards of a pattern been found in digs at a factory site where it was not made. Rose Cameo turned up on the site of Hazel Atlas. Maybe time will unravel this mystery. Of course, a yellow Cloverleaf shaker was dug up at the site of Akro Agate's factory in Clarksburg, West Virginia; and we know that Akro had nothing to do with making Cloverleaf. (Did you know some glass collectors dabble in archaeology in pursuit of glass?)

All three bowls are all difficult to find, with the smaller berry being the easiest.

Rose Cameo is not confusing new collectors as it once did. Cameo, with its dancing girl, and this cameo encircled rose were often mixed up in bygone times. An informed collecting public rarely makes those mistakes today.

The difference in two styles of tumblers is recognized by noticing the flaring of the rims. One does not flare.

	Green
Bowl, 4½" berry	10.00
Bowl, 5" cereal	15.00
Bowl, 6" straight sides	20.00
Plate, 7" salad	12.00
Sherbet	12.00
Tumbler, 5" ftd. (2 styles)	20.00

ROSEMARY, "DUTCH ROSE" FEDERAL GLASS COMPANY, 1935–1937

Colors: Amber, green, pink; some iridized.

The story of Rosemary's becoming a separate pattern redesigned from Federal's Mayfair can be read on page 124. The existence of Rosemary came about inadvertently because of Hocking's previous patent to the Mayfair name.

Pink Rosemary has begun to drive away those collectors who were searching for it. Many who saw this as a challenge have fallen by the wayside. Pink is not being seen any more!

Cereal bowls, cream soups, grill plates, and tumblers are seldom seen in any color. I might add for new collectors that grill plates are the divided plates usually associated with diners or grills (restaurants) in this time. Food was kept from running together by those raised divisions. These are especially tough to find in pink.

An amber set can be assembled, but it will take you some time to put a green set together. I can't remember when I have seen an amber cereal or a green cream soup! They are missing in my photo, I noticed!

The sugar has no handles and is often mislabeled as a sherbet. There is no sherbet known in Rosemary! Those sugars could serve as large sherbets and dessert lovers could get an extra helping if you used it that way.

Rosemary is an intriguing pattern whether you are a beginning collector or a collector looking for a new set to collect. Maybe, Mayfair's demise was a blessing!

	Amber	Green	Pink
Bowl, 5" berry	6.00	9.00	10.00
Bowl, 5" cream soup	15.00	20.00	28.00
Bowl, 6" cereal	27.50	30.00	35.00
Bowl, 10" oval vegetable	14.00	26.00	37.50
Creamer, ftd.	8.50	12.50	18.00
Cup	5.50	9.50	10.00
Plate, 6¾" salad	5.50	8.50	9.00
Plate, dinner	9.00	14.00	20.00
Plate, grill	7.50	14.00	20.00
Platter, 12" oval	15.00	22.00	30.00
Saucer	4.50	5.00	6.00
Sugar, ftd.	8.50	12.50	17.00
Tumbler, 4¼", 9 oz.	30.00	30.00	47.50

Please refer to Foreword for pricing information

ROSEMARY

ROULETTE, "MANY WINDOWS" HOCKING GLASS COMPANY, 1935–1939

Colors: Green, pink, and crystal.

Roulette was found to be the real name of this pattern which collectors previously had called "Many Windows." Several collectors have told me they prefer that descriptive term instead of the real name!

Cups, saucers, sherbets, and luncheon plates are easily found in green. Finding the 12" sandwich plate and fruit bowl will take more time as they are infrequently found. After acquiring those items, then comes the fun of looking for the six various tumblers! Juice tumblers and the old fashioned are the most elusive of all. I still have not found a juice tumbler or whiskey for my photograph.

Only beverage sets can be found in pink. Pink pitchers and tumblers are easier to find than green ones. Prices continue to be priced similarly because there are few collectors for the pink water set. All five sizes of pink flat tumblers are pictured, but I have never seen a pink footed tumbler. Have you?

Crystal tumbler and pitcher sets are rarely found; however, there is little demand for the few that have surfaced. Some crystal sets have been found decorated with colored stripes. In fact, this striped effect gives an art deco look. I am more impressed with these decorated crystal pitchers than with any other Roulette items I have seen!

	Crystal	Pink, Green
Bowl, 9" fruit	9.50	15.00
Cup	36.00	6.50
Pitcher, 8", 65 oz.	30.00	35.00
Plate, 6" sherbet	3.50	4.50
Plate, 8½" luncheon	5.00	6.00
Plate, 12" sandwich	11.00	14.00
Saucer	1.50	3.50
Sherbet	3.50	5.50
Tumbler, 3¼", 5 oz. juice	7.00	22.00
Tumbler, 3¼", 7½ oz. old fashioned	23.00	40.00
Tumbler, 4⅛", 9 oz. water	13.00	22.00
Tumbler, 5⅛", 12 oz. iced tea	16.00	27.50
Tumbler, 5½", 10 oz. ftd.	14.00	27.50
Whiskey, 2½", 1½ oz.	8.00	16.00

"ROUND ROBIN" MANUFACTURER UNKNOWN, Probably early 1930's

Colors: Green, iridescent, and crystal.

"Round Robin" is another of the smaller mystery patterns whose manufacturer has remained undetected. In all the years that glassware has been collected, it never fails to amaze me how little we have found out about many of the patterns. Why hasn't someone found a boxed set or a labeled piece?

The Domino tray is the unanticipated piece in this small pattern. Hocking's Cameo is the only other pattern in Depression Glass to offer a sugar cube tray. This tray has only been found in green. For new readers, the Domino tray held the creamer in the center ring with sugar cubes surrounding it. Sugar cubes were made by a famous sugar company, and the tray became synonymous with this name.

Sherbets and berry bowls are the hardest pieces to locate outside the Domino tray. I have not been able to round up one green berry bowl myself. Sherbets and berry bowls are particularly hard to find in green, but plentiful in iridescent.

Some crystal "Round Robin" is found today. Crystal was sprayed and baked to achieve the iridized look. Obviously, not all the crystal was sprayed, since we find it sporadically.

The "Round Robin" cup is one of the few footed ones found in Depression Glass. I have not found an iridescent cup and saucer. Have you seen one?

	Green	Iridescent
Bowl, 4" berry	5.00	5.00
Cup, ftd.	5.00	5.50
Creamer, ftd.	7.50	6.50
Domino tray	35.00	
Plate, 6" sherbet	2.50	2.50
Plate, 8" luncheon	4.00	4.00
Plate, 12" sandwich	7.50	7.00
Saucer	2.00	2.00
Sherbet	5.00	6.00
Sugar	6.50	6.00

ROXANA, HAZEL ATLAS GLASS COMPANY, 1932

Colors: "Golden Topaz," crystal, and some white.

You can see how Roxana was obtained in Michigan, at least, thanks to a couple of collectors there who found the information shown on page 193. If you ate Star Brand Oats, you were able to receive one piece of "Golden Topaz" table glassware in every package. This "Golden Topaz" is what we now know as Roxana. This may clear up why the deep 4½" bowl and the 5½" plate are so hard to find. They were not packed as a premium in these oats! I am assuming that the plate shown on the ad is the 6" one to go with the sherbet.

The "saucer" listed previously is actually a 5½" plate! All seven known pieces are shown; I also included a gold decorated plate in hopes it would expose the pattern a little better in the photograph. This delicate pattern is difficult to capture on film since the light shade of yellow has a tendency to disappear under bright lights. Notice that the pattern nearly evaporated in the original advertisement! Well, we do recognize shapes!

Roxana was only catalogued by Hazel Atlas for one year. It is a limited pattern when compared to thousands of pieces in many other patterns made over years. Unfortunately, there are so few pieces available that most collectors avoid it. If your name is Roxana, how could you avoid collecting this pattern?

Only the 4½" deep bowl has been found in white.

	Yellow	White
Bowl, 4½" x 2⅜"	11.00	14.00
Bowl, 5" berry	10.00	
Bowl, 6" cereal	15.00	
Plate, 5½"	8.50	
Plate, 6" sherbet	7.50	
Sherbet, ftd.	10.00	
Tumbler, 4¼", 9 oz.	18.00	

ROYAL LACE HAZEL ATLAS GLASS COMPANY, 1934–1941

Colors: Cobalt blue, crystal, green, pink; some amethyst.

Cobalt blue Royal Lace has always been one of the most alluring patterns in Depression Glass. I attended my first Depression Glass show in Springfield, Missouri, in May of 1971. The cobalt Royal Lace I delivered to a dealer at that show paid for my trip. There was a gas war in Missouri, so gas cost $.19⁹ a gallon and the motel room was $6.00. I made several hundred dollars on that trip after all expenses, and that was the introductory crash course of my glass buying and selling career. Royal Lace could be found in my area, and there was a ready market for it. Today, there still is!

There is something about cobalt blue that acts as a magnet for collectors. No matter how expensive it becomes, there is one more collector willing to pay the price to get that one piece he doesn't have in his set! This occurs in other patterns and colors, but it has always been evident in this pattern and color!

There are five different pitchers made in Royal Lace: a) 48 oz., straight side; b) 64 oz., 8", no ice lip; c) 68 oz., 8", w/ice lip; d) 86 oz., 8", no ice lip; e) 96 oz., 8½", w/ice lip. The ten ounce difference in the last two listed is caused by the spout on the pitcher without lip dipping below the top edge of the pitcher. This causes the liquid to run out before you get to the top. All spouted pitchers will vary in ounce capacity (up to eight ounces) depending upon how the spout tilts or dips. Always measure ounce capacities until no more liquid can be added without running out.

Crystal and pink pitchers can be found in all five styles. Green can only be found in four styles. There is no 68 oz. with ice lip in green. I have seen only four styles in blue. I have had reports of a blue 86 oz. without ice lip, but I have not seen one!

More water tumblers (9 oz.) without panels are found than with the panel. These paneled tumblers are more pronounced on crystal than any other color. Most collectors prefer the plain style to match their other tumblers.

The 4⅞",10 oz. tumblers remain the most elusive; but numbers of iced teas and juice tumblers are waning. This is true for all tumblers including crystal. Some collectors only purchase water tumblers and the straight sided pitcher strictly for economic reasons. This style of pitcher and water tumblers were prolific; but demand continues to drive up the price! Prices would soar if most collectors sought all four sizes of tumblers!

Green Royal Lace is being enthusiastically hunted again. Collecting green Royal Lace has always run in cycles for some reason; but so has cobalt blue. The prices will shoot up so fast that everyone stops buying for a while. When collectors realize that the law of supply and demand takes precedent over all else with this glass, they start to buy again; that pushes prices higher and everyone stops buying again because the prices are too high.

Both a rolled edge console bowl and rolled edge candlesticks have been found in amethyst! The console bowl was bought from a relative of a Hazel Atlas worker. I do not know the story on the candlesticks yet. The only other amethyst pieces are the sherbets in metal holders and the cookie jar bottom used for toddy sets. Years ago, there were reports of shakers, but they never materialized.

Collectors prefer all glass sherbets to the ones found in metal holders, which makes for higher prices on them. Be sure to check the inside rims for mould roughness and nicks. That inner rim is why mint condition pieces cost more. Even stacking bowls and plates will cause damage to rims if not carefully done. Many dealers place paper plates between their merchandise. It is also not a bad idea for stacking them at home!

	Crystal	Pink	Green	Blue
Bowl, 4¾" cream soup	12.00	22.00	30.00	38.00
Bowl, 5" berry	15.00	27.00	30.00	50.00
Bowl, 10" round berry	20.00	28.00	30.00	60.00
Bowl, 10", 3-legged straight edge	20.00	35.00	45.00	70.00
* Bowl, 10", 3-legged rolled edge	195.00	50.00	75.00	300.00
Bowl, 10", 3-legged ruffled edge	30.00	55.00	65.00	450.00
Bowl, 11" oval vegetable	22.00	33.00	35.00	60.00
Butter dish and cover	65.00	140.00	260.00	595.00
Butter dish bottom	42.50	90.00	170.00	400.00
Butter dish top	27.50	50.00	90.00	195.00
Candlestick, straight edge pr.	30.00	55.00	75.00	110.00
** Candlestick, rolled edge pr.	45.00	60.00	85.00	210.00
Candlestick ruffled edge pr.	28.00	65.00	70.00	225.00
Cookie jar and cover	32.00	55.00	80.00	365.00
Cream, ftd.	12.00	20.00	25.00	55.00
Cup	7.00	15.00	20.00	33.00
Nut bowl	195.00	375.00	375.00	1,000.00
Pitcher, 48 oz., straight sides	40.00	75.00	110.00	155.00

	Crystal	Pink	Green	Blue
Pitcher, 64 oz., 8", w/o/l	45.00	75.00	110.00	225.00
Pitcher, 8", 68 oz., w/lip	50.00	85.00		245.00
Pitcher, 8", 86 oz., w/o/l	50.00	85.00	135.00	
Pitcher, 8½", 96 oz., w/lip	65.00	95.00	145.00	275.00
Plate, 6", sherbet	5.00	8.00	10.00	12.00
Plate, 8½" luncheon	8.00	15.00	16.00	32.00
Plate, 9⅞" dinner	14.00	20.00	27.00	35.00
Plate, 9⅞" grill	11.00	20.00	27.00	32.00
Platter, 13" oval	20.00	35.00	40.00	50.00
Salt and pepper, pr.	42.00	65.00	125.00	265.00
Saucer	5.00	7.00	9.00	12.50
Sherbet, ftd.	16.00	18.00	25.00	40.00
*** Sherbet in metal holder	3.50			28.00
Sugar	8.50	15.00	22.00	25.00
Sugar lid	20.00	45.00	50.00	140.00
Tumbler, 3½", 5 oz.	15.00	26.00	30.00	42.00
Tumbler, 4⅛", 9 oz.	14.00	20.00	30.00	40.00
Tumbler, 4⅞", 10 oz.	25.00	65.00	62.00	110.00
Tumbler, 5⅜", 12 oz.	25.00	55.00	50.00	90.00
****Toddy or cider set: includes cookie jar metal lid, metal tray, 8 roly-poly cups and ladle				225.00

* Amethyst $900.00   ** Amethyst $900.00   *** Amethyst $35.00   **** Amethyst $150.00

ROYAL RUBY ANCHOR HOCKING GLASS COMPANY, 1938–1940

Color: Ruby red.

Anchor Hocking introduced the Royal Ruby color in 1938 by using their existing patterns. I am trying to include **only** pieces of Royal Ruby introduced **before 1940** in my list, but I am sure there will be others added as additional information is revealed. Pieces of Royal Ruby made after 1940 are now included in my book *Collectible Glassware from the 40's, 50's, 60's....*

The catalogue page reproduced on page 197 is from one of Anchor Hocking's first after the introduction of Royal Ruby. It shows both Oyster and Pearl and Coronation as two of the patterns used to launch this Royal Ruby campaign. Introductory pieces of Royal Ruby have been found in many of Anchor Hocking's lines including Colonial, Ring, Manhattan, Queen Mary, and Miss America. Most of these Royal Ruby pieces are rare in these patterns; so keep an eye out for them. There were other designs made in Royal Ruby, but my plan here is to show regular Depression Glass patterns that were issued and can be collected in Royal Ruby.

	Royal Ruby		Royal Ruby
Bonbon, 6½"	8.50	Creamer, ftd.	9.00
Bowl, 3¾" berry (Old Cafe)	5.50	Cup (Coronation)	6.50
Bowl, 4½", handled (Coronation)	6.50	Cup (Old Cafe)	8.00
Bowl, 4⅞", smooth (Sandwich)	12.50	Cup, round	5.50
Bowl, 5¼" heart-shaped, 1-handled (Oys & Prl)	13.00	Goblet, ball stem	10.00
Bowl, 5¼", scalloped (Sandwich)	20.00	Jewel box, 4¼", crys. w/Ruby cov.	12.50
Bowl, 5½" cereal (Old Cafe)	10.00	Lamp (Old Cafe)	25.00
Bowl, 5½", 1-handled (Oys & Prl)	13.00	Marmalade, 5⅛", crys. w/Ruby cov.	7.50
Bowl, 6½" deep-handled (Oys & Prl)	20.00	Plate, 8½", luncheon (Coronation)	8.00
Bowl, 6½", handled (Coronation)	12.00	Plate, 9⅛", dinner, round	11.00
Bowl, 6½", scalloped (Sandwich)	27.50	Plate, 13½" sandwich (Oys & Prl)	45.00
Bowl, 8", handled (Coronation)	15.00	Puff box, 4⅝", crys. w/Ruby cov.	9.00
Bowl, 8", scalloped (Sandwich)	37.50	Relish tray insert (Manhattan)	4.50
Bowl, 9", closed handles (Old Cafe)	14.00	Saucer, round	2.50
Bowl, 10½" deep fruit (Oys & Prl)	50.00	Sherbet, low ftd. (Old Cafe)	10.00
Candle holder, 3½" pr. (Oys & Prl)	50.00	Sugar, ftd.	7.50
Candle holder, 4½" pr. (Queen Mary)	65.00	Sugar, lid	11.00
Candy dish, 8" mint, low (Old Cafe)	11.00	Tray, 6" x 4½"	12.50
Candy jar, 5½", crys. w/Ruby cov. (Old Cafe)	15.00	Tumbler, 3" juice (Old Cafe)	10.00
Cigarette box/card holder, 6⅛" x 4" crys.		Tumbler, 4" water (Old Cafe)	18.00
w/Ruby top	65.00	Vase, 7¼" (Old Cafe)	16.00
		Vase, 9", two styles	16.00

9" Vase
A53—Royal Ruby
2 doz. ctn.—36 lbs.

CONSOLE SETS
(Candle Holders and Console Bowls and Plates)

PROMOTE CONSOLE SETS
Display Sets but price and sell both sets and individual pieces.

IN "ROYAL RUBY"
A881—3½" Candle Holder
    2 doz. ctn.—14 lbs.
A889—10½" Console Bowl
    1 doz. ctn.—30 lbs.
A890—13½" Console Plate
    1 doz. ctn.—28 lbs.

IN "POLISHED CRYSTAL"
881—3½" Candle Holder
    2 doz. ctn.—14 lbs.
889—10½" Console Bowl
    1 doz. ctn.—30 lbs.
890—13½" Sandwich Plate
    1 doz. ctn.—29 lbs.

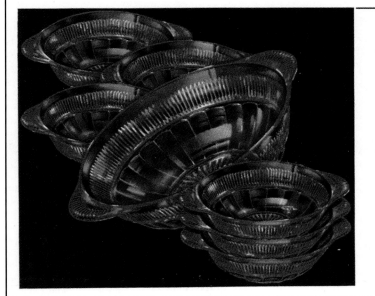

7-Pc. Dessert Set

BULK PACKED
IN "ROYAL RUBY" GLASS

A4400/8—7-Piece Set

Bulk Packed:

  1 Ctn., 1 doz. A4478—8" Bowl
      (Weight 16 lbs.)

  1 Ctn., 6 doz. A4474—4½" Dessert
      (Weight 26 lbs.)

  Minimum 12 Sets in 2 cartons—42 lbs.

"S" PATTERN, "STIPPLED ROSE BAND" MacBETH-EVANS GLASS COMPANY, 1930–1933

Colors: Crystal; crystal w/trims of silver, blue, green, amber; pink; some amber, green, fired-on red, Monax, and light yellow.

Decorated "S" Pattern, whether it be platinum trimmed crystal or pastel banded crystal, catches more attention than does the plain crystal. Notice how the green banded crystal pieces catch your eye in the photo on top of page 199. The predicament with collecting pastel banded crystal is that there is little of it available! Amber, blue, or green banded crystal was made; so, you might follow an ever growing trend in collecting and mix colors. You can find crystal, but you might have to mix some platinum trimmed with it to create a set.

Amber color variances make some pieces look more yellow than amber. The differences are almost as distinct as they are in Hocking's Princess; however, amber "S" Pattern collectors do have a dinner plate to use that has not yet been found in crystal.

A pink or green pitcher and tumbler set still turns up sporadically, but the demand for these has dwindled. Years ago, there were a number of pitcher collectors; rare pitchers sold fast. Today, there are fewer pitcher collectors still active and most of them already own the hard-to-find pitchers. Too, in those bygone days rare pitchers only sold in the $200.00–500.00 range. Today, some rarities are commanding prices of $1,500.00–5,000.00. One of the most stunning collections I ever saw displayed was of pitchers on lighted glass shelves with mirrors behind the glass. It made the room a show place!

Fired-on red and true red "S" Pattern items, like red American Sweetheart, both fit the rare category; however, like the pink and green pitchers, there are fewer collectors who are excited by them. For example, I sold the first red luncheon plates found for $65.00 each in the early 1970's which was the same price as those of American Sweetheart. Today, those red "S" Pattern plates are a tough sell at $40.00. Collector demand for red in this pattern is simply not as high as it was twenty years ago!

	Crystal	Yellow, Amber, Crystal W/ Trims		Crystal	Yellow, Amber, Crystal W/Trims
* Bowl, 5½" cereal	5.00	7.00	Plate, grill	6.50	8.00
Bowl, 8½" large berry	11.00	16.00	Plate, 11¾" heavy cake	40.00	45.00
* Creamer, thick or thin	6.00	7.00	*** Plate, 13" heavy cake	60.00	70.00
* Cup, thick or thin	3.50	4.50	Saucer	2.00	2.50
Pitcher, 80 oz. (like "Dogwood")			Sherbet, low ftd.	4.50	7.00
(green or pink 550.00)	52.50	100.00	* Sugar, thick and thin	5.50	6.50
Pitcher, 80 oz. (like "American			Tumbler, 3½", 5 oz.	4.50	6.00
Sweetheart")	60.00		Tumbler, 4", 9 oz. (green or		
Plate, 6" sherbet (Monax 8.00)	2.50	3.00	pink 50.00)	5.00	6.50
** Plate, 8¼" luncheon	4.50	5.00	Tumbler, 4¾, 10 oz.	5.00	7.50
Plate, 9¼" dinner		9.00	Tumbler, 5", 12 oz.	9.00	14.00

* Fired-on red items will run approximately twice price of amber   **Red – $40.00; Monax – $10.00   ***Amber – $77.50

SANDWICH INDIANA GLASS COMPANY, 1920's–1980's

Colors: Crystal late 1920's–today; teal blue 1950's–1980's; milk white mid-1950's; amber late 1920's–1980's; red 1933, 1969–early 1970's; Smokey Blue 1976–1977; pink, green 1920's–early 1930's.

Collecting Indiana's Sandwich pattern excites some people. Most dealers and even more collectors avoid it like a disease because of the company's total disregard for protecting old Indiana patterns by continually reissuing them. The pink and green shown here is from the Depression era, but Indiana has made a darker green in recent years.

Only six items in red Sandwich date from 1933, i.e., cups, saucers, luncheon plates, water goblets, creamers, and sugars. However, in 1969, Tiara Home Products marketed red pitchers, 9 oz. goblets, cups, saucers, wines, wine decanters, 13" serving trays, creamers, sugars, salad and dinner plates. Today, there is no difference for pricing the red color unless you have some red marked 1933 Chicago World's Fair. Crystal was made as early as the 1920's, but few people can tell it apart from the Tiara issues of the last 20 years. You, alone, will have to decide how seriously you want to collect Indiana's Sandwich.

Decanter stoppers are difficult to find as is indicated by their conspicuous absence in the photograph. Yes, the pattern is attractive! If you like it, buy it! I am just not certain this pattern has much investment possibility!

	Amber Crystal	Teal Blue	Red	Pink/ Green		Amber Crystal	Teal Blue	Red	Pink/ Green
Ash trays(club, spade, heart, diamond shapes, ea.)	3.25				Decanter and stopper	22.00		80.00	110.00
Basket, 10" high	35.00				Goblet, 9 oz.	13.00		45.00	
Bowl, 4¼" berry	3.50				Mayonnaise, ftd.	13.00			30.00
Bowl, 6"	4.00				Pitcher, 68 oz.	22.00		130.00	
Bowl, 6", hexagonal	5.00	14.00			Plate, 6" sherbet	3.00	7.00		
Bowl, 8½"	11.00				Plate, 7" bread and butter	4.00			
Bowl, 9" console	16.00			40.00	Plate, 8" oval, indent for cup	5.50	12.00		
Bowl, 11½" console	18.50			50.00	Plate, 8⅜" luncheon	4.75		20.00	
Butter dish and cover, domed	22.00	*155.00			Plate, 10½" dinner	8.00			20.00
Butter dish bottom	6.00	42.50			Plate, 13" sandwich	12.75	24.00	35.00	25.00
Butter dish top	16.00	112.50			Puff box	16.00			
Candlesticks, 3½" pr.	16.00			45.00	Salt and pepper pr.	17.50			
Candlesticks 7" pr.	26.00				Sandwich server, center	18.00		45.00	30.00
Creamer	9.00		45.00		Saucer	2.50	4.50	7.50	
Celery, 10½"	16.00				Sherbet, 3¼"	5.50	12.00		
Creamer and sugar on diamond shaped tray	16.00	32.00			Sugar, large	9.00		45.00	
					Sugar lid for large size	13.00			
Cruet, 6½ oz. and stopper	26.00	135.00		160.00	Tumbler, 3 oz. ftd. cocktail	7.50			
Cup	3.50	8.50	27.50		Tumbler, 8 oz. ftd. water	9.00			
					Tumbler, 12 oz. ftd. iced tea	10.00			
					Wine, 3", 4 oz.	6.00		12.50	25.00

*Beware recent vintage sell $22.00

SANDWICH

SHARON, "CABBAGE ROSE" FEDERAL GLASS COMPANY, 1935–1939

Colors: Pink, green, amber; some crystal. *(See Reproduction Section.)*

Pink and green Sharon prices are edging upward again. Amber prices are up on a few harder-to-find pieces. Of course, that upward trend tends to be true of all major patterns right now. That has not always been the case in recent times, but prices on rarely found items and collectable patterns have increased dramatically.

Sharon is a Depression pattern that has sustained loss of appeal for collectors in the past because of reproductions. Due to instruction of the differences between old and new, interest in Sharon has rejuvenated! It was not that people stopped collecting as much as new collectors did not start. Without new collectors, basic pieces stop selling and dealers stop buying them. It becomes a vicious cycle with only the rarely found and under priced pieces selling. Now, every dealer who stopped buying, is crying that he can't find enough pink or green Sharon to meet today's demand! This rising market is a great sign, unless you are an author trying to keep up with it!

I have pictured Sharon this time since I have a part of an ad showing a coupon exchange for amber Sharon. We only reproduced parts of this advertisement. The numbers in the right column under Golden Glow Tableware represent the number of coupons from large cans needed to order the item. Labels from small cans only were worth one-half. The problem being that I have no idea as to cans of what. This ad was given to me, and unfortunately I did not label or mark some pertinent information on the back as I usually do. In any case, most of the items shown were for amber Sharon or Golden Glow Dinnerware as listed. This ad featured pieces from Hocking (Manhattan), Jeannette (Jennyware), and McKee (Glass Bake). The major portion of the ad was for Federal glassware. If you have any idea what canned product manufacturer traded labels for glass, please let me know!

The price for a pink cheese dish continues to climb. The top for the cheese and butter dish are the same piece. The bottoms are different. The butter bottom is a 1½" deep bowl with a ledge while the cheese bottom is a salad plate with a raised band of glass on top of it. The lid fits inside this raised band! Amber cheese dishes can be found. There is no cheese dish in the original green.

Other pink pieces infrequently found include flat, thick iced teas and jam dishes. The jam dish is like the butter bottom except it has no indentation for the top. It differs from the 1⅞" deep soup bowl by standing only 1½" tall. I bought six jam dishes priced as soup bowls last year. You can still find a bargain if you keep your eyes peeled!

Green Sharon that is difficult to find include the pitchers and tumblers. Surprisingly enough, the green pitcher without ice lip is rarer than the one with an ice lip. There are no green soup bowls, only jam dishes.

There are two styles of flat tumblers. You have a choice of thick or thin. The heavy tumblers are easier to find in green; and the price reflects that. In amber and pink, the heavy iced teas are more rarely seen.

Amber footed teas are the most scarce of all Sharon tumblers; but few collectors of amber Sharon make this tumbler a priority at today's prices. Believe me, they are truly under priced for their scarcity! Amber Sharon pitchers are more difficult to find than the pink; but prices do not indicate that. There are many more collectors looking for pink Sharon, so demand pushes up the price.

		Amber	Pink	Green
	Bowl, 5" berry	8.50	12.50	15.00
	Bowl, 5" cream soup	27.50	45.00	50.00
	Bowl, 6" cereal	20.00	25.00	25.00
	Bowl, 7¾" flat soup, 1⅞" deep	50.00	50.00	
	Bowl, 8½" large berry	6.00	30.00	32.00
	Bowl, 9½" oval vegetable	20.00	30.00	32.00
	Bowl, 10½" fruit	21.00	37.50	37.50
	Butter dish and cover	46.00	50.00	85.00
	Butter dish bottom	23.00	25.00	37.50
	Butter dish top	23.00	25.00	47.50
*	Cake plate, 11½" ftd.	25.00	40.00	60.00
	Candy jar and cover	45.00	50.00	160.00
	Cheese dish and cover	190.00	850.00	
	Creamer, ftd.	14.00	18.00	20.00
	Cup	9.00	14.00	18.00
	Jam dish, 7½"	37.50	210.00	42.50
	Pitcher, 80 oz. with ice lip	135.00	145.00	395.00
	Pitcher, 80 oz. without ice lip	130.00	140.00	425.00
	Plate, 6" bread and butter	5.00	7.50	8.00
**	Plate, 7½" salad	15.00	22.50	22.50
	Plate, 9½" dinner	11.00	19.00	22.00
	Platter, 12½" oval	18.00	30.00	30.00
	Salt and pepper, pr.	40.00	50.00	67.50
	Saucer	6.50	12.00	12.00
	Sherbet, ftd.	12.00	15.00	35.00
	Sugar	9.00	14.00	15.00
	Sugar lid	22.00	30.00	38.00
	Tumbler, 4⅛", 9 oz. thick	27.00	37.50	65.00
	Tumbler, 4⅛", 9 oz. thin	27.00	40.00	70.00
	Tumbler, 5¼", 12 oz. thin	52.00	42.50	95.00
	Tumbler, 5¼", 12 oz. thick	65.00	80.00	90.00
***	Tumbler, 6½", 15 oz. ftd.	120.00	47.50	

* Crystal $8.00
** Crystal $13.50
*** Crystal $15.00

Golden Glow Tableware		
*101	Cup and Saucer	20
*102	Drinking Set, Ice Lip Jug and 6 Tumblers	110
*104	Salt and Pepper Shakers .... pair	22
*108	Bowl, 8½ inch	22
*113	Fruit Dish, 5 inch	8
*116	Plate, 6 inch	10
*117	Plate, 9½ inch	20
*118	Sherbet	10
*121	Sugar and Creamer	30
*122	Vegetable Dish, 9½ inch	22
*123	Meat Platter, 12½ inch	28
*124	Cream Soup, Handled	12
*127	Butter Dish	24

*Items not mailable. See page 31.
†Coupons from Small Cans count ½ Coupon.

"SHIPS" or "SAILBOAT" also known as "SPORTSMAN SERIES"
HAZEL ATLAS GLASS COMPANY, LATE 1930's

Colors: Cobalt blue w/white, yellow, and red decoration.

"Ships" shot glasses are still causing confusion for some collectors; so, I will try to explain them again. The "Ships" shot glass is shown in the top picture on page 203. It is the Lilliputian (2¼", 2 oz.) tumbler in front on the right. It is not the heavy bottomed tumbler shown to its left that holds 4 oz. and is 3¼" tall. I have letters from people who purchased the 4 oz. tumbler believing it to be a shot glass! You will notice there's a large price difference between the authentic 2 oz. shot and the 4 oz. tumbler!

"Ships" decorated Moderntone is not extensive. Search for unworn **white**, not beige, decoration on these pieces. Prices are for **mint** pieces. Worn and discolored items should fetch much less if someone should want to buy them. The "Ships" Moderntone decorated sherbet plate is as hard to find as the dinner plate, so don't sell them short!

The yellow "Ships" old fashioned tumbler is not a discoloration. It really is "raincoat" yellow rather than white! Observe the pieces with red and white "Ships" or crystal tumblers with a blue boat. These are the identical boats, so you can augment this pattern!

Pictured below are other items in the "Sportsman Series." People who collect Dutch related paraphernalia enjoy the "Windmills." There are "Nursery Rhymes," dogs, fish, horses, and whatever sports interest you — skiing, boating, fishing, golfing, dancing, or horse riding; you can surely find a drinking set to your preference!

The bottom photo on page 203 shows the cocktail shaker, ice tub, and several sizes of tumblers in a pattern Cathy likes to designate as "fancy" ships. The cloud formation differs. Also shown here are some accessory pieces that can go with this "Ships" pattern (that has its beginnings on the Moderntone blank). None of these are in the Hazel Atlas listing below; so I will put prices for these in parentheses as I mention them below.

The square or round ash trays ($55.00) and the three-sectional box ($185.00) on the right may have been manufactured by the same company since the designs are very similar. The ash tray with the metal ship ($95.00) is more than likely Hazel Atlas. I have seen a similar tray with a devil thumbing his nose! The smaller glass tray ($95.00), which has a tumbler with a sailor and matching anchor and rope design, and the larger glass tray ($120.00), which has a matching tumbler, are rarely seen. The crystal ash tray with light blue ship ($15.00 — set of 4) was a piece bought solely because it had a ship. The ceiling globe seems to match the ships found on McKee Ships pieces. I have seen many of these items priced even higher; but these are selling prices... not "dust them once a year" ones!

	Blue/White		Blue/White		Blue/White
Cup (Plain) "Moderntone"	11.00	Plate, 8", salad	23.00	Tumbler, 5 oz., 3¾", juice	12.00
Cocktail mixer w/stirrer	27.50	Plate, 9", dinner	30.00	Tumbler, 6 oz., roly poly	10.00
Cocktail shaker	32.50	Saucer	17.00	Tumbler, 8 oz., 3⅜", old fashion	16.00
Ice bowl	35.00	Tumbler, 2 oz., 2¼" shot glass	155.00	Tumbler, 9 oz., 3¾", straight water	14.00
Pitcher w/o lip, 82 oz.	50.00	Tumbler, 3½", whiskey	27.50	Tumbler, 9 oz., 4⅝", water	11.00
Pitcher w/lip, 86 oz.	47.50	Tumbler, 4 oz., heavy bottom	27.50	Tumbler, 10½ oz., 4⅞", iced tea	15.00
Plate, 5⅞", bread & butter	22.00	Tumbler, 4 oz., 3¼" heavy bottom	27.50	Tumbler, 12 oz., iced tea	22.00

SIERRA, "PINWHEEL" JEANNETTE GLASS COMPANY, 1931–1933

Colors: Green, pink, and some Ultramarine.

Sierra pitchers, tumblers, and oval vegetable bowls have all but disappeared in both pink and green. You could happen upon these pieces in pink a few years ago with tenacious shopping, but finding them now, at any price, is a major assignment! Ardent Sierra collectors have told me that obtaining the green oval vegetable is the most difficult task; but finding six or eight tumblers takes more time and a lot more money! A major problem is finding mint condition oval bowls. If they were much used, one of those pointed edges invariably got chipped, nicked, or chunked! The points have to be carefully inspected or you will often miss a "chigger bite" off one of these edges. Thankfully, most collectors can settle for having only one oval bowl in their sets.

Sugar bowls have become more difficult to find than the lids. It is the pointed edges on the sugar bowl (which chip so easily) that make this bowl so hard to get in mint condition. That is the one flaw in collecting any Sierra. You need to look carefully at all pink Sierra butter dishes. You might run into the Adam/Sierra combination. Be sure to read about this under Adam.

Frequently, the wrong cup is placed on Sierra saucers. You always have to be on your toes when you are buying! The cups, pitchers, and tumblers all have smooth edges instead of the serrated edges of the other pieces. Without smooth edges, these cups and tumblers would be the forerunners of dribble glasses.

There have been three Sierra ultramarine cups found, but no one has seen a saucer! Why? These must have been an experimental run or more would be surfacing! Possibly a batch of Sierra was made at the time Jeannette was making Doric and Pansy or Swirl in that color.

	Pink	Green		Pink	Green
Bowl, 5½" cereal	12.00	14.00	Platter, 11" oval	40.00	47.50
Bowl, 8½" large berry	28.00	28.00	Salt and pepper, pr.	37.50	37.50
Bowl, 9¼" oval vegetable	40.00	110.00	Saucer	6.00	7.00
Butter dish and cover	60.00	65.00	Serving tray, 10¼", 2 handles	15.00	18.00
Creamer	18.00	20.00	Sugar	18.00	24.00
Cup	11.00	14.00	Sugar cover	16.00	16.00
Pitcher, 6½", 32 oz.	75.00	110.00	Tumbler, 4½", 9 oz. ftd.	55.00	75.00
Plate, 9" dinner	18.00	22.00			

SPIRAL HOCKING GLASS COMPANY, 1928–1930

Colors: Green, crystal, and pink.

The Spiral platter is not often found. Observe that it is shaped like Hocking's Cameo platter. It has closed or tab handles as do many patterns made by Hocking. You might also notice several other pieces shaped like Cameo including the ice tub, creamer, and sugar. A luncheon set can be acquired rather inexpensively with the only problem being finding it! This is not a pattern that most dealers carry to glass shows; so you will have to ask for it.

Green Spiral is the color normally found, but there is some pink available. You might even find an occasional piece in crystal. I have never met a collector searching for any color other than green.

The Spiral center-handled server has a solid handle and the Twisted Optic center-handled server has an open handle if you have trouble distinguishing those from each other.

I have always included a Twisted Optic piece in my Spiral pictures for comparison to the Spiral. Can you spot it this time? Remember that Spiral swirls go to the left or clockwise while Twisted Optic spirals go to the right or counterclockwise.

Unfortunately, on a few pieces, whether the pattern spirals are placed inside or outside the design affect the left- or right-handed spiraling! This time the Twisted Optic piece is the covered candy on the left. You should be able to see spirals going counterclockwise on that lid!

	Green		Green
Bowl, 4¾" berry	5.00	Preserve and cover	30.00
Bowl, 7" mixing	8.50	Salt and pepper, pr.	35.00
Bowl, 8" large berry	12.50	Sandwich server, center handle	25.00
Creamer, flat or ftd.	7.50	Saucer	2.00
Cup	5.00	Sherbet	4.00
Ice or butter tub	26.00	Sugar, flat or ftd.	7.50
Pitcher, 7⅝", 58 oz.	30.00	Tumbler, 3", 5 oz. juice	4.50
Plate, 6" sherbet	2.00	Tumbler, 5", 9 oz. water	7.50
Plate, 8" luncheon	3.50	Tumbler, 5⅞" ftd.	15.00
Platter, 12"	27.50		

Please refer to Foreword for pricing information

STARLIGHT HAZEL ATLAS GLASS COMPANY, 1938–1940

Colors: Crystal, pink; some white, cobalt.

I have received several letters wanting to buy my Starlight punch bowl set. Evidently, these are rarer than I had previously thought. As with other Hazel Atlas sets, this punch bowl was made by putting a bowl in a metal holder and extending the metal to accommodate cups. The one pictured was bought for me in the St. Louis area; but it is the only one I have seen!

Some crystal Starlight prices are beginning to show signs of new collecting interest. This small pattern has never been collected by large numbers, but enough collectors are buying to show some inadequacies in supplies. Problems finding sherbets, cereals, and the large salad bowls are just commencing. Few 13" sandwich plates are being seen. Has anyone seen a pink 13" plate recently?

The 5½" cereal is handled and measures 6" including the handles. All measurements in this book do not include handles, unless specifically noted.

Starlight is another one of the smaller sets that can be collected without having to borrow money. The only difficulty (twenty-five years into Depression Glass mania) comes in finding it. Pink and blue bowls make nice accessory pieces that can be used alongside the crystal.

I have often wondered why Starlight shakers are found with a one hole shaker top. I have now found out! It was a specially designed top made to keep the salt "moisture proof." Airko shakers with these tops are often found in Florida and other southern areas where the humid air has caused shaker holes to clog. One of these moisture-proof shakers is pictured here with the original label.

	Crystal, White	Pink
Bowl, 5½" cereal, closed handles	7.00	9.00
* Bowl, 8½", closed handles	10.00	15.00
Bowl, 11½" salad	20.00	
Bowl, 12", 2¾" deep	25.00	
Creamer, oval	5.00	
Cup	4.00	
Plate, 6" bread and butter	3.00	
Plate, 8½" luncheon	5.00	
Plate, 9" dinner	7.50	
Plate, 13" sandwich	14.00	15.00
Relish dish	14.00	
Salt and pepper, pr.	22.50	
Saucer	2.00	
Sherbet	13.00	
Sugar, oval	5.00	

* Cobalt $30.00

STRAWBERRY U.S. GLASS COMPANY, Early 1930's

Colors: Pink, green, crystal; some iridized.

Strawberry and Cherryberry are now divided into two distinct patterns. For many years collectors lumped these patterns together regardless of the fruit on the piece. Today's sophisticated collectors consider these two patterns and not one. Strawberry does have more people appreciating its fruit than Cherryberry. See page 32 for the Cherryberry listing.

Green Strawberry commands more attention than pink. A diminutive problem exists in color tones of the green. Look at the shades of green in the photograph. Under sunlight or direct light, these color changes are more dazzling. Green or pink Strawberry can be collected in a set; however, as with other U.S. Glass patterns, there are no cups, saucers, or dinner sized plates.

Strawberry is another of those U.S. Glass patterns that has very rough mould seams. This occurs on the tumblers, pitchers, and even the plates. If mould roughness offends your collecting sensibilities, then this pattern needs to be avoided. Even pieces that are considered mint may have roughness on a seam.

Iridescent Strawberry pitchers and tumblers are quite rare! Carnival collectors prize this iridescent pitcher more highly than do Depression Glass collectors. One main criterion is that it has full, vivid color and does not have color fade out toward the bottom, as many do.

Crystal is priced along with iridescent because it is quite rare. There are few crystal Strawberry collectors; that is good since so few pieces are found! Strawberry sugar covers and the 6¼", 2" deep bowl are missing from most collections. Some dealers have mistakenly labeled the sugar with missing lid a spooner. It is a sugar bowl without handles that is often found in earlier glassware.

Strawberry has a plain butter dish bottom that is interchangeable with other U.S. Glass patterns. This is the pattern for which other U.S. Glass butter dish bottoms were borrowed to use with Strawberry tops, but that custom left many other butters bottomless! Strawberry butter dishes have always been coveted by collectors.

	Crystal, Iridescent	Pink, Green		Crystal, Iridescent	Pink, Green
Bowl, 4" berry	6.50	9.00	Olive dish, 5" one-handled	8.50	13.00
Bowl, 6¼", 2" deep	42.50	65.00	Pickle dish, 8¼" oval	8.50	12.50
Bowl, 6½" deep salad	15.00	18.00	Pitcher, 7¾"	160.00	150.00
Bowl, 7½" deep berry	16.00	20.00	Plate, 6" sherbet	5.00	7.00
Butter dish and cover	135.00	150.00	Plate, 7½" salad	10.00	13.00
Butter dish bottom	77.50	90.00	Sherbet	6.50	7.50
Butter dish top	57.50	60.00	Sugar, small open	12.00	17.50
Comport, 5¾"	14.00	19.00	Sugar large	22.00	32.00
Creamer, small	12.00	17.50	Sugar cover	38.00	50.00
Creamer, 4⅝" large	22.50	33.00	Tumbler, 3⅝", 8 oz.	20.00	30.00

"SUNBURST," "HERRINGBONE" JEANNETTE GLASS COMPANY, late 1930's

Colors: Crystal.

Jeannette made this smaller pattern from the same shaped moulds as it did Iris. I have received numerous requests to list this contemporary of Iris, so I have finally been coerced into doing that. I have been trying to find a catalogue or advertisement to ascertain the true name of this pattern that I have heard called both "Sunburst" and "Herringbone." I do not know which is correct, but more people use "Sunburst" so that will be the name until I find otherwise.

I am listing only pieces I have found or pieces that have been in photographs sent me over the years. I am sure there will be additional finds for future editions; so let me know what you have in your collection to embellish our listing.

As I have searched for this pattern for a few years, I have noticed that the candlesticks seem to be the most commonly found pieces. That is surprising because I can not think of any other pattern where candlesticks are seen more often.

Divided relish and the berry bowls would have made sensational pieces for Iris. This style rather outclasses those ruffled bowls of Iris. Look this pattern over carefully, since inner rims are easily nicked. Have fun searching; no one would probably have noticed "Sunburst" had it not been for Iris.

	Crystal
Bowl, 4¾", berry	6.00
Bowl, 8½", berry	15.00
Candlesticks, double, pr.	30.00
Creamer, footed	7.50
Cup	6.00
Plate, 5½"	3.50
Plate, 9¼", dinner	14.00
Plate, 11¾", sandwich	12.00
Relish, 2 part	12.00
Saucer	2.00
Sherbet	9.00
Sugar	7.50
Tumbler, 4", 9 oz., flat	17.50

SUNFLOWER JEANNETTE GLASS COMPANY, 1930's

Colors: Pink, green, some Delphite; some opaque colors.

Sunflower cake plates were packed in twenty pound bags of flour for several years during the 1930's when everyone bought flour in large quantities because home baking was necessary. A problem that occurs regularly with the green cake plate is that many are found in a deep, dark green that does not match any other pieces of green Sunflower. A pink cake plate is shown against the back of the picture. Those two "eyes" staring at you are the legs of the cake plate. Since it is standing on its side, those legs look strange. Sorry about that!

The 7" trivet has an edge that is slightly upturned and it is three inches smaller than the ever-present cake plate. These are often confused by novice collectors, but three inches is quite a difference! The trivet remains the most elusive piece of Sunflower. Collector demand for the trivet keeps prices increasing steadily. Green Sunflower pieces are found less often than pink; therefore, prices for green are surpassing prices in pink. Both colors make attractive sets.

After several collectors told me that Sunflower had a shortage of saucers, I have kept my eyes pealed and they are right! I have not found out why I see cups more often than saucers. Maybe the cups were a premium that never offered saucers. If you run into a stack of Sunflower saucers, remember that they might be a good buy!

The Ultramarine ash tray pictured is the only piece I have found in that color. Opaque colors show up occasionally. Only a creamer, cup, and saucer have been spotted in Delphite blue.

With the closing of my shop after the death of my Mom, Grannie Bear, I cannot write about Sunflower without relating a story about the ever-present Sunflower cake plates. It brings a smile to my face just thinking about it. A famous antique lecturer was in town for an exclusive antique show. People were charged $35.00 for admission on preview night and they could have one item appraised free with that admission. Days later a lady brought a Sunflower cake plate in to sell. Grannie Bear offered her our standard buying price of sixty percent of my book price or $3.60. She apprised Grannie Bear of the fact that she'd been informed by an "antique expert" that it was rare and she could only let it go for $35.00. (I guess she was trying to recoup her admission!) Mom then asked her how many she wished to buy for $6.00 since we had several at the time. The lady was indignant and stormed out of the shop. I have often wondered just how much she was told the cake plate was worth!

	Pink	Green		Pink	Green
* Ash Tray, 5", center design only	9.00	12.00	Saucer	8.00	10.00
Cake Plate, 10", 3 legs	15.00	15.00	Sugar (opaque 85.00)	18.00	19.00
** Creamer (opaque 85.00)	18.00	19.00	Tumbler, 4¾", 8 oz. ftd.	25.00	30.00
Cup (opaque 75.00)	12.00	14.00	Trivet, 7", 3 legs, turned up edge	285.00	300.00
Plate, 9" dinner	15.00	19.00			

* Found in Ultramarine $25.00   **Delphite $85.00

SWANKY SWIGS 1930's–early 1940's

I never set up with these at a show that someone doesn't see them and exclaim, "Why, I remember those! We used them when I was a child!" More often than not, they buy one or more for a grandchild.

See *Collectible Glassware from the 40's, 50's, 60's...* for later made Swankys.

Top Row	Band No.1	Red & Black	3⅜"	2.00–3.00
		Red & Blue	3⅜"	3.00–4.00
		Blue	3⅜"	3.50–5.00
	Band No.2	Red & Black	4¾"	4.00–5.00
		Red & Black	3⅜"	3.00–4.00
	Band No.3	Blue & White	3⅜"	3.00–4.00
	Circle & Dot:	Blue	4¾"	6.00–8.00
		Blue	3½"	5.00–6.00
		Red, Green	3½"	4.00–5.00
		Black	3½"	5.00–6.00
		Red	4¾"	6.00–8.00
	Dot	Black	4¾"	7.00–9.00
		Blue	3½"	5.00–6.00
2nd Row	Star:	Blue	4¾"	5.00–6.00
		Blue, Red, Green, Black	3½"	3.00–4.00
		Cobalt w/White Stars	4¾"	15.00–18.00
	Centennials:	W.Va. Cobalt	4¾"	20.00–22.00
		Texas Cobalt	4¾"	27.50–32.50
		Texas Blue, Black, Green	3½"	27.50–32.50
	Checkerboard	Blue, Red	3½"	22.50–25.00
3rd Row	Checkerboard	Green	3½"	25.00–27.50
	Sailboat	Blue	4½"	12.00–15.00
		Blue	3½"	10.00–12.00
		Red,Green	4½"	12.00–15.00
		Green, Lt. Green	3½"	10.00–15.00
	Tulip No.1	Blue, Red	4½"	12.50–15.00
		Blue, Red	3½"	3.00–4.00
4th Row	Tulip No.1	Green	4½"	12.50–15.00
		Green, Black	3½"	3.00–4.00
		Green w/Label	3½"	10.00–12.00
	*Tulip No.2	Red, Green, Black	3½"	22.50–27.50
	Carnival	Blue, Red	3½"	4.00–6.00
		Green, Yellow	3½"	4.00–6.00
	Tulip No. 3	Dk. Blue, Lt. Blue	3¾"	2.50–3.50

*West Coast lower price

210

SWIRL, "PETAL SWIRL" JEANNETTE GLASS COMPANY, 1937–1938

Colors: Ultramarine, pink, Delphite; some amber and "ice" blue.

The only new piece of Swirl to report is a small amethyst berry bowl. Five of these were found; so keep an eye out for the larger one, and I'll try to show you the small bowl next time. There have been no reports of Ultramarine Swirl 10½" rimmed flat soups other than the one found in the Pittsburgh area!

Swirl, along with other Ultramarine Jeannette patterns have some green-tinged pieces as well as the normally found color. This green tint is hard to match, and some collectors avoid this shade. Because of this, there are many times you can buy this green tint at a bargain price if you are willing to accumulate that shade. Who knows? In the future this color might be considered rare. The smaller tumbler in the picture below has this greener hue.

A few footed Ultramarine Swirl pitchers are in collections, but so far there has not been a pink one discovered. I say, so far, because some collectors of Swirl combine this pattern with Jeannette's "Jennyware" kitchenware line that does have a **flat**, 36 oz. pink pitcher in it! Others have confused the two patterns because they are similar in style and found in the same colors. If you find mixing bowls, measuring cups, or reamers, then you have crossed over into the kitchenware line and out of the Swirl dinnerware set. See *Kitchen Glassware of the Depression Years* for complete "Jennyware" listings.

Candy and butter dish bottoms are more abundant than are tops in Swirl. Remember that before you buy only the bottom! That fact holds true for ninety per cent of the butter and candy dishes in Depression Glass. Unless you are good at remembering color, buying an Ultramarine top or bottom separately can create a problem in matching hues. If you go to a Depression Glass show, it might be sensible to take your half with you to match the color.

Pink candle holders are not rare even though they were omitted from the price list last edition. Sometimes an error does creep into this book; hopefully, only a few! The pink coaster shown in the right foreground on page 212 is often found inside a small rubber tire. These tires were advertisements distributed by tire manufactures or neighborhood garages and have themselves become collectible. Those with a tire manufacturer's name on the glass insert are more in demand; but those with a nonadvertising glass insert (such as this coaster) are collected if the miniature tire is embossed with the name of a tire company.

Swirl was produced in several limited colors. A smaller set can be assembled in Delphite blue; it would only have basic pieces and a serving dish or two. Vegetable bowls (9") were made in several experimental colors. Notice the amber and "ice" blue shown on page 212. I have seen the ice blue vegetable **priced** at $100.00 and an amber one at $75.00. Did they sell?

Almost all pieces of Swirl can be found with two different borders, ruffled and plain. Pink comes mostly with plain borders while Ultramarine comes with both. This makes a difference if you mail order merchandise. It is **your** responsibility to specify what style you want if you place an order. Either style is acceptable to most collectors, but some do not mix shapes in their collections. If you only want plain edged pieces, please tell the dealer before he ships your order. This is not a problem when you can see the merchandise displayed at shows.

Please refer to Foreword for pricing information

SWIRL, "PETAL SWIRL" (Cont.)

	Pink	Ultra-marine	Delphite
Bowl, 5¼" cereal	10.00	14.50	13.00
Bowl, 9" salad	17.50	25.00	28.00
Bowl, 9" salad, rimmed	18.00	27.50	
Bowl, 10" ftd., closed handles	24.00	28.00	
Bowl, 10½" ftd. console	19.00	26.00	
Butter dish	180.00	250.00	
Butter dish bottom	32.50	40.00	
Butter dish top	147.50	210.00	
Candle holders, double branch pr.	40.00	45.00	
Candle holders, single branch pr.			115.00
Candy dish, open, 3 legs	11.00	17.50	
Candy dish with cover	100.00	150.00	
Coaster, 1" x 3¼"	9.50	13.00	
Creamer, ftd.	7.50	15.00	12.00
Cup	7.00	15.00	10.00
Pitcher, 48 oz. ftd.		1,650.00	

	Pink	Ultra-marine	Delphite
Plate, 6½" sherbet	4.50	6.50	6.00
Plate, 7¼"	6.50	12.00	
Plate, 8" salad	8.50	13.00	9.00
Plate, 9¼" dinner	12.50	18.00	12.00
Plate, 10½"		30.00	18.00
Plate, 12½" sandwich	12.00	27.00	
Platter, 12" oval			35.00
Salt and pepper, pr.		42.00	
Saucer	3.50	5.00	5.00
Sherbet, low ftd.	11.00	20.00	
Soup, tab handles (lug)	24.00	32.00	
Sugar, ftd.	10.00	15.00	12.00
Tray, 10½", two-handled			25.00
Tumbler, 4", 9 oz.	16.00	32.00	
Tumbler, 4⅝", 9 oz.	16.00		
Tumbler, 5⅛", 13 oz.	45.00	100.00	
Tumbler, 9 oz. ftd.	18.00	37.50	
Vase, 6½" ftd., ruffled	16.00		
Vase, 8½" ftd., two styles		26.00	

TEA ROOM INDIANA GLASS COMPANY, 1926–1931

Colors: Pink, green, amber, and some crystal.

Tea Room prices are not skyrocketing as they once did. This has occurred for several reasons, the main being lack of new quantities being offered for sale. New collectors are not buying Tea Room because they are not seeing any to buy. Rarely found pieces are not being offered at any price; so collectors with sets awaiting additions are not increasing their holdings either. Prices do not increase when sales are not being recorded.

Another major dilemma in collecting Tea Room when it is found is obtaining mint condition pieces. The underneath sides of flat pieces are prone to chip and flake on all the exposed points. There are numerous points on Tea Room items that need to be looked at when you buy a piece. I once saw an original box of Tea Room that had 32 each of cups, saucers, and luncheon plates. There were less than a dozen mint condition (as we define it today) pieces out of the 96 in the box. These had never been used; so, there must have been a mould problem with this pattern originally. Indiana had more than their share of mould problems!

There are more green Tea Room collectors than pink; and some people are even beginning to pursue crystal. Crystal pieces are fetching about seventy-five percent of the pink prices except for the commonly found 9½" ruffled vase and the rarely found pitcher, priced separately below.

There are two styles of banana splits. Look at the picture of pink on page 214. The flat banana split is in front and the footed banana split is behind it. Both styles of banana splits are very desirable pieces of Tea Room to own in any color! The green, flat one is the hardest to find.

The flat sugar and marmalade bottom are the same. The marmalade takes a notched lid; the sugar lid is not notched. Finding either of these is not an easy task! The mustard also comes with a plain or notched lid. As the name implies, Tea Room was intended to be used in the tea rooms and ice cream parlors of the day. That is why you find so many soda fountain type items in this pattern.

The pink bowl to the right of the mustard is a finger bowl. For such a utilitarian pattern, I find finger bowls an extraordinary piece. Maybe this pattern was used in some fancy soda fountains or tea rooms of the rich and famous.

Amber pitchers and tumblers always seem to turn up in the Atlanta metro area. Maybe they really were Coca-Cola premiums as one lady from Marietta, Georgia, once told me. Creamers and sugars appear occasionally in amber. After that, amber has not been seen in any other item. Some interesting lamps are showing up which used tumblers that had been frosted. The regular lamp (shown here in pink) is not as plentiful as it once was. It has been a while since I have seen one in green. Notice that unlike most pieces, the price on lamps have increased dramatically!

Prices are for mint items. These prices are high because mint condition items are difficult to obtain! Damaged pieces are often bought to supplement sets until mint items can be found. Not everyone can afford to buy only mint items, and they are more willing to accept Tea Room pieces with some minor flaws than to have no Tea Room at all.

Please refer to Foreword for pricing information

TEA ROOM INDIANA GLASS COMPANY, 1926–1931 (Cont.)

	Green	Pink		Green	Pink
Bowl, finger	50.00	39.00	Salt and pepper, pr.	55.00	50.00
Bowl, 7½" banana split, flat	85.00	80.00	* Saucer	28.00	28.00
Bowl, 7½" banana split, ftd.	70.00	62.50	Sherbet, low ftd.	23.00	20.00
Bowl, 8¼" celery	32.00	26.00	Sherbet, low flared edge	30.00	26.00
Bowl, 8¾" deep salad	80.00	67.50	Sherbet, tall ftd.	45.00	45.00
Bowl, 9½" oval vegetable	62.50	57.50	Sugar w/lid, 3"	100.00	95.00
Candlestick, low, pr.	48.00	43.00	Sugar, 4½" ftd. (amber $75.00)	17.00	16.00
Creamer, 3¼"	26.00	26.00	Sugar, rectangular	20.00	18.00
Creamer, 4½" ftd. (amber $75.00)	18.00	17.00	Sugar, flat with cover	195.00	160.00
Creamer, rectangular	19.00	17.00	Sundae, ftd., ruffled top	90.00	70.00
Creamer & sugar on tray, 4"	75.00	70.00	Tray, center-handled	195.00	155.00
* Cup	50.00	50.00	Tray, rectangular sugar & creamer	50.00	40.00
Goblet, 9 oz.	70.00	60.00	Tumbler, 8 oz., 4³⁄₁₆" flat	95.00	85.00
Ice bucket	57.50	50.00	Tumbler, 6 oz. ftd.	35.00	35.00
Lamp, 9" electric	85.00	75.00	Tumbler, 8 oz., 5¼" high, ftd.		
Marmalade, notched lid	195.00	160.00	(amber $75.00)	30.00	28.00
Mustard, covered	150.00	125.00	Tumbler, 11 oz. ftd.	45.00	40.00
Parfait	70.00	65.00	Tumbler, 12 oz. ftd.	60.00	55.00
** Pitcher, 64 oz. (amber $425.00)	140.00	125.00	Vase, 6½" ruffled edge	100.00	90.00
Plate, 6½" sherbet	32.00	30.00	***Vase, 9½" ruffled edge	100.00	100.00
Plate, 8¼", luncheon	35.00	30.00	Vase, 9½" straight	75.00	65.00
Plate, 10½", 2-handled	48.00	43.00	Vase, 11" ruffled edge	175.00	190.00
Relish, divided	25.00	20.00	Vase, 11" straight	100.00	90.00

  * Prices for absolutely mint pieces
 ** Crystal – $400.00
***Crystal – $16.00

THISTLE MacBETH-EVANS, 1929–1930

Colors: Pink, green; some yellow and crystal.

Thistle and Fire-King blue are the favorite patterns of every photographer that I have worked with in the last twenty-five years. One time we even used a blue bulb under the Plexiglas to enhance the Fire-King color. One photographer would see us unpacking either of these patterns and automatically inquire if we **really want a pattern to show** this time! Photography lights cause Thistle to do a vanishing act. That act is familiar to Thistle collectors. This pattern has been known to hide very well. Our new photographer seems to have captured Thistle on my transparencies; hopefully, the printer will too!

Green Thistle is more scarce than pink except for the large fruit bowl that is almost nonexistent in pink. I have owned the one shown here for twenty-two years, and I have only seen two others.

All Thistle pieces have the same mould shapes as the thin Dogwood; however, there is no Thistle creamer or sugar yet. The grill plate has the pattern on the edge only.

If you see thick butter dishes, pitchers, tumblers, and other heavy moulded pieces with Thistle designs, they are new! These pieces are being made by Mosser Glass Company in Cambridge, Ohio. They are not a part of this pattern, but copies of a much older pattern glass. If you have a piece of Thistle not in the photograph, then you probably do not have a piece of MacBeth-Evans Thistle pattern since all seven pieces known to have been made are shown.

	Pink	Green
Bowl, 5½" cereal	20.00	22.00
Bowl, 10¼" large fruit	295.00	185.00
Cup, thin	19.00	24.00
Plate, 8" luncheon	14.00	18.00
Plate, 10¼" grill	17.50	22.00
Plate, 13" heavy cake	115.00	145.00
Saucer	9.50	9.50

Please refer to Foreword for pricing information

TULIP DELL GLASS COMPANY, early 1930's

Color: Amber, amethyst, blue, crystal, green.

There are several new pieces to list in Tulip. Candle holders made from the 3¾" sherbet have turned up in several colors. These look like the sherbet, but have a candle cup in the middle. Another entertaining piece is a decanter that has a whiskey tumbler for a stopper. I have not been able to find one of these to buy, but candle holders are in the mail as I write. A juice tumbler has also been reported; keep an eye out for these.

I originally started buying Tulip about five years ago, when I found nine green sugar bowls for $10.00. I couldn't turn them down at that price, but it sure took a while to sell them since they were virtually unknown to most collectors.

Blue is the color that more collectors are asking for, but I have not been able to keep any color in stock. Basic pieces are available with searching, but there is a problem in finding other pieces in this pattern as you can see by my photographs on page 216 and 217.

I am not seeing amber in my travels. In the last four years of buying Tulip, I have found that the scalloped rims tend to have damage. Most of the damage occurs under the rim edge; be sure to turn the piece over and check each of the pointed scallops. Many times a scallop or two will be absent!

Many dealers selling this pattern do not know what it is, but because it is blue or amethyst, the price is usually less than reasonable. That price often doesn't reflect the damages on the pieces either. Points can be missing on plates and the price is still firm!

The little whiskey (shown in amethyst), the ice tub, and oval bowl are all scarce. You may find pieces of Tulip that I do not have listed; please keep me informed!

I have priced the crystal with the amber and green since you will not see much of it.

	Amethyst, Blue	Amber, Crystal, Green
Bowl, 6"	12.50	10.00
Bowl, oval, oblong, 13¼"	50.00	40.00
Candleholder, 3¾" (black sherbet)	25.00	20.00
Candy w/lid	40.00	30.00
Creamer	14.00	12.00
Cup	12.00	10.00
Decanter w/stopper	50.00	40.00
Ice tub, 4⅞" wide, 3" deep	30.00	20.00
Plate, 6"	5.00	4.00
Plate, 7¼"	7.50	6.00
Plate, 9"	17.00	14.00
Saucer	2.50	2.00
Sherbet, 3¾", flat	10.00	8.00
Sugar	14.00	12.00
Tumbler, juice	15.00	12.00
Tumbler, whiskey	20.00	16.00

TWISTED OPTIC IMPERIAL GLASS COMPANY, 1927–1930

Colors: Pink, green, amber; some blue and Canary.

All the pieces shown below belong to Twisted Optic. You can see an additional green piece of Twisted Optic under Spiral (page 205) placed there to help in differentiating these two confusing patterns. If you find a Spiral piece in some color besides pink or green, then it is most likely Twisted Optic since colored Spiral is only found in pink or green. You should understand that many glass companies made spiraling patterns besides Hocking and Imperial! There were many smaller glass factories that never issued catalogues and others that were in business for so short a duration that records were never kept or have long since disappeared.

Twisted Optic's spirals to the right and Spiral's go to the left!

On page 219 are two photographs of Canary. This color is often mislabeled Vaseline, but it is Imperial's Canary color. I was able to buy these pieces from a dealer who was selling a set. Thankfully, he had the pieces priced individually; so, I was able to obtain enough pieces to illustrate this color and pattern well. Powder jars and cologne bottles are in great demand due to so many collectors seeking only those items in every pattern that had dresser sets!

	Blue, Canary Yellow	*All Other Colors		Blue, Canary Yellow	*All Other Colors
Basket, 10", tall	75.00	40.00	Pitcher, 64 oz.		30.00
Bowl, 4¾" cream soup	16.00	11.00	Plate, 6" sherbet	4.00	2.00
Bowl, 5" cereal	10.00	5.50	Plate, 7" salad	6.00	3.00
Bowl, 7" salad	15.00	10.00	Plate, 7½" x 9" oval with indent	9.00	5.00
Bowl, 9"	25.00	15.00	Plate, 8" luncheon	8.00	3.50
Bowl, 10½", console	35.00	20.00	Plate, 10", sandwich	15.00	9.00
Bowl, 11½", 4¼" tall	45.00	22.50	Powder jar w/lid	65.00	35.00
Candlesticks, 3" pr. (2 styles)	40.00	20.00	Preserve (same as candy with slotted lid)		27.50
Candlesticks, 8", pr.	50.00	27.50	Sandwich server, open center handle	35.00	20.00
Candy jar w/cover, flat	50.00	25.00	Sandwich server, two-handled	18.00	12.00
Candy jar w/cover, flat, flange edge	55.00	30.00	Saucer	4.00	2.00
Candy jar w/cover, ftd., flange edge	55.00	30.00	Sherbet	10.00	6.00
Candy jar w/cover, ftd., short, fat	65.00	35.00	Sugar	12.50	6.50
Candy jar w/cover, ftd., tall	65.00	35.00	Tumbler, 4½", 9 oz.		6.00
Cologne bottle w/stopper	65.00	40.00	Tumbler, 5¼", 12 oz.		8.00
Creamer	12.50	7.50	Vase, 7¼", 2 handle, rolled edge	50.00	20.00
Cup	10.00	4.00	Vase, 8", 2 handle, fan	65.00	30.00
Mayonnaise	35.00	20.00	Vase, 8", 2 handle, straight edge	65.00	25.00

*Blue, Canary Yellow 50% more

U.S. SWIRL U.S. GLASS COMPANY, Late 1920's

Colors: Pink, green, iridescent, and crystal.

I have only been able to find one pink shaker in U.S. Swirl. Every other piece I run into seems to be green. Maybe the pink is as hard to find as iridescent. I see a few crystal sherbets along with the ever-present green; happily, green is the color that most collectors want.

Several iridescent butter dishes have been discovered, but that is the only piece being found regularly in that color. The tumbler listing 3⅝" corresponds with the only known size of Aunt Polly and Cherryberry/Strawberry tumblers, but the 12 oz. tumbler has only been found in this one U.S. Glass Company pattern. The footed piece in the back is a vase, although it has been incorrectly called a tumbler at times.

U.S. Swirl has the plain butter bottom that is interchangeable with all the other patterns made by U.S. Glass. The butter dish in this pattern is the one that many Strawberry collectors have purchased over the years to borrow the bottom for their Strawberry tops. This plundering has stressed butters in this pattern, particularly in pink.

I haven't found a green creamer. If you have an extra one, let me hear from you! In writing this copy I noticed an extra piece that was not in previous editions. Can you spot it? The 1¾" deep, 8⅜" oval bowl in front of the 2¾" deep, oval bowl is now listed.

	Green	Pink		Green	Pink
Bowl, 4⅜", berry	5.50	6.50	Pitcher, 8", 48 oz.	50.00	50.00
Bowl, 5½", 1 handle	9.50	10.50	Plate, 6⅛", sherbet	2.50	2.50
Bowl, 7⅞, large berry	15.00	16.00	Plate, 7⅞", salad	5.50	6.50
Bowl, 8¼", oval (2¾" deep)	40.00	40.00	Salt and pepper, pr.	45.00	45.00
Bowl, 8⅜", oval (1¾" deep)	50.00	50.00	Sherbet, 3¼"	4.50	5.00
Butter and cover	110.00	110.00	Sugar w/lid	32.00	32.00
Butter bottom	90.00	90.00	Tumbler, 3⅝", 8 oz.	10.00	10.00
Butter top	20.00	20.00	Tumbler, 4¾", 12 oz.	14.00	15.00
Candy w/cover, 2-handled	27.50	32.00	Vase, 6½"	18.00	20.00
Creamer	14.00	16.00			

"VICTORY" DIAMOND GLASS-WARE COMPANY, 1929–1932

Colors: Amber, pink, green; some cobalt blue and black.

Prices for "Victory" can be found on the next page. I squeezed in an additional page of Tulip pattern and got my format a little out of kilter. I have taken a few liberties with my format in order to maximize the space and still hold the size increase to sixteen pages. The price of paper has more than doubled in the last year; I want to make sure you get your money's worth before the price of the book has to increase.

Cobalt blue "Victory" is mostly found in the Northeast. It has been a while since I have shown that color in this book. The last time I had a set for sale, many of the pieces sold to collectors of cobalt blue rather than "Victory" collectors. Many rather politely asked what the pattern was, but I had the feeling that they really did not care what it was called — only that it was an attractive blue color!

That collecting concept applies to black "Victory," but not to the same extent that it does with cobalt blue. Collectors of black glass are more plentiful than collectors of black "Victory." Flat black pieces of "Victory" have to be turned over to see the pattern; and unless you have a strong light, the same is true for some cobalt blue pieces. The sherbet plate in the picture is an example. We turned it over so you can tell it is "Victory" and not a plain cobalt blue plate.

Sets of "Victory" can be completed in pink and green with much searching. Amber, cobalt blue, and black will take more hunting and some good fortune!

The "Victory" gravy boat and platter are the most desirable pieces to own in any color. I have only seen one amber set. A green gravy and platter can be seen on the bottom of page 222.

Goblets, cereal and soup bowls, candlesticks, as well as oval vegetable bowls will keep you looking long and hard in all colors of "Victory."

There are several styles of decorations besides the 22K gold trimmed pieces pictured on page 222. There are floral decorations and even a black decorated design that is very art deco looking. I have only seen this art deco design on pink and green. I have observed more floral decorated console sets (bowl and candlesticks) than anything. I assume that complete sets of gold decorated pink and green can be found. The black pieces decorated with gold may only be found in luncheon and console sets.

"VICTORY" DIAMOND GLASS-WARE COMPANY, 1929–1932 (Cont.)

	Amber, Pink, Green	Black, Blue
Bon bon, 7"	11.00	20.00
Bowl, 6½" cereal	11.00	27.00
Bowl, 8½" flat soup	20.00	45.00
Bowl, 9" oval vegetable	32.00	85.00
Bowl, 11" rolled edge	28.00	50.00
Bowl, 12" console	33.00	65.00
Bowl, 12½" flat edge	30.00	65.00
Candlesticks, 3" pr.	30.00	95.00
Cheese & cracker set, 12" indented plate & compote	40.00	
Comport, 6" tall, 6¾" diameter	15.00	
Creamer	15.00	45.00
Cup	9.00	33.00
Goblet, 5", 7 oz.	19.00	
Gravy boat and platter	175.00	325.00
Mayonnaise set: 3½" tall, 5½" across, 8½" indented plate, w/ladle	42.00	100.00
Plate, 6" bread and butter	6.00	16.00
Plate, 7" salad	7.00	20.00
Plate, 8" luncheon	7.00	30.00
Plate, 9" dinner	19.00	40.00
Platter, 12"	28.00	70.00
Sandwich server, center handle	29.00	70.00
Saucer	4.00	12.00
Sherbet, ftd.	13.00	26.00
Sugar	15.00	45.00

VITROCK, "FLOWER RIM" HOCKING GLASS COMPANY, 1934–1937

Colors: White and white w/fired-on colors, usually red or green.

Vitrock was Hocking's venture into the milk glass market. Platters and cream soups are pieces that are nearly impossible to find. Notice the Lake Como flat soup in the center. Lake Como was a decorated Vitrock pattern. Vitrock was not a pattern per se, but a mid-1930's white color of Hocking's. There are many different patterns found in this very durable line, but collectors have adopted the decorated Lake Como and the "Flower Rim" dinnerware sets as patterns to collect. If you find flat soups without the Lake Como design, you can enter them into this Vitrock line.

At the time, Vitrock vied with Hazel Atlas's Platonite; and by all the evidence found today, Platonite won the battle.

Vitrock is better known for its kitchenware line of reamers, measuring cups, and mixing bowls manufactured in this white color. Notice that the Vitrock Kitchenware items are also shown in this display of "The NEW Material" on page 224. I now understand why those large Vitrock mixing bowls are so hard to find. They sold for a quarter when a working man's wages were in the range of a $1.00 a day!

You can see more Vitrock in my book *Kitchen Glassware of the Depression Years*. Some collectors are gathering patterns that can cross-over into other fields. This is a very good example of a pattern that fits into both collecting areas. Hazel Atlas did the same with their Platonite. It made good business sense to sell accessory items that matched your everyday dishes.

I didn't receive as many letters on the Kresge's store window display of Vitrock as I did on the Old Colony. Then again, there are not as many collectors of Vitrock either! This mid-1930's store display photograph was found in Anchor Hocking's files. Note the emphasis that Vitrock "Will not craze or check" on the display sign. Crazing was a major flaw for many pottery wares of the time.

	White		White
Bowl, 4" berry	4.50	Cup	3.50
Bowl, 5½" cream soup	15.00	Plate, 7¼" salad	2.50
Bowl, 6" fruit	5.50	Plate, 8¾" luncheon	4.50
Bowl, 7½" cereal	6.00	Plate, 9" soup	13.00
Bowl, 9½" vegetable	14.00	Plate, 10" dinner	8.50
Bowl, flat soup	50.00	Platter, 11½"	27.50
Creamer, oval	4.50	Saucer	2.50
		Sugar	4.50

VITROCK

WATERFORD, "WAFFLE" HOCKING GLASS COMPANY, 1938–1944

Colors: Crystal, pink; some yellow, white; forest green 1950's.

Presently, there are more collectors buying crystal Waterford than pink. The quantity of pink is nearly depleted unless you find someone willing to sell you a set that was accumulated previously. The price of hard-to-find pink Waterford pieces is not a worry with collectors. Most would like to **see** some cereal bowls, a pitcher, or a butter dish sitting on a table or shelf for sale! Of these three pieces, the cereal is the most elusive. It has always been troublesome to find, and worse, difficult to find **mint!**

A crystal Waterford collection can be finished; but there are pieces less available than you can believe for this once bountiful pattern. Cereal bowls, pitchers, and even water goblets are vanishing.

Be sure to check the inside rims for roughness. A little roughness is normal; don't let that keep you from owning a hard-to-find piece. Because of the scalloped rim design, Waterford has been known to chip or flake.

There is a look-alike footed cup that is sometimes sold as a Waterford punch cup. This cup, and the larger lamps that are often displayed as Waterford, are only similar to Waterford. Waterford has a flattened (not rounded) "diamond" shape on each section of the design. There is also a large, pink pitcher with an indented, **circular design in each diamond** that is **not** Waterford. This pitcher was made by Hocking, but has more of a "bullseye" look. These only sell for $30.00; do not pay Waterford prices for one!

A few pieces of white Waterford and some Dusty Rose and Springtime Green ash trays turn up occasionally; these sell at crystal prices. Examples of rose and green colors can be seen in Oyster and Pearl on page 165. Forest green 13¾" plates in Waterford were made in the 1950's promotion; these are usually found in the $12.50 range. Some crystal has also been found trimmed in red. Unfortunately, you can not remove it to match the plain crystal. There is not enough of the red trim to collect a set unless you should happen upon a complete set at once.

Advertising ash trays, such as the "Post Cereals" shown below, are now selling for $15.00 to $20.00 depending upon the desirability of the advertising on the piece! An advertisement for Anchor Hocking itself will obtain $35.00.

The items listed below with Miss America style in parentheses are Waterford patterned pieces that have the same **mould shapes** as Miss America. You can see some of these in the seventh edition of this book or in the first *Very Rare Glassware of the Depression Years.* It seems likely that the first designs for Waterford were patterned on the shapes of Miss America that had been discontinued the year before Waterford was introduced. It is unlikely that a full set could be found, but one never knows!

Those yellow and amber goblets shown below are compliments of Anchor Hocking's photographer from items stored in their morgue. I haven't seen yellow ones for sale, but amber ones are hard to sell for $15.00.

	Crystal	Pink		Crystal	Pink
* Ash tray, 4"	7.50		Plate, 7⅛" salad	6.00	8.00
Bowl, 4¾" berry	6.50	15.00	Plate, 9⅝" dinner	11.00	20.00
Bowl, 5½" cereal	17.00	30.00	Plate, 10¼" handled cake	10.00	16.00
Bowl, 8¼" large berry	10.00	20.00	Plate, 13¾" sandwich	10.00	25.00
Butter dish and cover	25.00	220.00	Relish, 13¾", 5-part	16.00	
Butter dish bottom	6.00	30.00	Salt and pepper, 2 types	8.50	
Butter dish top	19.00	190.00	Saucer	3.00	6.00
Coaster, 4"	3.50		Sherbet, ftd.	4.00	11.00
Creamer, oval	5.00	10.00	Sherbet, ftd., scalloped base	4.00	
Creamer (Miss America style)	35.00		Sugar	5.00	10.00
Cup	6.50	14.00	Sugar cover, oval	5.00	24.00
Cup (Miss America style)		40.00	Sugar (Miss America style)	35.00	
Goblets, 5¼", 5⅝"	16.00		Tumbler, 3½", 5 oz. juice (Miss America style)		65.00
Goblet, 5½" (Miss America style)	35.00	90.00	Tumbler, 4⅞", 10 oz. ftd.	12.00	20.00
Lamp, 4" spherical base	26.00				
Pitcher, 42 oz. tilted juice	24.00				
Pitcher, 80 oz. tilted ice lip	32.00	145.00			
Plate, 6" sherbet	3.00	6.00			

* With ads $15.00

225

WINDSOR, "WINDSOR DIAMOND" JEANNETTE GLASS COMPANY, 1936–1946

Colors: Pink, green, crystal; some Delphite, amberina red, and ice blue.

Many crystal Windsor items turn up in unusual shapes that are not found in pink or green. There are numerous collectors of colored Windsor, but few presently collect crystal. Color was discontinued about 1940, but crystal pieces were made as late as 1946. A restyled Windsor butter and sugar were later transferred to Holiday when that pattern was introduced in 1947. I have placed the butter dish and the other style butter lid on the right in the photo below. There are two styles of sugars and lids. In that photograph, the crystal sugar bowl (shaped like Holiday) has no lip for the lid to rest against; at the top of page 229, the pink sugar represents the style with lip. The pink sugar and lid without the lip are hard to find.

Notice the flashed red edged cup at the bottom of this page. I had not seen this treatment of Windsor previously. Maybe someone decided to try a promotional set to compete with King's Crown.

Relish trays can be found with or without tab (closed) handles. Trays without handles appear in crystal. Pink trays without handles are much in demand! Two styles of sandwich plates were made. The normally found one is 10¼" and has open handles. The newly discovered tray is 10" and has closed handles.

Green Windsor tumblers are evasive. Even the water tumbler (which is commonly found in pink) is scarce. As with many patterns, there is an unusual amount of mould roughness on seams of tumblers; and Windsor tumblers have an inclination to chip on the sides. The diamond pattern protrudes outward, making the sides an easy target of abuse. Check these seams carefully before you buy! There are color variances in green; be aware of that if you see a piece that looks darker than you are used to seeing! It might just be!

The pink 13⅝" plate is often found as a beverage set with a pitcher and six water tumblers. That may have been a premium item since so many pitchers and water tumblers are available today. Green pitcher and tumbler sets do not suffer this copiousness.

The 10½" pointed edge bowl is hard to find in pink. This bowl in crystal, along with the comport, make up a punch bowl and stand. The upended comport fits inside the base of the bowl to keep it from sliding. In recent years, there have been newly made comports in crystal and sprayed-on, multicolored ones that have a beaded edge. That recently made crystal comport will not work as a punch stand because of the beaded edge. This beaded edge comport was made in the late 1950's in Jeannette's Shell Pink, one of the patterns shown in *Collectible Glassware from the 40's, 50's, 60's….*

A new style pink ash tray and a tab handled berry bowl can be seen in the *Very Rare Glassware of the Depression Years, Second Series*. While looking there, check out the blue Windsor butter dish!

I hope you enjoy the additional photographs of Windsor! This pattern always brings a sigh of relief when it comes up on my computer screen since the light begins to shine at the end of the writing tunnel!

WINDSOR, "WINDSOR DIAMOND" JEANNETTE GLASS COMPANY, 1936–1946 (Cont.)

	Crystal	Pink	Green		Crystal	Pink	Green
* Ash tray, 5¾"	13.50	36.00	45.00	** Plate, 9" dinner	5.00	24.00	23.00
Bowl, 4¾" berry	4.00	9.00	11.00	Plate, 10", sandwich, closed handle		22.00	
Bowl, 5" pointed edge	5.00	18.00		Plate, 10¼", sandwich open handle	6.00	16.00	16.00
Bowl, 5" cream soup	6.00	20.00	25.00	Plate, 13⅝" chop	9.50	45.00	45.00
Bowls, 5⅛, 5⅜" cereal	8.50	20.00	22.00	Platter, 11½" oval	6.00	20.00	22.00
Bowl, 7⅛", three legs	7.50	25.00		**** Powder jar	15.00	55.00	
Bowl, 8" pointed edge	9.00	45.00		Relish platter, 11½" divided	10.00	200.00	
Bowl, 8", 2-handled	7.00	16.00	22.00	Salt and pepper, pr.	16.00	36.00	48.00
Bowl, 8½" large berry	6.50	17.00	18.00	Saucer (ice blue $15.00)	2.50	5.00	6.00
Bowl, 9½" oval vegetable	7.00	20.00	25.00	Sherbet, ftd.	3.50	11.00	14.00
Bowl, 10½" salad	12.00			Sugar & cover	8.00	25.00	30.00
Bowl, 10½" pointed edge	25.00	120.00		Sugar & cover (like "Holiday")	12.00	110.00	
Bowl, 12½" fruit console	24.00	100.00		Tray, 4", square, w/handles	5.00	10.00	12.00
Bowl, 7" x 11¾" boat shape	18.00	32.00	35.00	Tray, 4", square, wo/handles	6.00	40.00	
Butter dish (two styles)	26.00	50.00	85.00	Tray, 4⅛" x 9", w/handles	4.00	10.00	16.00
Cake plate, 10¾" ftd.	8.50	20.00	21.00	Tray, 4⅛" x 9", wo/handles	9.00	50.00	
Candlesticks, 3" Pr.	20.00	80.00		Tray, 8½" x 9¾", w/handles	6.50	24.00	35.00
Candy jar and cover	16.00			Tray, 8½" x 9¾", wo/handles	13.00	85.00	45.00
Coaster, 3¼"	3.50	14.00	18.00	** Tumbler, 3¼", 5 oz.	8.00	24.00	32.00
Comport	8.50			** Tumbler, 4", 9 oz. (red 55.00)	6.00	20.00	30.00
** Creamer	4.50	11.00	12.00	Tumbler, 5", 12 oz.	8.00	28.00	50.00
Creamer (shaped as "Holiday")	7.50			Tumbler, 4⅝", 11 oz.	7.50		
** Cup	3.50	9.50	11.00	Tumbler, 4" ftd.	7.00		
Pitcher, 4½", 16 oz.	20.00	110.00		Tumbler, 5" ftd., 11 oz.	10.00		
*** Pitcher, 6¾", 52 oz.	13.00	28.00	55.00	Tumbler, 7¼" ftd.	15.00		
Plate, 6" sherbet	2.50	5.00	8.00				
Plate, 7" salad	4.50	16.00	20.00				

* Delphite – $45.00   ** Blue – $65.00   *** Red – $450.00   **** Yellow – $175.00; Blue – $185.00

Please refer to Foreword for pricing information

REPRODUCTIONS

NEW "ADAM" PRIVATELY PRODUCED OUT OF KOREA THROUGH ST. LOUIS IMPORTING COMPANY
ONLY THE ADAM BUTTER DISH HAS BEEN REPRODUCED!

The recent Adam butter is finally off the market as far as I can determine. Identification of the reproduction is easy.
Top: Notice the veins in the leaves.
New: Large leaf veins do not join or touch in center of leaf.
Old: Large leaf veins all touch or join the center vein.
A further note in the original Adam butter dish: the veins of all the leaves at the center of the design are very clear cut and precisely moulded; in the new, these center leaf veins are very indistinct — and almost invisible in one leaf of the center design.
Bottom: Place butter dish bottom upside down for observation. Square it to your body.
New: Four (4) Arrowhead-like points line up in northwest, northeast, southeast, and southwest directions of compass. There are very bad mould lines and a very glossy light pink color on the butter dishes I have examined; but these have been improved.
Old: Four (4) Arrowhead-like points line up in north, east, south, and west directions of compass.

NEW "AVOCADO" INDIANA GLASS COMPANY Tiara Exclusives Line, 1974

Colors: Pink, frosted pink, yellow, blue, red, amethyst, and green.

In 1979 a green Avocado pitcher was produced. It was darker than the original green and was a limited hostess gift item. Yellow pieces that are beginning to show up are all recently made! Yellow was never made originally!
The original pink Indiana made was a delicate, attractive pink. The new tends to be more orange than the original color. The other colors shown pose little threat since none of these colors were made originally.
I understand that Tiara sales counselors told potential customers that their newly made glass was collectible because it was made from old moulds. I don't share this view. I feel it's like saying that since you were married in your grandmother's wedding dress, you will have the same happy marriage for the fifty-seven years she did. All you can truly say is that you were married in her dress. I think all you can say about the new Avocado is that it was made from the old moulds. **Time, scarcity,** and **people's whims** determine collectability in so far as I'm able to determine it. It's taken nearly fifty years or more for people to turn to collecting Depression Glass — and that's done, in part, because **everyone** remembers it; they had some in their home at one time or another; it has universal appeal. Who is to say what will be collectible in the next fifty years. If we knew, we could all get rich!
If you like Tiara products, then of course buy them; but don't do so **depending** upon their being collectible just because they are made in the image of the old! You have an equal chance, I feel, of going to Las Vegas and **depending** upon getting rich at the blackjack table.

NEW "CAMEO"

Colors: Green, pink, cobalt blue (shakers); yellow, green, and pink (child's dishes).

I hope you can still see how very weak the pattern is on this reproduction shaker. It was made by Mosser Glass Company in Ohio originally, but is now being made overseas. Also, you can see how much glass remains in the bottom of the shaker; and, of course, the new tops all make this easy to spot at the market. These were to be bought wholesale at around $6.00 but did not sell well. A new **importer** is making shakers in pink, cobalt blue, and a terrible green color. These, too, are weakly patterned! They were never originally made in the blue, but **beware of PINK**!
Children's dishes in Cameo pose no problem to collectors since they were never made originally. These, also made by Mosser, are scale models of the larger size. This type of production I have no quarrel with since they are not made to dupe anyone. There are over forty of these smaller pieces; thus, if you have a piece of glass that looks like a smaller (child's) version of a larger piece of Cameo, then you probably have a newly manufactured item!

NEW "CHERRY BLOSSOM"

Colors: Pink, green, blue, Delphite, cobalt, red, and iridized colors.

Please use information provided only for the piece described. Do not apply information on tumbler for pitcher, etc. Realize that with so many different importers now involved, there are more variations than I can possibly analyze for you. Know your dealer and hope he knows what he is doing!

Due to all the different reproductions of the same pieces over and over, please realize this is only a guide as to what you should look for when buying! We've even enjoyed some reproductions of those reproductions! All the items pictured on the next page are extremely easy to spot as reproductions once you know what to look for with the possible exception of the 13" divided platter pictured at the back. It's too heavy, weighing 2¾ pounds, and has a thick, ⅜" of glass in the bottom; but the design isn't too bad! The edges of the leaves aren't smooth; but neither are they serrated like old leaves.

There are many differences between old and new scalloped bottom, AOP Cherry pitchers. The easiest way to tell the difference is to turn the pitcher over. The branch crossing the bottom of my old Cherry pitchers **looks** like a branch. It's knobby and gnarled and has several leaves and cherry stems directly attached to it. One variation of the new pitcher just has a bald strip of glass cutting the bottom of the pitcher in half. Further, the old Cherry pitchers have a plain glass background for the cherries and leaves in the bottom of the pitcher. In the new pitchers, there's a rough, filled in, straw-like background. You see **no plain glass**.

As for the new tumblers, the easiest way to tell old from new is to look at the ring dividing the patterned portion of the glass from the plain glass lip. The old tumblers have three indented rings dividing the pattern from the plain glass rim. The new has only one. Again, the pattern at the bottom of the new tumblers is brief and practically nonexistent in the center curve of the glass bottom. The pattern, what there is of one on the new tumblers, mostly hugs the center of the foot.

2 handled tray — old: 1⅞ lb.; ³⁄₁₆" glass in bottom; leaves and cherries east/west from north/south handles **(some older trays were rotated so this is not always true)**; leaves have real spine and serrated edges; cherry stems end in triangle of glass. new: 2⅛ lb.; ¼" glass in bottom; leaves and cherries north/south with the handles; canal type leaves (but uneven edges; cherry stem ends before canal shaped line).

cake plate — new: color too light pink, leaves have too many parallel veins that give them a "feathery" look; arches at plate edge don't line up with lines on inside of the rim to which the feet are attached.

8½" bowl — new: crude leaves with smooth edges; veins in parallel lines.

cereal bowl — new: wrong shape, looks like 8½" bowl, small 2" center. old: large center, 2½" inside ring, nearly 3½" if you count the outer rim before the sides turn up.

plate — new: center shown close up; smooth edged leaves, fish spine type center leaf portion; weighs 1 pound plus; feels thicker at edge with mould offset lines clearly visible. old: center leaves look like real leaves with spines, veins, and serrated edges; weighs ¾ pound; clean edges; no mould offset.

cup — new: area in bottom left free of design; canal centered leaves; smooth, thick top to cup handle (old has triangle grasp point).

saucer — new: offset mould line edge; canal leaf center.

The Cherry child's cup (with a slightly lopsided handle) having the cherries hanging upside down when the cup was held in the right hand appeared in 1973. After I reported this error, it was quickly corrected by re-inverting the inverted mould. These later cups were thus improved in design but slightly off color. The saucers tended to have slightly off center designs, too. Next came the "child's butter dish" that was never made by Jeannette. It was essentially the child's cup without a handle turned upside down over the saucer and having a little glob of glass added as a knob for lifting purposes.

Pictured are some of the colors of butter dishes made so far. Shakers were begun in 1977 and some were dated '77 on the bottom. Shortly afterward, the nondated variety appeared. How can you tell new shakers from old — should you get the one in a million chance to do so?

First, look at the tops. New tops could indicate new shakers. Next, notice the protruding edges beneath the tops. **In the new they are squared off juts rather than the nicely rounded scallops on the old** (which are pictured under Cherry Blossom pattern). The design on the newer shakers is often weak in spots. Finally, notice how far up inside the shakers the solid glass (next to the foot) remains. The newer shakers have almost twice as much glass in that area. They appear to be ¼ full of glass before you ever add the salt!

In 1989, a new distributor began making reproduction glass in the Far East. He's making shakers in cobalt blue, pink, and an ugly green, that is no problem to spot! These shakers are similar in quality to those made before, but the present pink color is good; yet the quality and design of each batch could vary greatly. Realize that **only two original pairs of pink Cherry shakers have been found** and those were discovered before any reproductions were made in 1977!

Butter dishes are naturally more deceptive in pink and green since those were the only original colors. The major flaw in the new butter is that there is **one band** encircling the bottom edge of the butter top; there are **two bands** very close together along the skirt of the old top.

REPRODUCTIONS (Continued)

NEW "MADRID" CALLED "RECOLLECTION" Currently being made.

I hope you have already read about Recollection Madrid on page 120. The recent rage of Indiana Glass is to make Madrid in teal after making it in **blue, pink, and crystal.** This teal is a very greenish color that was never made originally, so there is no problem of it being confused with old! The teal color is being sold through all kinds of outlets ranging from better department stores to discount catalogues. In the past couple of years we have received several ads stating that this is genuine Depression Glass made from old moulds. None of this is made from old glass moulds unless you consider 1976 old. Most of the pieces are from moulds that were never made originally.

The light blue was a big seller for Indiana according to reports I am receiving around the country. It is a brighter, more fluorescent blue than the soft, original color.

Look at the top picture on page 235! None of these items were ever made in the old pattern Madrid. The new grill plate has one division splitting the plate in half, but the old had three sections. A goblet or vase was never made. The vase is sold with a candle making it a hurricane lamp. The heavy tumbler was placed on top of a candlestick to make this vase/hurricane lamp. That candlestick gets a workout. It was attached to a plate to make a pedestal cake stand and to a butter dish to make a preserve stand. That's a clever idea, actually. You would not believe the mail generated by these two pieces!

The shakers are short and heavy and you can see both original styles pictured on page 121. The latest item I have seen is a heavy 11 oz. flat tumbler being sold in a set of four or six called "On the Rocks." The biggest giveaway to this newer pink glass is the pale, washed out color.

The only concerns in the new pink pieces are the cups, saucers, and oval vegetable bowl. These three pieces were made in pink in the 1930's. None of the others shown were ever made in the 1930's in pink; so realize that when you see the butter dish, dinner plate, soup bowl, or sugar and creamer. These are new items! Once you have learned what this washed-out pink looks like by seeing these items for sale, the color will be a clue when you see other pieces. My suggestion is to avoid pink Madrid except for the pitcher and tumblers.

The most difficult piece for new collectors to tell new from old is the candlestick. The new ones all have **raised ridges inside** to hold the candle more firmly. All old ones do not have these ridges. You may even find new candlesticks in black.

NEW "MAYFAIR"

Colors: Pink, green, blue, cobalt (shot glasses), 1977… Pink, green, amethyst, cobalt blue, red (cookie jars), 1982…
cobalt blue, pink, amethyst, red, and green (odd shade), shakers 1988, green, cobalt, pink, juice pitchers, 1993.

Only the pink shot glass need cause any concern to collectors because that glass wasn't made in any other color originally. At first glance, the color of the newer shots is often too light pink or too orange. Dead giveaway is the stems of the flower design, however. In the old that stem branched to form an **"A"** shape; in the new, you have a single stem. Further, in the new design, the leaf is hollow with the veins moulded in. In the old, the leaf is moulded in and the veining is left hollow. In the center of the flower on the old, dots (anther) cluster entirely to one side and are rather distinct. Nothing like that occurs in the new design.

As for the cookie jars, at cursory glance the base of the cookie has a very indistinct design. It will feel smooth to the touch it's so faint. In the old cookie jars, there's a distinct pattern that feels like raised embossing to the touch. Next, turn the bottom upside down. The new bottom is perfectly smooth. The old bottom contains a 1¾" **mould circle rim** that is raised enough to catch your fingernail in it. There are other distinctions as well; but that is the **quickest** and **easiest** way to tell old from new.

In the Mayfair cookie lid, the new design (parallel to the straight side of the lid) at the edge curves gracefully toward the center "V" shape (rather like bird wings in flight); in the old, that edge is a flat straight line going into the "V" (like airplane wings sticking straight out from the side of the plane as you face it head on).

The green color of the cookie, as you can see from the picture, is not the pretty, yellow/green color of true green Mayfair. It also **doesn't glow** under black light as the old green does.

The corner ridges on the old shaker rise half way to the top and then smooth out. The new shaker corner ridges rise to the top and are quite pronounced. The measurement differences are listed below, but the **diameter of the opening is the critical and easiest way to tell old from new!**

	OLD	NEW
Diameter of opening	¾"	⅝"
Diameter of lid	⅞"	¾"
Height	4¹⁄₁₆"	4"

Mayfair juice pitchers were reproduced in 1993. The old pitchers have a distinct mould circle on the bottom that is missing on the newly-made ones.

NEW "MISS AMERICA"

Colors: Crystal, green, pink, ice blue, red amberina, cobalt blue.

I am still receiving reports of cobalt blue sugars and creamers. Since no cobalt was ever found in Miss America, I am inclined to believe these are new! Cobalt blue is a favorite color of these rip-off artists.

The reproduction butter dish in "Miss America" design is probably the best of the newer products; yet there are three distinct differences to be found between the original butter top and the newly made ones. Since the value of the butter dish lies in the top, it seems more profitable to examine it. **There is a new importer who is making reproductions of the reproductions.** Unfortunately, these newer models vary greatly from one batch to the next. The only noticeable thing I have seen on these butters is how the top knob sticks up away from the butter caused by a longer than usual stem on the knob. All the other characteristics still hold true, but the paragraph in bold below explains the best way to tell old from new!

In the new butter dishes pictured, notice that the panels reaching the edge of the butter bottom tend to have a pronounced curving, skirt-like edge. In the original dish, there is much less curving at the edge of these panels.

Second, pick up the top of the new dish and feel up inside it. If the butter top knob is filled with glass so that it is convex (curved outward), the dish is new; the old inside knob area is concave (curved inward).

Finally, from the underside, look through the top toward the knob. In the original butter dish you would see a perfectly formed multi-sided star; in the newer version, you see distorted rays with no visible points.

Shakers have been made in green, pink, cobalt blue, and crystal. The latest copies of **shakers are becoming more difficult to distinguish from the old!** The new distributor's copies are creating havoc with new collectors and dealers alike. **The measurements given below for shakers do not hold true for all the latest reproductions.** It is impossible to know which generation of shaker reproductions that you will encounter, so you have to be careful on these! Know your dealer and **if the price is too good to be true,** there is likely a good reason! **It's NEW!**

The shakers most likely will have new tops; but since some old shakers have been given new tops, that isn't conclusive at all. Unscrew the lid. Old shakers have a very neatly formed ridge of glass on which to screw the lid. It overlaps a little and has rounded off ends. Old shakers stand 3⅜" tall without the lid. **Most new** ones stand 3¼" tall. Old shakers have almost a forefinger's depth inside (female finger) or a fraction short of 2½". **Most new** shakers have an inside depth of 2", about the second digit bend of a female's finger. (I'm doing finger depths since most of you will have those with you at the flea market, rather than a tape measure). In men, the old shaker's depth covers my knuckle; the new shaker leaves my knuckle exposed. **Most** new shakers simply have more glass on the inside of the shaker — something you can spot from twelve feet away! The hobs are more rounded on the newer shaker, particularly near the stem and seams; in the old shaker these areas remained pointedly sharp!

New Miss America tumblers have ½" of glass in the bottom, have a smooth edge on the bottom of the glass with no mould rim and show only two distinct mould marks on the sides of the glass. Old tumblers have only ¼" of glass in the bottom, have a distinct mould line rimming the bottom of the tumbler and have four distinct mould marks up the sides of the tumbler. The new green tumbler doesn't glow under black light as did the old.

New Miss America pitchers (without ice lip only) are all perfectly smooth rimmed at the top edge above the handle. All old pitchers that I have seen have a **"hump"** in the top rim of the glass above the handle area, rather like a camel's hump. The very bottom diamonds next to the foot in the new pitchers "squash" into elongated diamonds. In the old pitchers, these get noticeably smaller, but they retain their diamond shape.

NEW "SHARON" Privately Produced 1976...(continued page 238)

Colors: Blue, dark green, light green, pink, cobalt blue, opalescent blue, red, burnt umber.

A blue Sharon butter turned up in 1976 and turned my phone line to a liquid fire! The color was Mayfair blue — a fluke and dead giveaway as far as real Sharon is concerned. The original mastermind of reproductions did not know his patterns very well and mixed up Mayfair and Sharon!

When Sharon butters are found in colors similar to the old pink and green, you can immediately tell that the new version has more glass in the top where it changes from pattern to clear glass, a thick, defined ring of glass as opposed to a thin, barely defined ring of glass in the old. The knob of the new dish tends to stick up more. In the old butter dish there's barely room to fit your finger to grasp the knob. The new butter dish has a sharply defined ridge of glass in the bottom around which the top sits. The old butter has such a slight rim that the top easily scoots off the bottom.

In 1977 a cheese dish appeared having the same top as the butter and having all the flaws inherent in that top which were discussed in detail above. However, the bottom of this dish was all wrong. It's about half way between a flat plate and a butter dish bottom, **bowl** shaped; and it is over thick, giving it an awkward appearance. The real cheese bottom was a **salad plate** with a rim of glass for holding the top. These round bottom cheese dishes are but a parody of the old and are easily spotted. We removed the top from one in the picture so you could see its heaviness and its bowl shape.

REPRODUCTIONS (Continued)

NEW "SHARON" (Continued)

Some of the latest reproductions in Sharon are a too-light pink creamer and sugar with lid. They are pictured with the "Made in Taiwan" label. These retail for around $15.00 for the pair and are also easy to spot as reproductions. I'll just mention the most obvious differences. Turn the creamer so you are looking directly at the spout. In the old creamer the mould line runs dead center of that spout; in the new, the mould line runs decidedly to the left of center spout.

On the sugar, the leaves and roses are "off" but not enough to **describe** it to new collectors. Therefore, look at the center design, both sides, at the stars located at the very bottom of the motif. A thin leaf stem should run directly from that center star upward on **both** sides. In this new sugar, the stem only runs from one; it stops way short of the star on one side; **or** look inside the sugar bowl at where the handle attaches to the bottom of the bowl; in the new bowl, this attachment looks like a perfect circle; in the old, its an upside down "v" shaped teardrop.

As for the sugar lid, the knob of the new lid is perfectly smooth as you grasp its edges. The old knob has a mould seam running mid circumference. You could tell these two lids apart blind folded!

While there is a hair's difference between the height, mouth opening diameter, and inside depth of the old Sharon shakers and those newly produced, I won't attempt to upset you with those sixteenths and thirty-seconds of a degree of difference. Suffice it to say that in physical shape, they are very close. However, as concerns design, they're miles apart.

The old shakers have true appearing roses. The flowers really **look** like roses. On the new shakers, the roses appear as poorly drawn circles with wobbly concentric rings. The leaves are not as clearly defined on the new shakers as the old. However, forgetting all that, in the old shakers, the first design you see below the lid is a **rose bud**. It's angled like a rocket shooting off into outer space with three leaves at the base of the bud (where the rocket fuel would burn out). In the new shakers, this "bud" has become four paddles of a windmill. It's the difference between this 🌿 and this 🌿.

Candy dishes have been made in pink, green, cobalt blue, red, and opaque blue that goes to opalescent. These candy jars are among the easiest items to discern old from new. Pick up the lid and look from the bottom side. On the old there is a 2" circle knob ring; on the new the ring is only ½". This shows from the top also but it is difficult to measure with the knob in the center. There are other major differences but this one will not be mould corrected easily. The bottoms are also simple to distinguish. The base diameter of the old is 3¼" and the new only 3". On the example I have, quality of the new is rough, poorly shaped and moulded; but I do not know if that will hold true for all reproductions of the candy. **I hope so!**